FOOTSTEPS

The New York Times

Introduction by Monica Drake

FOOTSTEPS

From Ferrante's Naples
to Hammett's San Francisco, Literary Pilgrimages
Around the World

THREE RIVERS PRESS
NEW YORK

Published in the United States by Three Rivers Press, an imprint of the Crown Publishing Group, a division of Penguin Random House LLC, New York.
crownpublishing.com

Three Rivers Press and the Tugboat design are registered trademarks of Penguin Random House LLC.

All of the essays in this book were previously published in the Travel section of *The New York Times.*

Library of Congress Cataloging-in-Publication Data
Title: Footsteps : from Ferrante's Naples to Hammett's San Francisco, literary pilgrimages around the world.
Other titles: At head of title: The New York Times | New York times.
Description: New York : Three Rivers Press, 2017.
Identifiers: LCCN 2016041783 | ISBN 9780804189842 (paperback) | ISBN 9780804189859 (ebook)
Subjects: LCSH: Travelers' writings. | Travel writing. | Authors—Travel | BISAC: TRAVEL / Essays & Travelogues. | LITERARY COLLECTIONS / Essays. | TRAVEL / Special Interest / General.
Classification: LCC PN56.T7 F66 2017 | DDC 808.8/032—dc23
LC record available at https://lccn.loc.gov/2016041783

ISBN 978-0-8041-8984-2
Ebook ISBN 978-0-8041-8985-9

Printed in the United States of America

Book design by Elina Nudelman
Maps and illustrations by Gracia Lam
Cover design by Michael Morris
Cover illustration by Gracia Lam

10 9 8 7 6 5 4 3 2 1

First Edition

Contents

BEYOND

Introduction

Monica Drake

Back when travel was just my passion and not yet my profession, I went to the French Riviera for the party scene and instead found myself dazzled by the otherworldly light of day. I was marveling at how it made every waking moment dreamlike when I noticed a small plaque on a building indicating that Henri Matisse had lived inside. Whatever I'd read about Matisse and Nice before that moment hadn't mattered: it was then that I understood how the city had challenged him to make art as sublime as the setting.

All of us have experienced a moment in our travels when we stray onto turf that an artist, including those who paint pictures with words, once trod. It surprises us, this statue in the middle of a park, a street named for a luminary, or the small museum that at one point was her home. But it shouldn't be unexpected.

All the world is a reliquary, filled with fields, forests, and city plazas that lead visionaries among us to create work that endures the ages. We travelers are but devotees who touch these monuments and in place of prayers meditate on how someone else came to be who they are and create what they did. We inevitably look about and wonder. Did the sweep of this hill and the mist of the morning somehow ignite a spark? Was this place more incidental than inspirational? Examining these questions has been the defining task of Footsteps since 1981, when *The New York Times* ran it as a short-lived series. It appeared sporadically in the intervening years until it emerged as a full-fledged feature.

Regardless of provenance, the conceit in these pages is nearly as old as the *Times* itself. An article from 1860 chronicles a visit to Stratford-upon-Avon to see the birthplace and tomb of the "world's master-genius," William Shakespeare. That report, a faithful recounting of a voyage in the footsteps of someone universally revered, assumed the best of the Bard: "Calm, quiet and beautiful were all the surroundings, and I thought it was not strange that one whose early childhood was passed amid such scenes as this should have partaken of their beauty, and been gentle, kind and loving." In aspiring to capture the interplay of a writer's real identity, work, and setting, this was an early version of what would become Footsteps.

As the breadth of the stories in this collection indicates, our approach varies as much as the literary giants that they profile. "Mark Twain's Hawaii," for example, examines the four-month stretch in which the writer sent letters from the island, rather than tracing any of his fictional works. Yet it suffuses the place with the spirit of Twain. "Orhan Pamuk's Istanbul" is on the other end of the spectrum, using the Nobel laureate as a tour guide who leads us through the city that he has called home for nearly six decades.

What unifies them is a single guiding principle: each story should leave the reader with a new perspective on an artist and the place that has somehow been a muse. Often an unusual pairing is enough to supply the novelty—as with Rimbaud in Ethiopia, a lesser-examined point in the poet's life. But occasionally—as with Dashiell Hammett and San Francisco—the setting and star go hand in hand until the story of the city's transformation is taken into account. There is little hard-boiled left in a city awash in venture capital, it turns out.

As Footsteps evolves, the *Times* has been venturing farther afield to choose the settings. Inspiration comes from America and Europe and also from Argentina (Borges), Martinique (Césaire), and Vietnam (Duras). We've also added contemporary personalities such as Jamaica Kincaid and Elena Ferrante to those whose trails we trace.

At the same time, we seek contributors who are able to view the place and the person they are profiling with equal fervor. The best of our Footsteps capture their passion for specific authors and places in time.

These escapes immerse travelers in a setting by providing a purpose while on the road. A fixed mission forces us to be present rather than meander, refreshing our social feeds and lamenting the cost of international roaming. Studying the world this way pushes away workaday life that much more efficiently. These accounts can make us travelers instead of tourists.

And that they do, even if you do not take a trip. "That was a pleasant journey into the real Wonderland," a reader wrote in response to the description of Lewis Carroll's Oxford. It isn't rare for readers to send e-mails and comments and letters that refer to a Footsteps essay as if it had been a vacation.

True literature itself is a flight of fancy, and appreciators of it are all too familiar with the discombobulating feeling of finishing a novel and being slightly surprised to be at home in a recliner rather than hundreds of miles—and hundreds of years—away. Above all, Footsteps essays are for the avid readers who can travel by simply turning a page. Turn these, and they'll take you around the world.

United States

JACK KEROUAC
VLADIMIR NABOKOV
M. F. K. FISHER
DASHIELL HAMMETT
MARK TWAIN
Poet of the Appetites
Portnoy's Complaint
Last House

RACHEL CARSON
H. P. LOVECRAFT
MARY OLIVER
PHILIP ROTH
FLANNERY O'CONNOR
Red Harvest

Mark Twain's Hawaii

Lawrence Downes

Like any paradise, Hawaii walks the fine line between blissful and boring. David Lodge noted this in his satirical novel *Paradise News,* imagining the predicament of tourists in fanny packs walking up and down the sidewalks of Waikiki like heavenly pilgrims with no place left to go. They seem contented, but a half-formed question lingers in their eyes:

"Well, this is nice, but is this all there is? Is this it?"

Actually, it's not. Hawaii's blandly sunny face hides a turbulent history, an extra dimension of sadness and beauty. This is what separates Hawaii from the beach-and-beer nowheres like Fort Lauderdale and Cancún: a complicated soul.

Finding it means getting out of Waikiki, peeling back layers to uncover the stories behind the scenery. It means having the right guide, a writer to annotate the loveliness.

Hawaii has seen its share of famous storytellers. Robert Louis Stevenson, Jack London, and Herman Melville passed through on their way to other frontiers. But what little they wrote about Hawaii was fictionalized, heavily metaphorical, and is now mostly forgotten. James Michener, on the other hand, wrote way too much: his 1959 novel, *Hawaii,* covers nearly the whole thing, from the volcanoes to the missionaries, a span of forty million years, or maybe pages, it's hard to tell. Neither is what you want if you're looking for something to enrich your visit.

What you want is Mark Twain.

Twain spent four months on the islands in 1866, when he was thirty-one and working on becoming famous. His twenty-five letters from the Sandwich Islands, written on assignment for *The Sacramento Union,* are still fresh and rudely funny after almost a century and a half—a foretaste of genius and the best travel writing about Hawaii I have ever read.

Twain's Hawaii teemed with ship captains, whalers, missionaries, mosquitoes, fragrant thickets of flowers, and thousands of cats. France, Britain, and the United States were competing for influence, making the usual colonial mischief. The population and ancient ways of native Hawaiians, the Kanaka Maoli, were in catastrophic decline, beset by disease and cultural pressures. But Hawaii was still in its sovereign glory, with an elected legislature and a thirty-five-year-old king: stately, plump Kamehameha V, the last of his family dynasty. It was a land of royal pageantry, tropical splendor, and a fair amount of squalor.

Determined to "ransack the islands" for his dispatches, Twain rented a horse and rode until he was laid up with saddle sores. He rode by moonlight through a ghostly plain of sand strewn with human bones, the remains of an ancient battlefield. He scaled the summit of Kīlauea during an eruption, standing at the crater's edge on a foggy night, his face made crimson by lava glow. He hiked through misty valleys. He surfed.

That's right, Huck: America's greatest writer took a wooden surfboard and paddled out to wait, as he had seen naked locals do, "for a particularly prodigious billow to come along," upon which billow he prodigiously wiped out.

"None but natives ever master the art of surf-bathing thoroughly," he wrote.

He also tried swimming with nude native women, but when he got into the surf, they got out.

He might have tasted poi, eaten with the fingers in those days from a communal calabash, but after reading this passage, I suspect not: "Many a different finger goes into the same bowl and many a different kind of dirt and shade and quality of flavor is added to the virtues of its contents. One tall gentleman, with nothing in the world on but a soiled and greasy shirt, thrust in his finger and tested the poi, shook his head, scratched it with the useful finger, made another test, prospected among his hair, caught something and ate it; tested the poi again, wiped the grimy perspiration from his brow with the universal hand, tested again, blew his nose—'Let's move on, Brown,' said I, and we moved."

That passage is from *Mark Twain's Letters from Hawaii,* which along with *Mark Twain in Hawaii: Roughing It in the Sandwich Islands* is the starting point for tracing Twain's footsteps. The trail begins in downtown Honolulu, which is far less wild than it once was, but architectural traces of the kingdom survive among the groves of mirrored office towers. The grandest is Iolani Palace, a Victorian dollhouse of fluted columns and wrought iron that is the only royal residence in the United States, not counting Graceland.

Twain never saw it—it went up in 1882—but on the palace lawn, now shaded by an immense kapok tree, he watched two thousand Hawaiians grieving by torchlight for Princess Victoria Kamāmalu, the king's sister, on the eve of her funeral.

"Every night, and all night long, for more than thirty days," he wrote, "multitudes of these strange mourners have burned their candle-nut torches in the royal inclosure, and sung their funeral dirges, and danced their hula hulas, and wailed their harrowing wail for the dead."

All you hear now is the droning of cars; the palace is in Honolulu's business district, next to the state capitol. Nuuanu Valley, however, the princess's burial place, is a far more haunting experience. On the day of her funeral, Twain galloped there to await the procession.

The Royal Mausoleum of Hawaii consists of several crypts and a coral-block chapel on a lawn lined with palms. It may be the most history-drenched place in the islands. The mausoleum's curator, or *kahu,* is William Kaiheekai Maioho, who lives in a cottage on the grounds and is the sixth in his family to hold the position. After opening the windows to the sun, he sat in a pew to tell the story.

Speaking gently, he recited a long history of royal funerals and renovations, then took me to the family crypt of the Kalakauas, successors to the Kamehamehas. The gold inscriptions on its white marble walls are as familiar to Hawaii schoolchildren as those of presidents: *Kalakaua, Kapiolani, Kaiulani, Kalanianaole,* and *Liliuokalani,* Hawaii's last monarch.

Visiting their graves made me eager to plunge deeper into Hawaii's royal past, following Twain's footsteps to the Big Island, where Kamehameha the Great was born and where an eruption of Kīlauea that began in 1983 is still sending lava down gentle slopes into the boiling sea.

Twain spent weeks covering the Big Island on horseback, but a rental car makes it possible to hit the highlights in two days or three. The highway to Kīlauea's summit is a straight, slow climb out of Hilo, past tin-roofed frame houses in tidy yards planted with ti, banana, and torch ginger, and the more recent development: a gridlocked shopping-mall sprawl. That side of the island also has an end-of-the-road Alaska feel, with lots of blond dreadlocks and holistic massage salons. One Adopt-A-Highway sponsor is the Raelians, the sect that promotes human cloning and believes the first humans were created by visiting space aliens.

If so, the upper slopes of Kīlauea are a likely landing area. The lush, broad-leaved lowlands give way to scrubby ohia trees poking out of an understory thick with ginger and *uluhe* ferns. Soon you are in the chill and splendid desolation of Hawaii Volcanoes National Park, where rangers give daily briefings on the air quality—the sulfurous fumes can be thick and dangerous—and the state of the lava flow.

Perched at the rim of the steaming caldera is the old Volcano House hotel. Twain stayed here, but when it was a primitive hostel, not this imposing structure with a large fireplace in a lobby lined with portraits of Hawaii's kings and queens.

The Volcano House has crater-view rooms, but the hotel's tidy wooden cabins in the Nāmakanipaio Campground provide an experience much closer to Twain's. In a grove of towering koa, ohia, and eucalyptus trees, they are a perfect base for a Twain-style expedition to the eruption.

For the last twenty-three years, the lava has been flowing not from Kīlauea's summit but from the Pu'u 'Ō'ō vent, a crack in its southern slopes. The lava has buried miles of mountainside—as well as streets, subdivisions, and beaches—in crunchy black lacquer. Chain of Craters Road winds down the mountain like a lazily draped ribbon on a pillow. Roadcuts through old lava flows are marked with dates, and even those from the 1950s are still desolate—just craggy, brownish-black rock, like strewn coffee grounds.

Night falls like an anvil in these latitudes. The flowing lava is invisible by day, but at night it becomes a shimmering strip of orange, running up the mountainside and coloring the clouds above. A steam plume rises at the ocean's edge. Tourists who wisely take walking sticks, boots, and flashlights can clamber up to where the lava has overrun the road, for a long hike over cool lava to get closer to the glowing rock and steam.

But the view from the road—especially through the rangers' telescope—is also excellent. It is a staggering sight, though not, sadly, as spectacular as the bubbling lava lake Twain lucked upon:

> *The greater part of the vast floor of the desert under us was as black as ink, and apparently smooth and level; but over a mile square of it was ringed and streaked and striped with a thousand branching streams of liquid and gorgeously brilliant fire! It looked like a colossal railroad map of the State of Massachusetts done in chain lightning on a midnight sky. Imagine it—imagine a coal-black sky shivered into a tangled network of angry fire!*

A long drive out of Volcanoes National Park winds down around the United States' southernmost point, then up the coast to Kailua-Kona. In Waiohinu, a roadside marker points out Mark Twain's monkeypod tree, planted by the man himself.

Pu'uhonua o Hōnaunau National Historical Park, commonly called the City of Refuge, is a centuries-old religious sanctuary that provides a surreal plunge into deep history. Twain marveled at its hulking stonework, which was built in the 1500s without mortar and stands to this day just as he described it, above tidal pools full of foraging sea turtles.

It's a short drive from there to Kealakekua Bay, where native Hawaiians brought Captain James Cook's celebrated career to a sudden halt. "Plain unvarnished history takes the romance out of Captain Cook's assassination, and renders a deliberate verdict of justifiable homicide," wrote Twain, ever the provocative American. "Wherever he went among the islands he was cordially received and welcomed by the inhabitants, and his ships lavishly supplied with all manner of food. He returned these kindnesses with insult and ill-treatment."

Heading from there to Kailua-Kona, the Big Island's main tourist enclave, I concluded that Cook's defeat was only a temporary setback. Twain described it as "the sleepiest, quietest, Sundayest looking place you can imagine." But today the main drag, Ali'i Drive, is a tacky cousin to Kalakaua Avenue in Waikiki, a ruthlessly efficient operation for the concentration and extraction of tourist money.

It looks like a highly unlikely place for Hawaiian authenticity, but there it is at King Kamehameha's Kona Beach Hotel, the city's main hotel for locals—the one that caters to a mom-and-pop, wedding, and luau crowd. Its '70s decor is pleasing, but even more so are the lobby and hall exhibits of old Hawaiian art and artifacts. It is a museum doubling as hotel, complete with portraits of royalty and a wooden bust of King Kamehameha I himself over the front desk.

The dinner buffet is a paradise of Hawaiian food: poi, kalua pig, rice, and poke, a traditional dish of marinated raw fish. At the poolside bar that night, a table of local guys in tank tops and sunglasses downed pitchers of beer and played ukuleles. I listened while floating on my back in the pool, staring up at Orion in the inky sky and thinking: it doesn't get much more Hawaiian than this.

But it does: there is a restored Hawaiian temple, or *heiau,* on the grounds. I walked there after dark, following a row of gas torches to the water's edge, a grass hut, and a lava-rock platform. The platform, a marker says, is the very one used by William Kaiheekai Maioho's distant ancestor to prepare Kamehameha I for burial. Twain, quoting from an 1844 history volume, gives a detailed account of the events surrounding Kamehameha's death, which prompted, among other things, the sacrifice of three hundred dogs "in lieu of human victims."

On a lawn beyond the platform an outdoor reception was breaking up. Musicians were packing up instruments, lingerers were chatting, the dark waters were rippling in the orange glow of torchlight. There was a table with a guest book and photo album—this had been a baby luau, celebrating a child's first birthday. It was about as old and genuine as Hawaiian traditions get.

And so, two true stories of the real Hawaii; one nearly lost to time, the other just beginning, and both hidden in plain sight among the tiki torches of a tourist ground zero. Twain would have appreciated it.

Originally published in May 2006.

Lawrence Downes is an editorial writer at *The New York Times*.

Climbing a Peak That Stirred Kerouac

Ethan Todras-Whitehill

I passed through a stand of fir and out onto the bare ridge, and there it was: the squat white structure where Jack Kerouac spent sixty-three days as a fire lookout in the summer of 1956. I had assumed that the Desolation Peak lookout would be empty, a silent monument to the Voice of the Beat Generation. But the shutters were propped open on all four sides, the door was ajar, and inside, a small, seated silhouette was visible against the hazy late-afternoon sky.

I grew giddy as the figure stood and came into the doorway. Surely this was Kerouac's spiritual brother, a man uniquely qualified to speak about the solitary days and nights that inspired major portions of *Desolation Angels, The Dharma Bums,* and *Lonesome Traveler.* A compact man with dark hair, he introduced himself as Daniel Otero, a Marine reservist who had served two tours of duty in Iraq. Kerouac, I remembered, was thirty-four during his time on Desolation Peak, and did stints in the navy and the merchant marine.

Otero, who had been up there all summer and was leaving in only a few days, invited me into the shack, which felt like the cabin of a ship with its desk, kitchen, bed, and astrolabe-like fire-finder tool all squeezed into the single, tiny room. My eyes latched onto the corner bookshelf, lined with Kerouac paperbacks.

We made small talk for a few minutes before I finally asked about Otero's famous predecessor. He took a deep breath, obviously having gotten the question before. "I tried, but . . ." he said, gesturing toward the books. Those books, I now realized, did not belong to Kerouac's spiritual brother. They looked new, untouched, as if they had just come out of an Amazon box. "Me and that guy just don't see eye-to-eye."

I knew exactly how he felt. For my college graduation, my uncle gave me a copy of *On the Road* with the heartfelt wish that I would find it as life-changing as he had. I was a likely candidate to do so: avid traveler, a student of English and political science in college, and, later, a writer. Instead, I found Kerouac's "masterpiece" rambling and frivolous; it took me two years to get through it.

But when I moved to Seattle last year, I started hearing about Desolation Peak. Ten years older than the last time I read him, I decided to give Kerouac's "spontaneous prose" another shot. I picked up a biography and the relevant novels, organized a few friends for a fall weekend, and set out for the North Cascades.

The nice part about the Desolation Peak hike is that it can be as easy or as hard as you please. The trailhead is about three hours from Seattle, and day hikers can pay for a boat ride up Ross Lake to the base of the mountain from the Ross Lake Resort; the lakeside camp at nearby Lightning Creek offers the option to tack on a night in the wilderness. But for those looking to sleep atop Kerouac's mountain, as we planned to do, the price of admission is steep: a 3,500-foot climb carrying all the water you will need for the next day (not to mention camping gear), as Desolation Peak is bone-dry once the snowfields melt in August.

And although Kerouac himself got boat rides both ways, my wife, buddies, and I opted to go farther and hike in from the highway, taking the boat only on the return trip. After all, Kerouac had two months in the northwestern woods; even with the extra mileage (almost thirty for the whole trip) we would have only three days.

The first day we hiked sixteen miles across slopes of sword ferns and Oregon grape shrubs, stopping occasionally to peer into the clear depths of Ross Lake, whose contours we followed. But pretty views don't make sixteen miles any shorter, and we stumbled into Lightning Creek Camp with feet in full rebellion.

Many people forget that the publication of *On the Road* in 1957 came almost a decade after the events that inspired it. In the summer of 1956, Kerouac was still an anonymous wandering soul looking for truth in America's boxcars, bars, and wildernesses. Nature as a subject was new to him, having been introduced to hiking and the mountains by his brief but intense friendship with the Buddhist poet Gary Snyder, an experience recounted in *The Dharma Bums.* Snyder was a Pacific Northwest native who himself had twice been a fire lookout in the Cascades; it was he who suggested the Desolation posting to Kerouac.

Kerouac arrived at the base of Desolation by boat on a wet July morning and rode up the mountain in his poncho, a "shroudy monk on a horse" with mules carrying the supplies. For our hike, we were the mules. Although hundreds of people a day hike up Desolation Peak every summer, according to Otero, fewer than a half dozen groups stay at Desolation Camp, one mile down the ridge from the summit with many of the same views. I can't blame them; with the extra water our packs weighed over forty pounds. But the reward was having Kerouac's mountain to ourselves.

I especially couldn't wait to see Hozomeen, the unbelievably symmetrical, four-peaked prominence to the north. "Hozomeen, Hozomeen, most beautiful mountain I ever seen," Kerouac wrote. The peak was his constant companion, his friend and tormentor. "Stark naked rock, pinnacles and thousand feet high protruding from . . . immense timbered shoulders . . . awful vaulty blue smokebody rock."

The mile-long climb up the ridge brought ever grander views of fjord-like Ross Lake and moody Jack Mountain 7,000 feet above. At a couple of points, snatches of Hozomeen were visible, but it wasn't until we were in calling distance of the lookout tower that we felt the mountain's full impact. It wasn't much for elevation, at 8,071 feet—only 2,000 above Desolation—but, oh my, Hozomeen wasn't human-looking, but rather monstrous. Kerouac frequently connected it to the Abominable Snowman, but to me it looked like the back of some Cascadian dragon, wings folded as it waited until night to hunt.

Up at the peak, I met Otero. Like most fire lookouts—Kerouac included—Otero had little to do up there but watch for fires, sleep, and read. While he was indifferent to Kerouac, he was pretty enthusiastic about visitors who had climbed his peak because of the writer. All of his Kerouac books were gifts from hikers; other hiker-pilgrims would slip poems—Kerouac's or their own—between the pages when Otero wasn't looking. There was no explicit record of Kerouac in the shack, formal or informal, but Otero showed me air force forms of the sort described in *Desolation Angels,* given to Kerouac to record aircraft sightings, but used by the writer to roll cigarettes. If I wanted to get in touch with Kerouac's spirit, he suggested, "you could stand on your head and look at Hozomeen. Lots of people do that."

After talking with Otero for a while, we drifted down the north face to soak in the slanted rays cut for us by peaks with names like Prophet, Redoubt, and Terror. Taking full advantage of our nearby camp, we stayed up on the mountaintop until almost dark, drinking in one of Desolation's "mad raging sunsets pouring in sea foams of cloud through unimaginable crags like the crags you grayly drew in pencil as a child, with every rose-tint of hope beyond" (*Lonesome Traveler*).

We hustled down the ridge in the windy dusk and zipped into our sleeping bags. As the night was fine, we slept in the open beneath a black blanket of sky pierced with winking stars.

When I started planning this trip, I had imagined this night as my last chance to "get" the Beat writer. But in reality, I was already a Kerouac convert. Not to his writing—the guy needed an editor after *Desolation Angels* possibly more than he needed a bath—but to the story of his life, as recounted in Dennis McNally's biography and other places. It reads like a classical tragedy, or at least a high-minded Hollywood screenplay: a sensitive young man seeks truth in order to change his world; he doesn't find that truth, not in any real, sustained way, but his quest makes him famous and inspires a generation to follow in his footsteps, even as he cannot cope with his fame and drinks himself to death.

Three months after Kerouac came down from Desolation, he learned that Viking would finally publish *On the Road*—ostensibly his greatest triumph, but in reality the beginning of his end. Kerouac's time on the mountain was a literal and figurative apex for him, his last truth-seeking adventure before he was transformed by the hostile media into first a caricature of himself, and later a shadow. Of Kerouac's major works (all of which are unabashedly autobiographical), only *Big Sur* describes events that took place wholly in the years after Desolation; it chronicles the writer's descent into alcoholism and mental instability.

The next day, before we headed down to catch our boat, I climbed back up the ridge before sunrise, this time with only my friend Josh for company. We quickly separated once we hit the peak. The air felt cold and mystical, so I brought out the pages of *Desolation Angels* I had ripped from their binding for the trip. In the purpling dawn, I read Kerouac's good-bye to his mountain. "No clock will tick, no man yearn, and silent will be the snow and the rocks underneath and as ever Hozomeen'll loom and mourn without sadness evermore," Kerouac wrote. He concluded the valedictory with a sentiment that echoes deep in the core of any hiker about to leave the wilderness: "Farewell, Desolation, thou hast seen me well . . . All I want is an ice cream cone."

Originally published in November 2012.

Ethan Todras-Whitehill is a writer who lives in Western Massachusetts with his wife and daughter.

A House Built to Feed Body and Soul

Michelle Green

Sheltered by a grove of bay trees, madroños, and live oaks, the white stucco house in Sonoma County's Valley of the Moon hugs a meadow where wildflowers bloom in slabs of yellow and sprinklings of rich purple. The barbed-wire fences and cattle guards are still in place, though the cows that feasted on M. F. K. Fisher's grapevines are gone. Gone, too, is the sign warning drop-ins away from the ranch where Last House, as Fisher called her retreat, was built for her in 1971. TRESPASSERS, it announced, WILL BE VIOLATED.

One hundred years after the birth of Mary Frances Kennedy Fisher, the author and culinary seer whose sensuous, deeply personal work defined a genre, her former cottage near Glen Ellen is a landmark visible only to those who know how to look. Though it's easy to spot from Highway 12, a road lined by vineyards, half-finished housing developments, and the occasional vintage barn, nothing defines the house where Fisher died in 1992 as the lair of a literary grande dame.

It's a paradox that the author who helped liberate the American palate left such a small mark in this vineyard-rich, food-mad terroir, where a bottle of local olive oil commands as much as an unassuming cabernet sauvignon. *Poet of the Appetites,* a biography by Joan Reardon, is on offer in an Italianate wine-tasting room in leafy Glen Ellen, but the Historical Society's town map takes no note of Fisher.

In Sonoma Valley recently, I wanted to get closer to Fisher, the woman who had lived so well. In her accounts of her cultural awakening in France and her memories of great love and transformative meals, she had helped me see the link between seizing the moment and feeding the soul. "It seems to me," she wrote,

> *that our three basic needs, for food and security and love, are so mixed and mingled and entwined that we cannot straightly think of one without the others. So it happens that when I write of hunger, I am really writing about love and the hunger for it, and warmth and the love of it and the hunger for it . . . and then the warmth and richness and fine reality of hunger satisfied . . . and it is all one.*

Once widowed, twice divorced, Fisher bore a child between marriages and acknowledged having "several good affairs." As a screenwriter in Hollywood, she dated Groucho Marx; later, she and the *Esquire* editor Arnold Gingrich were a bicoastal item. She understood the culinary subtleties of seduction, and she explained her tactics in one of her most charming essays.

In a piece called "W Is for Wanton," Fisher describes toying with a prospect before pouncing: "I would tease and excite him by bewilderment, and serve him what he thought he hated . . . I would quarrel with him on a celestially gentle plane." For the denouement: "Good Scotch and water for him, a very dry Martini for me," followed by three moderate courses. Rich food and copious alcohol? Only if you want to "rest inviolate."

Along with that cheeky advice, the image of her in a cottage of her own has never left me. On the cover of *Last House,* a collection published after her death, is a photo of Fisher on her balcony wearing a Cheshire-cat smile. In the book, she meditates on the pleasures of living in a "palazzino" amid wildflowers like the "small blue coarse kind of daisy" that evoked vineyards in France and stirred erotic memories of her second husband, Dillwyn Parrish, who died two years after they wed.

Elsewhere, she noted that her guests were captivated by the sensory pleasures around her: "The air is very sweet . . . when people walk out to their cars their feet crush the falling eucalyptus buds, and they look almost dazed for a minute. I put some buds in their hands."

The ranch where Last House sits is different now. In 1979, the author's friend David Pleydell-Bouverie, an architect, donated the 535-acre property to Audubon Canyon Ranch. Since his death in 1994, bobcats, gray foxes, and rattlesnakes have roamed freely at the Bouverie Preserve of Audubon Canyon Ranch. Educational programs are targeted at third- and fourth-graders in Napa and Sonoma Counties; others who want to observe the pileated woodpeckers and red-bellied newts must compete for places on guided walks.

A renovated barn, now a nature center, is open to the public, but the Mediterranean-style house where Pleydell-Bouverie lived is off-limits. So, too, is Last House, a short walk down the hill past an imposing bell tower. Thirty years ago, a ranch hand rang the enormous bell at sunset. Now, the tower serves as an annual nesting place for Canada geese whose hatching dramas are recorded on a discreet "goose cam."

Since the preserve is private, I couldn't just pop in; instead, after many phone calls, I made an appointment at the nature center. Driving up the lane by the meadow, I slowed to a rubber-necker's creep. A sweet sense of déjà vu set in when I neared Fisher's cottage: with its flared roof and arched balconies, it looked much as it had in Fisher's day, but Nancy Trbovich, the administrative coordinator of the preserve, warned me against investigating. "The man who lives there," she said, "doesn't like people knocking on his door."

What she did allow me to see was so evocative, though, that I felt guilty about the nudging that got me into the writer's home. After I surveyed the nature center, we strolled down the hill to Pleydell-Bouverie's hacienda.

She led me through high-ceilinged rooms filled with touches from the historic homes where the owner (a grandson of the fifth Earl of Radnor) spent his childhood: rich fabrics, formal portraits, glittering chandeliers. Gleaming copperware and gilt-framed landscapes caught the light in the moss-green kitchen. Outside was a pool that perfectly mimicked a pond; it was framed by trellises trailing wisteria.

Socially eclectic, Pleydell-Bouverie (who was divorced from Alice Astor) entertained friends, including the Queen of Jordan and Maya Angelou, in Glen Ellen. After he wrote a note introducing himself in 1968, Fisher invited him to lunch at her Victorian house in Saint Helena—a jasmine-scented town in the Napa Valley. Her two daughters were grown, and she was ready to streamline her life; two years later, she proposed building on his compound.

Fisher lent Pleydell-Bouverie $39,400 to build what she called "a shack" inspired by her "eccentric specifications." He gave her domed redwood ceilings, black tile floors, and a decadent bathroom the size of a second bedroom: its Chinese-red walls served as her art gallery.

Open to the living space, the kitchen was galley-simple. Its focus was a window above the sink where anyone sudsing and rinsing—once, an assembly line comprising Chuck Williams, Julia Child, and James Beard—could meditate on light and shadow in the grove.

Fisher's serene bedroom had its own balcony with a view of the bell tower and endless reminders of her travels: a poster from Venice, nativity figures from France. Throughout the house were bookcases whose scarlet interiors echoed the red of the entranceway, which was dominated by a daybed that looked like an empress's throne.

It all worked. "She seemed to wear her house—it was classic and simple as the perfect dress," wrote the novelist Anne Lamott, who was a friend.

Like Fisher, the house continued to evolve; artworks were moved continually to keep the eye engaged.

"Mary Frances' house was full of vitality—just really stimulating," said Marsha Moran, the author's assistant for twelve years. "When you entered her space you came alive."

When Fisher moved to Glen Ellen, she was sixty-two and independent. In the next two decades, eye problems, arthritis, and Parkinson's disease turned her into an invalid. At the same time, the success of books, including *Two Towns in Provence,* brought the masses to her door; colleagues, including Alice Waters, visited, and Bill Moyers came to talk about love, loss, and aging.

Pilgrims brought food, so the house was alive with the aromas of herbs and bread and ripe cheeses. Entertaining was simple; Fisher often served what she called "go down easy wines" from local vineyards, accompanied by toasted almonds or tomatoes with olive oil and basil. Her drink: a pinkish cocktail of gin, vermouth, and Campari.

"She never turned anyone away," Moran recalled. "She loved talking with people. Even at the end, she was always generous with her spirit and she shared it even when she was shutting down."

As it happens, one of Fisher's biggest admirers was John Martin, who now lives in Last House. The ranch foreman for Pleydell-Bouverie and now the preserve's land manager, he moved into the cottage three months after she died.

"She was the nicest woman," said Martin, a dynamic Scotsman with close-cropped white hair. "I counted her as a friend. I came here in 1986 and lived in the bunkhouse; she said, 'You end up in jail, you call me first.' "

When I first phoned him from a market in Glen Ellen, Martin was polite but wary. He listened to my pitch and then invited me to come by.

His terrier, Fergus, was yipping at his side when he opened the door. Wearing shorts and a polo shirt, he led the way into the front room, with its arresting views of gold meadow and cloudless sky. A raptor sailed past a north-facing window. "Turkey vulture," he said.

Like many sideswiped by fame, Martin guards his privacy. About twice a month, he said, Fisher cultists "come up here and I chase them away."

In any case, the house is his now: Fisher's Chinese-red cabinets are blue, Virginia Woolf and Brillat-Savarin are gone, and the closet that was the author's wine cupboard is stacked with board games. A patio umbrella and Astroturf have been added to the balcony where she held court in a fan-backed chair.

Martin was leaving that evening to celebrate his birthday, and after he showed me through the cottage, Fergus began to bark more urgently. So I kept going: What was it like to be with M. F. K. Fisher in this house?

"Mary Frances would send a card with a matchstick girl on the front to invite me to come over," he said, leaning on the rail of the balcony and squinting into the sunset. "I used to watch movies with her. She called it our 'Shut Up and Eat Your Popcorn Club.' "

As Martin told it, the author's work continues to offer sustenance to readers who imagine her living at Last House, writing about love and warmth and "hunger satisfied." Even now, he receives letters addressed to her or to her family and friends.

"I opened one recently from a woman who was extremely ill," he said. "She wanted to come visit because she'd always found Mary Frances inspiring."

Which brought to mind something Fisher wrote about her legacy: "The only real thing to leave in the world is one's spirit . . . the leavings of me, murking up the atmosphere, smogging the air, sprinkling a sort of mist over things so perhaps they will twinkle a bit."

We were in his kitchen when I asked Martin whether he sensed that twinkling. Another man with a tattooed forearm might have laughed, but not one who had known the entrancing Fisher.

"Oh, yes," he answered, as though we were talking about the cactuses in his garden or the tiny black frogs that Fisher found in her sink or the owl that she once called "my familiar." Martin turned and led me into her sumptuous bathroom.

"Every time I go through this door into the bedroom, it closes behind me," he said. "I know it's Mary Frances."

Originally published in August 2008.

Michelle Green is a freelance journalist who lives in New York City and Columbia County, New York.

San Francisco Noir

Dan Saltzstein

San Francisco is well known for its transformations, the most recent one fueled by tech money that has seemingly scrubbed much of the city clean. Evidence of it tends to be easy to mock: the $4 artisanal toast, the shuttle buses carrying workers from the city interior to Silicon Valley, the preponderance of reclaimed wood. But for almost a century, the city has been indelibly linked with an enigmatic genre that might be considered an antidote to all of that: noir.

Like the characters that populate it, noir can be tough to put your finger on: a fog rolling in from the bay and coating city streets; a lonely sort of glamour perched on a bar rail; a sense of menace just over your shoulder. It is a genre that revels in ambiguity.

And so perhaps a search for noir in San Francisco was bound to yield some mysteries. Was an apartment at the edge of the Tenderloin, one lovingly restored in the decor of a bygone era, actually home not just to the writer Dashiell Hammett but to his most famous creation, Sam Spade? Who was the enigmatic woman from the 1920s whose name adorns a nearby cocktail bar, lovingly made, speakeasy style, in an actual speakeasy? And what about that doorway at the end of the alley, a pivotal location in Hammett's best-known book, *The Maltese Falcon*?

Above all: Could this city still be home to noir?

The search—through the Tenderloin, neighboring Union Square and Nob Hill, and up into North Beach—led me to a handful of disparate but passionate individuals, dedicated, in one way or another, to celebrating an era when the idea of darkness held a certain romance, when corrupted heroes lost out at the end of the tale. If noir, or at least the appreciation of it, is still alive in San Francisco, it's largely due to them. And it turns out that, though it may have gone dormant for a time, there's a broad sense of gratitude in the city for their efforts.

My guide through this urban landscape, in spirit and inspiration, was Hammett. Though he lived in San Francisco for less than a decade, his association with both the city and noir is inarguable; his early stories and novels are the urtexts of noir, and Spade its antiheroic face.

I met Don Herron, one of Hammett's preeminent appreciators, in front of the Flood Building in Union Square. The structure used to house the San Francisco offices of Pinkerton's National Detective Agency, where Hammett was an operative during the early 1920s, and is one of the few landmarks to have survived the great earthquake of 1906. It has, however, undergone a transformation: it is now home to well-trafficked outlets of the Gap and Anthropologie.

Nevertheless, it is a regular stop on the noir tours that Herron, a genial man with a slightly disheveled look and a wild white beard, has conducted in San Francisco since 1977. But soon after we started chatting, Herron said something that, as a devotee, made my heart sink. Hammett's writing, Herron said, wasn't really noir.

"Hammett is almost a precursor," he said. "He's proto-noir."

His work, which at the time was called hard-boiled or pulp, would come to encapsulate noir, a genre with a dizzying timeline. The term was coined and popularized in the late 1940s and early '50s by French film critics who used it to describe American films from that era (the 1941 John Huston adaptation of *The Maltese Falcon* is generally considered the first major noir release), many of which were, in turn, based on books written in the '20s and '30s. Hence, proto-noir.

It was hard to imagine that the building in its current incarnation could have figured into the origin story of anything besides a modest credit card debt. But when Hammett was a Pinkerton operative, the experience informed and honed his writing in a way no other mystery writer could claim. He left the agency by early 1922, soon after his arrival in the city, and turned his efforts to fiction. By 1923, he had placed a few stories in *Black Mask,* a popular pulp magazine.

Out of those stories came Hammett's two greatest books, *Red Harvest,* which featured a nameless detective called the Continental Op, and *The Maltese Falcon,* which introduced the Op's better-known successor, Sam Spade. Still, what first drew Herron to Hammett had more to do with the sheer power of his writing. In a staccato as direct as a passage out of early Hammett, he said: "I really like the stories. The fiction."

Herron and I headed from now-touristy Union Square into the Tenderloin, the notoriously seedy neighborhood where Hammett lived and set many of his stories. Of all of old San Francisco, it may be the neighborhood most intact. Many buildings date to the '20s; notable Art Deco touches appear occasionally. Demographics have changed, but its sense of character remains. On Post Street we passed a Chinese coffee shop where locals of all races lined the sidewalk, half a block from a homeless family decamped in a doorway. Crime is still a major presence in the Tenderloin, these days largely fueled by an active drug culture.

Herron stopped occasionally to point out intact spots from Hammett's life and work. Still a stunner is the Geary Theater (now home to the American Conservatory Theater), where Joel Cairo, a *Falcon* villain, attends a performance of *The Merchant of Venice*—a tidbit, Herron noted, that turned out to be the forensic evidence necessary to place the exact time of the novel's events: in the book, the British actor George Arliss is playing Shylock, a fact that dates the story to early December 1928.

We continued up through the Tenderloin, Herron pointing out probable hotel stand-ins from *Falcon,* and 891 Post Street, where Hammett lived and wrote.

The young author must have cut a striking figure walking into that building. He was tall and rail thin; tuberculosis contracted stateside while in the army during World War I made his weight a constant struggle. He had a long, handsome face topped by a gray pompadour.

In his writing, Hammett was obsessive, almost comically so, about San Francisco geography. Locations pile up like elements in a chemical equation: "Pine Street, between Leavenworth and Jones"; "the Garfield Apartments on Bush Street"; "walking over to California Street."

But no location holds a more essential place than our next stop, Burritt Street, where, in *The Maltese Falcon,* Sam Spade's partner, Miles Archer, is shot and killed by the book's femme fatale, Brigid O'Shaughnessy. (Twenty-five years ago, Herron told me, he talked the poet Lawrence Ferlinghetti, who was tasked with naming streets after prominent area literary figures, out of renaming Burritt for Hammett. He redirected him to a different alley across the street, where Hammett had lived briefly.)

A plaque does decorate Burritt, though, rather delightfully not mentioning the book by name: "On approximately this spot, Miles Archer, Sam Spade's partner, was done in by Brigid O'Shaughnessy."

As we approached the alley, Herron became more animated and narrated the pivotal scene. Like Spade in the book, he "went to the parapet, and, resting his hands on the damp coping, looked down into Stockton Street." He noted that the fog that damps the parapet—"thin, clammy, and penetrant," Hammett wrote—wasn't added just for atmosphere. "It was wintertime, remember," he said. "Everything is intentional."

We descended onto Stockton. Herron had noted a door at the end of Burritt and said he had always wondered where it led—and thought he had it figured out. A half-block away was the newly rebranded Mystic Hotel, at the tail end of a restoration. We headed up a flight of stairs and were ushered into the Burritt Room, a speakeasy-style bar fronting a tavern room in a space that was indeed once a speakeasy. The bar wasn't open yet, but we were taken up a couple more flights, out an unmarked door—and into the back end of Burritt Street. (I would later find out that denizens of the speakeasy would enter through that door.) One mystery explained.

Back at the bar, Herron and I sat down over a beer (him) and a glass of rye (me). We discussed, among dozens of other topics, what defines noir. He began by listing some essential ingredients from *The Maltese Falcon.*

"The femme fatale, the murder, the city—a lot of it at night," he said. "They coalesce into this perfect thing."

The key ingredient, though, was an unhappy ending.

"Sam Spade kind of loses," he said. "There's a sense of failure."

On our way out, a bartender, setting up for the evening rush, asked about the Hammett connection, about which he knew little. "He wrote about that alley, right?" he asked.

The Burritt Room is just one of seemingly endless spots around town housed in former speakeasy spaces. In just the first day of my trip, I hit three places that, at least in theory, Hammett could have visited during his San Francisco days.

The House of Shields is a charming spot in the Financial District that opened in 1908; during Prohibition, the drinking moved down to the basement. I made an early visit, and the crowd seemed to be a mix of after-work imbibers, cocktail enthusiasts, and tourists. The bar was renovated a few years ago, but plenty remains intact. A soaring but narrow interior features a substantial bar rail, gorgeous carved lighting fixtures, and the namesake shields, which surround a huge mirror—all original, except the mirror. I ordered a Green Point, a brooding variation on the Manhattan, with yellow chartreuse; it's a modern concoction, but felt about right.

Hammett was an alcoholic, and almost certainly spent his share of time in speakeasies. Mentions of liquors of all sorts are peppered throughout his stories and letters—but mostly straight stuff, and he apparently wasn't too picky. The rare cocktail references are as simple as could be; in *The Maltese Falcon,* Sam Spade imbibes from an apparently premixed bottle of "Manhattan cocktail" he stores in an office desk drawer.

I wandered across the street to the Palace Hotel and its stunningly elegant Garden Court restaurant, where Sam Spade stopped for lunch ("he ate hungrily without haste"), then headed up in the lovely early-evening light to North Beach, best known as home to San Francisco's Italian American community and as the heart of the Beat culture that dominated the area in the '50s.

On Columbus Avenue, across from City Lights bookstore, where many of those Beat writers congregated, is Tosca Cafe. Tosca was brand-new when Hammett came to town, having opened in 1919, and over the years became a destination dive bar, host to local regulars and celebrities alike. After it faced eviction last year, the chef April Bloomfield and Ken Friedman, her business partner, took over the space and renovated it—but with careful attention to maintaining its period feel.

The banquettes may no longer be torn, but they are intact (and generally full—the place has become one of the city's hottest spots since its renovation). The House Cappuccino, a booze-infused concoction born during Prohibition, has been updated to include Armagnac, bourbon, artisanal chocolate, and organic milk (and, by the way, no coffee). I instead sampled a pleasantly fruity Zamboanga cocktail, and dishes like the chicken liver spiedini, one of a few that are indicative of Bloomfield's nose-to-tail approach. (It's possible Sam Spade would have approved; in *The Maltese Falcon,* Hammett has him snacking on pickled pigs' feet.)

I headed behind Tosca, into the warren of alleys that blankets North Beach. They afford great views of the city, but also a what's-around-the-corner nervousness. If you are looking for the shadowy, atmospheric side of noir, this spot might capture it best. (The area also makes a cameo as the site of a rooftop chase scene in Hammett's Continental Op story "The Big Knockover.")

Back down Columbus is Comstock Saloon. The space dates to 1907 and has been continuously operating as a bar ever since. In 2010, new owners reopened it as Comstock, including the original bar, complete with a tiled urinal at its base—a not-uncommon sight in the men-only saloons of the pre-Prohibition era. The menu is peppered with classics, including my selection: a boozy '20s-era cocktail called Twelve-Mile Limit, its name a reference to the seafaring parameters of the Volstead Act.

A couple of days later, I visited the spot that has most benefited from an association with Hammett: John's Grill, in Union Square, which features portraits of local police officers, not celebrities, on its walls, and on its signage the phrase HOME OF THE MALTESE FALCON. It's not—at least not literally. The falcon behind glass on the restaurant's second floor is an oversize replica (one of a number scattered around town; the actual movie prop, likely one of two, sold at auction in 2013 for an astounding $4 million). But John's is indeed featured in the book, though briefly: Sam Spade eats a hurried lunch while waiting for a car to pick him up.

Perhaps no spot better celebrates the San Francisco–noir association better than a speakeasy-style bar secreted within another speakeasy-style bar—and in the Tenderloin, no less. Heading down Jones Street toward O'Farrell, I passed a pane of frosted glass labeled WILSON AND WILSON PRIVATE DETECTIVE AGENCY. With a password, I gained entry to Bourbon & Branch, a dimly lit and bustling cocktail bar. After a quick right through a fake wall, I headed into Wilson and Wilson, a love letter to noir, Prohibition-era drinking, and, as the name indicates, the detective trade.

Said letter is from Brian Sheehy, who owns five bars around the city—with two more opening soon, including an apothecary-themed spot next to Tosca—and is obsessive about research; what might otherwise feel gimmicky feels passionately thought-out. With the Tenderloin spots, that research, he said, included Hammett.

"The two cornerstones of his writing were reality and

authenticity," Sheehy said over the strains of '20s-era swing and jazz. "And, of course, it's hard-boiled."

The Tenderloin, he continued, "would probably be considered the hardest of all hard-boiled eggs in San Francisco."

He added, "And then when it comes to the reality, you can just step outside the door."

All that research lead Sheehy to identify the authenticity: during the Prohibition era, the space had briefly been a "beverage parlor" owned by one Frank Ipswitch, and then, for the bulk of the '20s, J. J. Russell's "cigar shop."

"These guys," Sheehy said, gesturing at the bartenders, who served drinks to a mostly youthful crowd, some dressed up for the occasion, "are our detectives. They're investigating the history of cocktails."

The result of those investigations have yielded cocktails more complex than Hammett is ever likely to have seen—as we chatted, I sipped on a Truth Serum (Scotch, *amaro,* brown-sugar-cinnamon syrup, sarsaparilla bitters, licorice root tincture). Still, the place shows a spirited attention to detail, from the elaborate theatrics of entry to a menu that includes a dossier, complete with photos and artifacts, exploring the bar's name.

That name is a playful nod to what turns out to be a mystery in progress—one that may never be fully solved. When contractors were doing construction for Bourbon & Branch, Sheehy explained, they came upon a variety of items: papers, lace underwear, cartons of Lucky Strikes. But the most mysterious and richest find was a bloodstained bag (yes, bloodstained), probably lost in May 1931. Inside were items indicating that the bag belonged to one Lorraine Adeline Wilson. Many of the items are amazingly intact, including lipstick, rouge, food stamps, and her bank ID card.

Sheehy said they have not yet been able to locate her descendants.

The night before, I found myself back at 891 Post Street, Hammett's home. I was led into the building and up a creaky antique elevator by Eddie Muller, a San Francisco native, author, and self-proclaimed "noirchaeologist." We headed to the fourth floor and entered apartment 401; I was immediately struck by a sensation of having traveled through time.

The apartment has been restored to be a simulacrum of what it might have looked like in the '20s, outfitted with all things vintage: a gramophone, a frosted-glass door, and a desk topped with a typewriter and lamp—and yet another replica falcon.

As we sat down to chat over a bottle of bourbon, Muller, a pleasantly gregarious man clad in a checkered beige suit, blue tie, and pocket square, began to explain the story of the apartment's revival. (The apartment is not open to the public; I got lucky in that Muller is one of only a couple of people with access. "It is more like a shrine than a museum," he told me, with evident pride.)

Hammett had sent letters from 891 Post Street, where he wrote three of his five novels, but the apartment's exact location had to be teased out of clues, ones embedded in *The Maltese Falcon,* by the apartment's onetime resident Bill Arney, who had taken Herron's tour years before. Spade, too, lived on Post Street, and a few further details—it's a fourth-floor apartment in proximity to the elevator; there's an unusual bend in the hallway—left only one suspect: apartment 401.

After Arney gave up the apartment, Muller contacted a friend, Robert Mailer Anderson, an acclaimed writer and philanthropist, who had the resources to make the restoration happen. The idea, Muller said, was "so that it looks like Hammett just went out for a pack of cigarettes."

Muller's love for the genre extends well beyond Hammett's work. For twelve years he has run the Noir City Film

Festival. When it started, he said, it was mostly driven by his personal passions. Now the audience is so enthusiastic that some attendees—many of them of a younger generation—dress up in period costume.

"I don't think it's a kitschy thing or a retro thing," he said. "I think people are drawn to social interaction in an age where social interaction is almost meaningless."

I asked Muller why Hammett wrote about San Francisco with enormous specificity but little emotion.

"Because he was a detective," he said. "He's writing reports." That approach became highly influential on what would eventually be called noir.

As the light began to fade and shadows crept across the room, Muller said he believed that the appeal of noir can be summed up in his three-word description of the genre: "suffering with style." Noir, he said, "presupposes the worst aspects of human nature," yet its birth "coincided with the pinnacle of American style." That juxtaposition all began with Hammett.

Part of Muller's take on noir is that, in the end, it's not about solving mysteries. The Maltese Falcon is—spoiler alert—not the Maltese Falcon. It's a fake. As I headed down Post back toward Union Square, I realized that my search for noir was itself based on a red herring. Noir is a state of mind. I thought back to a phrase Herron had used.

"It's almost a magic spell," he said.

Originally published in June 2014.

Dan Saltzstein is an editor in the Travel section of *The New York Times*. He has also written for Arts & Leisure, the Book Review, and Food.

On the Trail of Nabokov in the American West

Landon Y. Jones

For the last fifteen years my wife, Sarah, and I have driven every summer with our golden retriever from New Jersey to the Northern Rockies. I used to say that I felt like Humbert Humbert, the notoriously unreliable narrator of *Lolita,* who made a similar trip, but instead of traveling with a precocious preteen girl, I was traveling with a wife and a dewy-eyed dog.

But then I learned that Vladimir Nabokov himself had done the same thing. Nabokov wrote his disturbingly compelling classic over the course of five breathless years, from 1948 to 1953, filling five-by-seven-inch cards with notes he took riding shotgun while his designated driver, his wife, Véra, drove their black Oldsmobile from Ithaca, New York, to Arizona, Utah, Colorado, Wyoming, and Montana.

In other words, at the height of the Cold War, an expatriate Russian novelist with the resonant name of Vladimir was roaming through the reddest of red states, researching a book about a jaded aristocrat's sexual obsession with "nymphets" (a coinage the book put in the *Oxford English Dictionary*). The wonder is that Nabokov survived at all.

Today we revere *Lolita* for Nabokov's bold, multilayered subject matter and his dazzling and allusive prose. But Nabokov's most enduring contribution may be his portrait of the brash, kitschy, postwar America he observed on his cross-country journeys. Nabokov never learned to drive, and so he estimated that between 1949 and 1959 Véra drove him 150,000 miles—almost all of them on the two-lane blue highways that preceded the interstates.

Measured by the sheer number of miles covered, Nabokov is the most American of authors. He saw more of the United States than did Fitzgerald, Kerouac, or Steinbeck, and what he saw was back-roads America: personal, intimate, ticky-tack, and yet undeniably authentic. It took a Russian-born writer to awaken us to what Mark Twain knew: America is not a place; it is a road.

Nabokov went west because he was chasing butterflies. He was a passionate lepidopterist who wrote the definitive scholarly study of the genus Lycaeides and had several species named after him, such as Nabokov's wood nymph. His travels over the years took him from the Bright Angel Trail in the Grand Canyon to Utah, Colorado, and Oregon. But one of the best places to find many different species of butterflies congregating at one time was at nosebleed-high altitudes along the Continental Divide in Wyoming. Along the way, the shape of the novel took root, and he started to take notes during his butterfly hunts and write them up back in his motel rooms.

Like a twenty-first-century version of Humbert's nemesis, Clare Quilty, who pursued Humbert and Lolita across the country, I went west to chase Nabokov chasing butterflies and to piece together the plot of his most popular novel. It became a tale of three overlapping journeys: Humbert's with Lolita, Vladimir with Véra, and mine with Sarah and my retriever, Mack.

The physical geographies of *Lolita* are still there—not only Humbert's "distant mountains," "oatmeal hills," and "relentless peaks," but also the daisy chain of Kumfy Kabins, Sunset Motels, Pine View Courts, U-Beam Cottages, and Skyline Courts where Humbert took the captive Dolores Haze (Lolita's given name). Among them are some of the same motels where Vladimir and Véra checked in more than a half-century ago.

We traveled the same basic route the Nabokovs did, leaving the East, descending into Ohio, and across the Midwest—or, as Humbert put it, "We crossed Ohio, the three states beginning with 'I' and Nebraska—ah, that first whiff of the West!" We stayed in motels, too, though they lacked the cheesy allure of Humbert's "countless motor courts [proclaiming] their vacancy in neon lights, ready to accommodate salesmen, escaped convicts, impotents, family groups, as well as the most corrupt and vigorous couples." Mack was no Lolita, either, licking my hand affectionately, unlike the frequently disdainful Lolita, whose contempt only made Humbert more crazed in his obsession.

I had assumed that the sight of a man of Humbertesque age carrying a well-worn copy of *Lolita* might raise some eyebrows, but never once during my pursuit of Nabokov did I find a motel owner who had heard of the writer or his most famous work.

Like Humbert, and presumably Vladimir, we observed "that curious roadside species, Hitchhiking Man, Homo pollux of science." There are fewer hitchhikers on the interstates these days—I saw only one east of the Mississippi—but just as many roadside wonders. Like Humbert and Lolita, we stopped in restaurants festooned with EAT signs and sticky counters with sugar-drunk flies wobbling off them.

Humbert and Lolita toured "the crazy-quilt of forty-eight states"—Bourbon Street, Carlsbad Caverns, Yellowstone, Crater

Lake, fish hatcheries, cliff dwellings, and "thousands of Bear Creeks, Soda Springs, and Painted Canyons." My wife and I saw picturesque red barns in Pennsylvania Dutch country, developments of Monopoly-style bungalows, double-wides, casinos everywhere, Victorian farmhouses with double-hung windows that look like Bette Davis eyes. Huge cell towers looming like the alien creatures from the 1953 movie *War of the Worlds,* out of scale with the environment of telephone poles and road signs observed by Vladimir and Véra.

And the road signs! PASSIONS: COUPLES ADULT SUPERSTORE. GUN CONTROL MEANS USING BOTH HANDS. Both Nabokov and Humbert would have been alternatively appalled and delighted by these: COLLECTABLES SIN-A-BAR CREEK, BADLAND'S REST STOP, DICK'S TOE SERVICE. (I asked Sarah if she thought that Dick had a foot fetish. She replied that he more likely runs a service station.)

When Humbert and Lolita made their trip, religious icons on the roadside were mostly confined to the South. They saw a "replica of the Grotto of Lourdes in Louisiana." Today there are crosses everywhere—little white ones memorializing highway fatalities, gigantic ones like the 198-foot "world's largest cross" at the intersection of I-70 and I-57 in Effingham, Illinois.

And what would Nabokov have made of this sign: IF YOU DIE TONIGHT HEAVEN OR HELL? Followed by this one: GARY'S GUN SHOP.

As it happens, Véra Nabokov once packed a Browning pistol in her purse. When she applied for her license to carry one, she explained primly that it was "for protection in traveling in isolated parts of the country in the course of entomological research." She wasn't kidding. Nabokov killed a large rattlesnake during their 1953 trip to Portal, Arizona.

The state Nabokov returned to for the third time in 1952

was Wyoming. I imagine that Vladimir and Véra approached the mountains cautiously at night, cringing as trucks thundered past them "studded with colored lights, like dreadful giant Christmas trees." We knew the West had begun when we began seeing not eighty-pound hay bales in the fields but the huge, rolled-up behemoths that only a tractor can lift.

Once in Wyoming, Vladimir and Véra stayed at the now-defunct Lazy "U" Motel in Laramie, at the edge of the Medicine Bow Mountains in southeastern Wyoming. Traveling with them was their Harvard-student son, Dmitri, driving his new 1931 Model A Ford. From Laramie, the family drove over the Snowy Range, passing "a remarkably repulsive-looking willowbog, full of cowmerds and barbed wire" where Vladimir immediately stopped to pursue butterflies. They eventually arrived in Riverside, Wyoming, a dusty hamlet with "one garage, two bars, three motor courts and a few ranches, one mile from the ancient and obsolete little town Encampment (unpaved streets, wooden sidewalks)."

If Nabokov was hunting butterflies, I set about hunting for trout in the North Platte River, which flows through the same remote Saratoga Valley. Our base was the A Bar A Ranch, an upscale guest ranch that offers tennis, par-3 golf, and massages along with the traditional riding and fishing. The Nabokovs most likely checked into the present-day Riverside Garage and Cabins, on the banks of the Encampment River. Each log cabin wears its name on a shingle: COWBOY, SODBUSTER, WILDCATTER, MOUNTAINMAN, MULESKINNER.

Nabokov, who spent July 4, 1952, in Riverside, must have made note of the Independence Day festivities that day, which found a second life in *Lolita* when the European Humbert is mystified by "some great national celebration in town judging by the firecrackers, veritable bombs, that exploded all the time."

From Riverside, Vladimir and Véra took a day trip into the nearby Sierra Madre mountains to hunt butterflies, taking an "abominable local road" to the Continental Divide. Sixty-three years later, I traveled up Wyoming State Highway 70 to the same pass with Justin Howe, second-generation manager, with his wife, Lissa, of the A Bar A Ranch. The highway goes through a checkerboard of timbers and lakes to reach Battle Pass, a wide spot in the highway on the Continental Divide at 9,955 feet. From there, Howe and I bounced over a dirt Forest Service road in his truck to a pristine alpine lake where he had camped as a boy with his parents.

On the way up to the pass, as Nabokov later described it in an article for *The Lepidopterists' News,* he found the "best hunting grounds" in Wyoming and captured a number of "curious" specimens of butterflies, including the Speyeria egleis, that he later gave to collections at Cornell, Harvard, and the American Museum of Natural History.

The Nabokovs next drove north to the Wyoming town of Dubois (pronounced "Dew-BOYS"), where they hunted for butterflies along the gorgeous Wind River and stayed in a log-cabin unit at the then Red Rock Motel, now doing business as the Longhorn Ranch Lodge and RV Resort. Located under buttes on the Wind River, flecked with reds and browns, the Longhorn pays enthusiastic homage to a Western aesthetic by way of Hollywood. Attached to the office is a museum-shrine to Harley-Davidson motorcycles.

We camped in a room outfitted in knotty pine and drove into Dubois for dinner at the Cowboy Cafe, a stacked-log restaurant whose breakfast specials include spicy elk served with two eggs, hash browns, and toast. On the way we found ourselves on a busy, motel-strewn street called Ramshorn—the name Nabokov modified into Ramsdale, the name of Lolita's fictional hometown. In front of a filling station at one end of town is a heroic ten-foot-tall polymer statue of a rabbit with antlers, the mythological creature called a jackalope.

After Dubois, Vladimir and Véra went north over the dramatic Togwotee Pass, overlooking Jackson Hole, which Humbert must have had in mind when he described "heart and sky-piercing snow-veined gray colossi of stone" of the high-mountain West. They wound up in Jackson Hole and eventually Star Valley and what Nabokov called the "altogether enchanting little town" of Afton, Wyoming, a place with 2,500 people and many more elk and trout.

The motel the Nabokovs stayed in, the Corral Lodges, is still there in the center of town. Built in the 1940s, the Corral Lodges is a semicircle of fifteen single-unit log cabins huddled around a log office that used to be a gas station. In *Lolita,* it turns up as any one of the log hideaways with "glossily browned" pine logs that remind the thirteen-year-old Dolores Haze "of fried-chicken bones."

Checking in, I resisted the urge to register under a Nabokovian anagram of my own name, as Humbert and Quilty might have done. Still, I could look straight out my cabin window at the view Humbert saw: "the mysterious outlines of tablelike hills, and then red bluffs ink-blotted with junipers, and then a mountain range, dun grading into blue, and blue into dream."

On their journey west, Humbert and Lolita had gone sightseeing in a cave advertising the "world's largest stalagmite." Right down the street from the Corral Lodges we saw the "world's largest elkhorn arch," a triumphant gateway spanning the four-lane main street built entirely of more than three thousand antlers, shed every year by bull elk.

Nabokov hunted for his beloved butterflies in the nearby

mountain tributaries of the Salt River, including "the world's largest intermitting spring" on Swift Creek. The logs that had been used to build the Corral Lodges were floated down Swift Creek to be handcrafted in the distinctive "Swedish cope" style of cutting corners and chinking. Something about the Rocky Mountain West reminded Nabokov of his youth in Russia. "Some part of me must have been born in Colorado," he wrote to the critic Edmund Wilson, "for I am constantly recognizing things with a delicious pang."

The Nabokovs made their return trip through Jackson Hole, where Dmitri would vacation with the Harvard Mountaineering Club. In 1951, they had stayed at the Teton Pass Ranch, a few miles west of tiny Wilson, Wyoming. It no longer exists, but one of its cabins has been moved to the nearby Trail Creek Ranch, founded in 1946 by Betty Woolsey, captain of the first American women's ski team. A working ranch, it offers weekly cabin rentals and deep-powder skiing. A few miles away is Nora's Fish Creek Inn, built in the 1930s, a popular hangout with locals like the celebrity lawyer Gerry Spence.

Our final stop on the Nabokov Trail in Wyoming was the Battle Mountain Ranch on the Hoback River, southeast of Jackson. A working guest ranch when Véra and Vladimir visited on their butterfly quest, it has since moved downriver and is now the Broken Arrow Ranch, home of the nonprofit City Kids Wilderness Project. Every summer it hosts a camp for inner-city children and teenagers from Washington, D.C. During the off-season, the cabins are rented out to help cover the costs of the camp. It seems fitting that the guest ranch where Nabokov stayed while writing *Lolita* is now operating as a resource for disadvantaged children.

A year after his 1952 trip across Wyoming, Nabokov finished the "great and coily thing" that had haunted him for a half-century. Concerned about a negative reaction, he had tried at least twice to burn the cards on which he had written the manuscript. Each time, Véra rescued them from the fire. Rejected in the United States, *Lolita* was first published in 1955 in France, and the *London Sunday Express* called it "sheer unrestrained pornography." But the novelist Graham Greene praised it, rescuing it from the critical flames.

It was published then, to a tumultuous reception, in the United States in 1958. It became an instant No. 1 *New York Times* best seller, and the movie rights were grabbed up by Stanley Kubrick for $150,000. It has been in print ever since, and today Nabokov's reputation has never been higher, with new books published about him seemingly every year, most recently Robert Roper's insightful biography, *Nabokov in America*.

Reader, please allow me to give Mr. Humbert Humbert the last word. On the final pages of the novel, Humbert finds himself back in the Rocky Mountain West. In a scene Nabokov himself anticipated in a letter written in 1951 to Edmund Wilson, Humbert walks to a cliff on the edge of a mountain where he rhapsodically and perhaps ruefully reports hearing "a melodious unity of sounds rising like a vapor from a small mining town that lay at my feet, in a fold of the valley . . . all these sounds were of one nature, that no other sounds but these came from the streets of the transparent town, with the women at home and the men away. Reader! What I heard was but the melody of children at play . . ."

That was exactly what my wife and I heard as we drove out of the Broken Arrow Ranch on the Hoback River. The happy melody of children at play.

Originally published in May 2016.

Landon Y. Jones is the former managing editor of *People* and *Money* magazines and the author of *William Clark and the Shaping of the West*.

In Search of Flannery O'Connor

Lawrence Downes

The sun was white above the trees, and sinking fast. I was a few miles past Milledgeville, Georgia, somewhere outside of Toomsboro, on a two-lane highway that rose and plunged and twisted through red clay hills and pine woods. I had no fixed destination, just a plan to follow a back road to some weedy field in time to watch the sun go down on Flannery O'Connor's Georgia.

Somewhere outside Toomsboro is where, in O'Connor's best-known short story, "A Good Man Is Hard to Find," a family has a car accident and a tiresome old grandmother has an epiphany. The fog of petty selfishness that has shrouded her life clears when she feels a sudden spasm of kindness for a stranger, a brooding prison escapee who calls himself the Misfit.

Of course, that's also the moment that he shoots her in the chest, but in O'Connor's world, where good and evil are as real as a spreading puddle of blood, it amounts to a happy ending. The grandmother is touched by grace at the last possible moment, and she dies smiling.

"She would of been a good woman," the Misfit said, "if it had been somebody there to shoot her every minute of her life."

O'Connor's short stories and novels are set in a rural South where people know their places, mind their manners, and do horrible things to one another. It's a place that somehow hovers outside of time, where both the New Deal and the New Testament feel like recent history. It's soaked in violence and humor, in sin and in God. He may have fled the modern world, but in O'Connor's he sticks around, in the sun hanging over the treeline, in the trees and farm beasts, and in the characters who roost in the memory like gargoyles. It's a land haunted by Christ—not your friendly hug-me Jesus, but a ragged figure who moves from tree to tree in the back of the mind, pursuing the unwilling.

Many people—me, for instance—are in turn haunted by O'Connor. Her doctrinally strict, mordantly funny stories and novels are as close to perfect as writing gets. Her language is so spare and efficient, her images and characters' speech so vivid, they burn into the mind. Her strange Southern landscape was one I knew viscerally but, until this trip, had never set foot in. I had wondered how her fictional terrain and characters, so bizarre yet so blindingly real, might compare with the real places and people she lived among and wrote about.

Hence my pilgrimage to Milledgeville, and my race against the setting sun.

O'Connor's characters shimmer between heaven and hell, acting out allegorical dramas of sin and redemption. There's Hazel Motes, the sunken-eyed army veteran who tries to reject God by preaching "the Church of Christ Without Christ, where the blind don't see, the lame don't walk and what's dead stays that way." Hulga Hopewell, the deluded intellectual who loses her wooden leg to a thieving Bible salesman she had assumed was as dumb as a stump. The pious Mrs. Turpin, whose heart pours out thank-yous to Jesus for not having made her black or white trash or ugly. Mrs. Freeman, the universal busybody: "Besides the neutral expression that she wore when she was alone, Mrs. Freeman had two others, forward and reverse, that she used for all her human dealings."

People like these can't be real, and yet they breathe on the page. And there is nothing allegorical about the earthly stage they strut on: it's the red clay of central Georgia, in and around Milledgeville, where O'Connor spent most of her short life. She lived with her widowed mother on the family farm, called Andalusia, just outside Milledgeville, writing and raising peacocks and chickens from 1951 until her death in 1964 at age thirty-nine, of lupus.

O'Connor was a misfit herself, as a Roman Catholic in the Bible Belt, a religiously devout ironist writing for nonbelievers. She liked to gently mock the redneckedness of her surroundings. "When in Rome," she once wrote, "do as you done in Milledgeville."

But Milledgeville is not the backwoods. It's a city of 19,000, on the Oconee River in Baldwin County, thirty miles from Macon. It is the former capital of Georgia, trashed by General Sherman on his March to the Sea. It has a huge state psychiatric hospital and a prominent liberal-arts college, Georgia College and State University. The old capitol building is now home to a military school. There is a district of big antebellum homes with columns and fussy flowerbeds. Oliver Hardy lived here when he was young and fat but not yet famous.

Milledgeville now looms huge beyond these modest attributes because of O'Connor, or Mary Flannery, as she was known in town. Her output was slender: two novels, a couple dozen short stories, a pile of letters, essays, and criticism. But her reputation has grown steadily since she died. Her *Complete*

Stories won the National Book Award for Fiction in 1971. Her collected letters, *The Habit of Being,* banished the misperception that she was some sort of crippled hillbilly Emily Dickinson. They revealed instead a gregarious, engaged thinker who corresponded widely and eagerly, and who might have ranged far had illness not forced her to stay home and write.

O'Connor's own trail begins about two hundred miles southeast of Milledgeville, in Savannah, where she was born and spent her childhood among a community of Irish Roman Catholics, of whom her parents, Edward and Regina Cline O'Connor, were prominent members. The O'Connor home, on a mossy historic square downtown, is landmarked. The Roman Catholic Cathedral of Saint John the Baptist is across the square, although nothing in it informs a visitor that one of the country's most prominent apologists for the Catholic faith worshipped and went to parochial school there.

O'Connor learned her craft at the University of Iowa and at Yaddo, the writers' colony in Saratoga Springs, New York. She lived for a while in Connecticut with the poet Robert Fitzgerald and his wife, Sally, and thought she was leaving the South behind.

But she got sick, and went home to Andalusia, four miles north of Milledgeville.

Andalusia was a working dairy farm run by Flannery's mother, Regina, who as a prominent widow-businesswoman was something of a novelty in town. No one has lived there since O'Connor died in 1964 and Regina moved back into downtown Milledgeville.

Strip malls have long since filled the gap between town and farm, and you now find Andalusia by driving past a Walmart, a Chick-fil-A, and a Lowe's Home Improvement Warehouse, where a man shot his wife and killed himself a few days before I arrived. You pass a billboard for Sister Nina, a fortune-teller who reads palms in a home office cluttered with votive candles and pictures of Catholic saints. (To judge from one consultation, she is capable of divining that a visitor is a bearer of dark sorrows, but not exactly skilled at pinpointing what those sorrows might be.)

Across the highway from an America's Best Value Inn, a tiny sign marks the dirt road to Andalusia. I turned left, went through an open gate, and there it was, a two-story white frame house with columns and brick steps leading up to a wide screened porch. Through the screens I could see a long, tidy row of white rocking chairs.

I drove around back, between the magnolia and pecan trees, parked on the grass, and walked back to the house past a wooden water tower and an ancient garage, splintered and falling in on itself.

I was met at the door by Craig R. Amason, the executive director of the Flannery O'Connor–Andalusia Foundation, the nonprofit organization set up to sustain her memory and preserve her home. When the affable Amason, the foundation's sole employee, is not showing pilgrims around, he is raising money to fix up the place, a project that is a few million dollars short of its goal. The foundation urgently wants to restore the house and outbuildings to postcard perfection, to ensure its survival. In 2006, the Georgia Trust for Historic Preservation placed Andalusia on its list of most endangered places in the state.

For now, the twenty-one-acre property is in a captivating state of decay.

There is no slow buildup on this tour; the final destination is the first doorway on your left: O'Connor's bedroom and study, converted from a sitting room because she couldn't climb the stairs. Amason stood back, politely granting me silence as I gathered my thoughts and drank in every detail.

This is where O'Connor wrote, for three hours every day. Her bed had a faded blue-and-white coverlet. The blue drapes, in a 1950s pattern, were dingy, and the paint was flaking off the walls. There was a portable typewriter, a hi-fi with classical LPs, a few bookcases. Leaning against an armoire were the aluminum crutches that O'Connor used, with her rashy swollen legs and crumbling bones, to get from bedroom to kitchen to porch.

There are few opportunities for so intimate and unguarded a glimpse into the private life of a great American writer. Amason told me that visitors sometimes wept on the bedroom threshold.

The center hall's cracked plaster walls held a few family photographs: an adorable Flannery, age three, scowling at a picture book, and her smiling older self on an adjacent wall. There was a picture of Edward O'Connor, but none of Regina, who died in 1995 at ninety-nine. In the kitchen, an old electric range with fat heating elements sat near a chunky refrigerator, the very one Flannery bought for her mother after selling the rights to "The Life You Save May Be Your Own" for a TV movie in which Gene Kelly butchered the role of the con man Tom T. Shiftlet. In the center of the room, a small wooden table was set for two.

A walk around the grounds summoned all manner of O'Connor images. In a field of goldenrod, a lone hinny, a horse-donkey hybrid named Flossie, with grotesque clumps of fat on her rump, kept a reserved distance. I followed a path below the house down to a pond buzzing with dragonflies. Amason had told me to keep to the mowed areas to avoid snakes, so I wasn't too surprised to encounter a black rat snake, stretched out like a five-foot length of industrial cable, by a footbridge at the far edge of the pond. I tickled it with a turkey feather and it curled to strike faster than I could blink.

Back in Milledgeville's tidy downtown, I went to Georgia College and State University, which was the Georgia State College for Women when O'Connor went there. The library displays her desk, paintings, and other artifacts, and a librarian took me in the back to see her papers and books—a daunting array of fiction, classics, and Catholic theology. The book of Updike's poetry looked well read, but not as much as the Kierkegaard (*Fear and Trembling* and *The Sickness Unto Death*), whose bindings were falling off.

I found Sacred Heart Church, where Flannery and Regina worshipped, and was amazed when the pastor, the Reverend Michael McWhorter, suggested that I come back the next morning for the funeral service of O'Connor's first cousin Catherine Florencourt Firth, whose ashes were coming home from Arizona. At the funeral, I sat quietly in a back row, then shrank into my jacket when Father McWhorter announced my presence from the pulpit. But the mourners, clearly accustomed to Flannery admirers, nodded graciously at me. The pastor had a shiny round head and tidy beard, and applied incense with medieval vigor, sending curls of sweet smoke around Firth's urn until the tiny sanctuary was entirely fogged in.

I am not accustomed to crashing funerals, so I did not linger afterward. I was grateful for the kind offers from Mrs. Firth's relations to come back and visit longer next time.

My last stop was also O'Connor's: Memory Hill Cemetery, in the middle of town, where mother, father, and daughter lie side-by-side-by-side under identical flat marble slabs. A state prison detail was prowling the grounds, trimming hedges. They had sloppily strewn oleander branches on Flannery's grave, which I brushed clean. I found a plastic bouquet to place at its head. I looked at the dates:

MARCH 25, 1925–AUGUST 3, 1964

She died young, but not without saying what she wanted to say. I thought back to my journey the night before, when I captured the O'Connor sunset I had been looking for. I found a road that led down to the edge of a kaolin mine. Standing beside huge mounds of white chalky dirt, surrounded by deep treads left in the red clay by earth-moving machinery, I watched as a sentence from one of my favorite stories, "A Temple of the Holy Ghost," slowly unfolded, as if for me alone:

"The sun was a huge red ball like an elevated Host drenched in blood and when it sank out of sight, it left a line in the sky like a red clay road hanging over the trees."

By the road's edge I spied an unusual-looking vine. It was a passionflower, with purple blossoms that looked like a crown of thorns, and the nails for Christ's hands and feet. I picked a bunch of strands, with their immature fruit, like little green boiled eggs, and got back onto the road to Milledgeville, under a blackening sky, to put them in some water.

Originally published in February 2007.

Walking the Streets of Roth's Memory

David Carr

It is a school day. Kids swarm from Weequahic High School and the adjacent elementary school into an epic October afternoon, shouting plans and see-you-laters into the bluest sky possible. With eyes slightly crossed, you can see what Philip Roth saw six decades ago as a young man.

In Roth's novel *The Plot Against America,* the Weequahic neighborhood of the 1930s and '40s is a bootstrap paradise—a cultural preserve to some, a ghetto to others. Walk across the street from the school to the tidy block of Summit Avenue today, and you will find almost identical two-and-a-half-story, wood-frame houses, topped by gabled roofs and redbrick stoops, including the second one in from Keer Avenue, Roth's old home. Ring the bell and the door opens.

"The lady of the house is not home," said a polite, somewhat startled elderly black woman. "Come back when she is and you can talk to her."

And Philip Roth?

"I know nothing of him," she said.

Who can blame her? The Weequahic Jews—the conflicted, foot-in-both-worlds strivers of Roth's fiction and his youth—are gone, propelled first by their own upward mobility and then by the riots of 1967. The neighborhood avoided the worst of it, but the riots wiped out much of the merchant class when stores elsewhere in Newark were looted to the walls in a burst of atavistic rage. White people, including the Jews, were scared and left, and black people gradually became the majority. What remains is still a neighborhood of people with hopes of mobility, but Chancellor Avenue, the heart of the Weequahic neighborhood, no longer has any commercial viability. Turn down the wrong block, some locals say, and commerce of another sort, furtive and transitory, is under way.

On the south side of Newark, hard behind the airport, Weequahic was once a place to be attained. The recently arrived Jews scrimped along in the cold-water flats in Newark's old Third Ward, and then grabbed at the bottom rung of the middle class by moving up the hill to Weequahic.

In *The Plot Against America,* a dark fantasy of what might have been, their purchase on a version of the American dream is threatened and all but severed when Charles Lindbergh, a transatlantic hero known for admiring Hitler, improbably defeats Franklin Roosevelt for the presidency in 1940. An accommodationist who cuts a deal with the Nazis, Lindbergh keeps America out of World War II and puts American Jewry on the run. Newark, with more than 70,000 Jews and more than fifty synagogues, is immediately imperiled, most notably by one of its own, the fictional Rabbi Lionel Bengelsdorf, who sells out in grand style. Seen through the wide eyes of a preteen version of Philip Roth himself, his hermetic little neighborhood is beset by fear of a pogrom storming in from those middle places in America, where Jews are often viewed as aliens or worse. In the book, he and his family fight, sacrificing nearly everything, to stay in a neighborhood they love, a place that very much loved them back.

Phil watches much of the grim future unfold at the Newsreel Theater in sixty-minute increments. There, sitting in the dark next to his father, he sees Hitler roll across Europe unopposed in this nightmarish rewrite of American history. The Newsreel Theater was at the nexus of Market and Broad, an intersection that was among the world's busiest in the '30s and '40s. Much of the traffic is gone, and the building has been broken up into three storefronts, the middle of which is host to an array of discounted shoes. Hyo Kang, the owner of Golden Shoes, said he had heard it was once a movie theater, but that was before his time.

Most Jews in the city lived on the large, low hill on the southern side, while Italians were in the old First Ward to the north, and Irish and German immigrants down in the Ironbound. In the book, Phil sees his Newark unfold as the bus grinds its way up the hill on Clinton Avenue. The Riviera, the fancy hotel where his mother and father had spent their wedding night and where machers and wise guys cut deals down in the bar, rears into view. It is now a fairly rundown hotel, the Divine Hotel Riviera, named after Father Divine, a religious leader who founded a sect in the first part of the last century. Higher on the hill behind it sits Hopewell Baptist Church, but the Torah relief topping the structure suggests the worshipers it once held, the reform members of Temple B'nai Jeshurun.

Farther up Clinton, Temple B'nai Abraham stuns with its size, a massive oval that overpowers even the biggest churches in the neighborhood. Nat Bodian, a dogged historian of old Newark, used to take his wife there when they were courting, making a date out of a night of listening to Rabbi Joachim

Prinz. It, too, has been repurposed, now serving as the Deliverance Temple.

Up on the edge of Clinton Hill, the Roosevelt Theater, a former gathering place for the neighborhood, has become a Christian religious storefront, its marquee gone and its architectural filigree painted over. Across the street, a once-glorious mansion, built by one of the prosperous Jewish merchants and professionals who remade the neighborhood, is a portrait of entropy, its Victorian details gradually being pulled back down to earth by Newton's laws.

Some parts of the neighborhood remain unchanged. Weequahic Park, designed by Frederick Law Olmsted, has an urban lake and a golf course. At sunset on an autumn day, a few people traced its paths through light dappled by the overhanging trees.

Present-day Newark has its charms—a relatively new performing arts center, a minor-league baseball team, and the incomparable carnivorous feasting in the Ironbound section—but the Newark of Roth's books is nothing more than a memory held in common by people who once lived there.

"In some places around my neighborhood, I am still able to see what used to be there," Roth said in an interview. "But the further I get out into the city, it is just a desert. I can only vaguely remember what was there."

Newark has served as a backdrop for many of Roth's books—*Portnoy's Complaint, American Pastoral, I Married a Communist*—and Roth says its evocation is more than a trick of memory.

"It is part and parcel of each book," he said. "I want those places to seem true, and I want to be as precise as I can in laying out the social landscape."

He succeeds, often to eerie effect, given how profoundly

the city and his former neighborhood have changed. Someone retracing the steps of the young protagonist in the book does not have to strain much to hear echoes. Saint Peter's Orphanage, a Catholic facility that took up almost four blocks in a Jewish neighborhood, is gone, replaced by ball fields and a park. But walk down Goldsmith Avenue near where the orphanage stood, and you can almost hear Phil's bitter cousin Alvin, disabled after serving with the Canadian army in the war that Lindbergh's America turned its back on, chanting at the dice in a game of craps.

Take a right onto Hobson Street, and a scene in the book in which an FBI investigator quizzes Phil about his cousin springs to memory. Stop by the fence on the old orphanage property and you can almost picture the horses that used to graze there.

Elliot B. Sudler, a retired pharmacist, remembers the Roths, and he remembers those horses. On a dare, he once climbed the fence and mounted one. "I couldn't get off," he recalled. "I was on that horse for fifteen minutes before I finally slid off."

In one of the book's key inflection points, the young Roth wanders into that horse enclosure in the dark and pays dearly.

Sudler was a few years ahead of Roth at Weequahic High School, but he remembers him well. "He was a dreamy, creamy kind of guy," Sudler said. "He didn't go by facts, but he always seemed to know what was going to happen."

At the very top of the hill on Chancellor Avenue are the grade school, where Roth's mother served on the PTA, and the high school that served as the community's claim on the future. On a recent Saturday, Joe Komp, a custodian at the high school, was waiting for some sports teams to come in from the athletic field. He opened the school door and revealed an Art Deco marvel, built in 1932, with WPA murals, marble facing, and stunning tile floors. A plaque dedicated to men who died in World War II—men with names like Pollack and Greenberg—testifies that Roth's novel was a flight of horrid fancy.

The school was renowned for a good basketball team and ferocious scholarship. In its yearbook, the *Legend,* Philip Roth, at sixteen, was described as "a boy of real intelligence, combined with wit and common sense." He is the most famous graduate, but the alumni also include many successful executives, judges, doctors, and rabbis.

Jack Kirsten, a retired judge, did well for himself and his family, and now lives in Short Hills, New Jersey. But he lived below the Roths when they moved down to Leslie Street in 1942, after their landlord raised the rent on Summit.

"When I read *Portnoy's Complaint,* everything was familiar to me," Judge Kirsten said. "I gave it to my mother, and she said, 'I can't understand why such a nice Jewish boy would write such a dirty book.' Philip wrote a letter to her and told her that his bark is worse than his bite."

After Roth's parents moved to Elizabeth, he used to drive through the old neighborhood on the way to visit them, and he went back for more looks at it before writing *The Plot Against America.*

Roth said the neighborhood does not cohere the way it used to because massive ribbons of I-78 and the Garden State Parkway now dissect its streets. "The neighborhood was destroyed by the highways as much as anything else," he said.

Up on Summit, memory lingers. In *The Plot,* Phil sees his neighborhood with new eyes after a rain, causing him to pledge a childish fealty that will not last:

> *Tinged with the bright after-storm light, Summit Avenue was as agleam with life as a pet, my own silky, pulsating pet, washed clean*

by sheets of falling water and now stretched to its full length to bask in the bliss.

Nothing would ever get me to leave here.

Originally published in October 2004.

David Carr (1956–2015) was the media columnist for *The New York Times* and author of the memoir *The Night of the Gun.*

The Land and Words of Mary Oliver, the Bard of Provincetown

Mary Duenwald

By half-past five on a morning in early May, the sun rising over Blackwater Pond had already brightened the pinewoods. I stood in a wide natural path, carpeted with brown-red needles, that rises up the forested dune from the southwest side of the pond. In the high branches of the pines and beeches and honeysuckles, the birds were carrying on their racket—warblers, goldfinches, woodpeckers, doves, and chickadees. But on the sandy ground among the trunks, nothing moved. Perfect stillness. Could this have been where Mary Oliver had seen the deer?

She had written about them in more than one poem, but most famously in "Five A.M. in the Pinewoods":

I'd seen
their hoofprints in the deep
needles and knew
they ended the long night

under the pines, walking
like two mute

and beautiful women toward
the deeper woods, so I

got up in the dark and
went there. They came
slowly down the hill
and looked at me sitting under

the blue trees, shyly
they stepped
closer and stared
from under their thick lashes . . .
. . . . This
is not a poem about a dream,
though it could be . . .

If the deer hadn't been at this particular spot, they must have been no farther than a mile or two away, because this small patch of earth, a two-mile-long smattering of a dozen or so freshwater ponds on the northwest tip of Cape Cod, is where Mary Oliver, a Pulitzer Prize–winning poet who has a devoted audience, has set most of her poetry since she arrived in Provincetown in the 1960s.

She moved to Provincetown to be with the woman she loved, and to whom she has dedicated her books of poetry, Molly Malone Cook. As Oliver explained it in *Our World,* a collection of Cook's photographs that she published two years after Cook's death in 2005, the two of them had met at Steepletop, the home of Edna Saint Vincent Millay, when both of them were there in the late 1950s visiting Norma Millay, the late poet's sister, and her husband. "I took one look and fell, hook and tumble," Oliver said.

Cook was drawn to Provincetown, where she ran a gallery and later opened a bookstore, and once Oliver was there with her, "I too fell in love with the town," she recalled, "that marvelous convergence of land and water; Mediterranean light; fishermen who made their living by hard and difficult work from frighteningly small boats; and, both residents and sometime visitors, the many artists and writers. . . . M. and I decided to stay."

Before long, she had discovered the Province Lands: 3,500 acres of national parkland tucked away on the other side of Route 6 from Provincetown itself. The tract was named the Province's Lands in 1691, when the Massachusetts Bay Colony became a royal province as it absorbed Plymouth Colony and the land that had belonged to the Pilgrims (and absorbed Maine as well). This is not the Cape Cod of beaches and sailboats, shops and art galleries, but rather a small, shady, and cool wilderness quietly teeming with life—a geological and biological wonder that stands in relative obscurity on the Cape.

"Most people think of Cape Cod as beaches and ocean, but quite a bit of it is forested, and there are all types of different freshwater ponds," said Robert Cook, a wildlife ecologist for the Cape Cod National Seashore. This part of the Cape is relatively new land. It is made not of glacial moraine, as the rest of Cape Cod is, but of sand that eroded from cliffs farther south, and was shaped into parabolic dunes by the Atlantic winds and currents. As this sand settled, ponds were formed in depressions in the dunes, and a rich deciduous forest mixed with strands of pine grew up from the sandy soil.

This is what the Pilgrims beheld in 1620, when they landed at the future site of Provincetown. The ponds and forests of the Province Lands are, Cook said, a small "undisturbed remnant" of Cape Cod's ancient past. Oliver's poems draw vivid pictures of all manner of life in this tightly contained ecosystem: blacksnakes swimming, foxes running, goldfinches singing, blue herons wading, and lilies that "break open over the dark water."

At Blackwater Pond the tossed waters have settled
after a night of rain.
I dip my cupped hands. I drink
a long time. It tastes
like stone, leaves, fire. It falls cold
into my body, waking the bones. I hear them
deep inside me, whispering
oh what is that beautiful thing
that just happened?

Follow Oliver's lead to the edges of Blackwater Pond and you can have something approaching a primal experience of Cape Cod. You won't be alone, especially in summer, when crowds gather to see the locally beloved water lilies that blanket the ponds. But that's why it pays to go at dawn, as the poet prefers to do.

Finding your way through her stomping grounds without a guide is not simple. Her 2004 collection, *Why I Wake Early,* is sold in the shop at the Province Lands Visitor Center nevertheless, and although she is well loved in Provincetown and sometimes gives readings at the town library, the rangers who were there on the day I stopped in had not heard of her. Nor had they heard of her beloved Blackwater Pond, which is not even marked on the Cape Cod National Seashore map.

This is especially odd, given that Blackwater is the only one of the ponds in the area that is encircled by a well-groomed and marked trail, the Beech Forest Trail. This can be reached by car, less than half a mile up Race Point Road from Route 6, on the left, and there is a roomy parking lot at the trailhead. Most pedestrian visitors to the Province Lands ponds confine their walks to this trail. But there are ways to get deeper into the woods and see the other ponds.

You can make your way toward Great, Pasture, Bennett, and the ponds to the southwest of Blackwater on the bicycle path, though when I was there, it was flooded and impassable by foot at some points. Also, there are a couple of very subtly marked fire roads leading into the pond area from Route 6, between Race Point Road and Route 6A to the west. Once on the fire lanes, you come across smaller paths leading here and there, dead-ending as often as not at a swampy edge of a pond, blocked by weeds and trees. If you can find your way to Clapps Pond, you can take a footpath all the way around. But this is not easy to find; it's not marked on the park maps, and in the woods, it's easy to get lost.

"It's one of the secret places the locals know," said Polly Brunnell, an artist who lives in Provincetown and calls herself a pond walker. "Tourists don't know about it at all. I don't tell too many people about it. It's our townie place."

But even if you don't find a particular pond, the paths leading away from the fire road allow for a nice walk. The climbs are gentle, and in most places the sandy soil is so cushy you can go barefoot, which helps set the proper pace. You'd need to spend a long time here, probably several hours each morning for at least a year, to see all the life Oliver describes and the annual rhythms she chronicles—cattails rising in spring, water lilies opening in summer, goldenrod rustling in the fall breezes, and vines frozen in winter. Or you can simply take her poetry along with you for a long walk in the woods. Based as they are on her patient and scientifically informed observations, her poems allow you to see the deeper life of this little American wilderness.

Down at Blackwater
blacksnake went swimming, scrolling
close to the shore, only
his head above the water, the long
yard of his body just beneath the surface,
quick and gleaming. . . .

I carried a handful of paperback collections of her poems, and I also downloaded her hour-long CD *At Blackwater Pond,* on which Oliver reads forty-two of her poems, and listened as I sought out the places and creatures she describes. (Oliver herself has said that "poetry is meant to be heard.")

To follow in Oliver's footsteps is not to power walk, but to stroll and stop often to take in sights and sounds and feelings. As she told an interviewer fifteen years ago: "When things are going well, you know, the walk does not get rapid or get anywhere: I finally just stop, and write. That's a successful walk!"

Once, she added, she found herself in the woods with no pen and so later went around and hid pencils in some of the trees.

In her back pocket, Oliver carries a three-by-five-inch, hand-sewn notebook for recording impressions and phrases that often end up in poems, she explained in 1991. In that same essay, she also revealed a few of the entries, including these:

"The cry of the killdeer / like a tiny sickle."

"little myrtle warblers / kissing the air"

"When will you have a little pity for / every soft thing / that walks through the world, / yourself included?"

After some hours in the quiet Province Lands, Provincetown itself, with its busy shopping and eating district, exerts a pull. I drove back into the town, parked on Commercial Street, and stopped at the Mews Café for brunch. Seated in the beach-level dining room, I watched the waves smooth the harbor sand while I ate lobster Benedict. Some of the other patrons walked through an open door into the breezy sunshine, where people were strolling on the sand. Oliver still lives on Commercial Street, on the eastern side of Provincetown, in a building that backs onto the harbor. She has described it as being "about 10 feet from the water"—unless there is a storm blowing from the southeast, and then it is "about a foot from the water." A child of the Midwest, she grew up in Maple Heights, Ohio, outside Cleveland, where her father was a social studies teacher and an athletics coach in the Cleveland public schools. She began writing poetry at the age of fourteen, and in 1953, at seventeen and just out of high school, she got the idea to simply drive off to Austerlitz in upstate New York to visit the home of the late Edna Saint Vincent Millay.

She and Norma, the poet's sister, became friends, Oliver recalled in *Our World,* and so she "more or less lived there for the next six or seven years, running around the 800 acres like a child, helping Norma, or at least being company to her." Eventually she moved to Greenwich Village, and it was on a return visit to the Millay house that she met Cook.

From 1963 to October 2014, when her most recent collection, *Blue Horses,* came out, she had published twenty volumes of poetry, plus seven books of prose; all but two of her books are still in print. Her Pulitzer Prize came in 1984, and in 1992 she won the National Book Award. From time to time over what she has called her "40-year conversation" with Cook, she or the couple would go off to places like Sweet Briar, Virginia, and Bennington, Vermont, where

Oliver would teach poetry writing. But their home base was always Provincetown.

"People say to me: wouldn't you like to see Yosemite? The Bay of Fundy? The Brooks Range?" she wrote in *Long Life,* a book of essays. "I smile and answer, 'Oh yes—sometime,' and go off to my woods, my ponds, my sun-filled harbor, no more than a blue comma on the map of the world but, to me, the emblem of everything."

She does give some of her time to the sea, walking along the shore—especially, it seems, along Herring Cove, just northwest of Provincetown, below the curled top of Cape Cod. She has told in her poetry of picking up an ancient eardrum bone from a pilot whale, and has written about the whelks: "always cracked and broken— / clearly they have been traveling / under the sky-blue waves / for a long time."

Herring Cove is a peaceful stretch of sand for a morning walk, one of the rare beaches on the East Coast that faces west. And it comes with two large parking lots. A stroll from the car northwest to where the ocean water was streaming onto the beach, and back, took about forty minutes.

Another day, wanting a different kind of exercise, I tried my hand—or rather, my feet—at crossing the Provincetown breakwater, a half-mile-long row of enormous cubes of stone. The Army Corps of Engineers constructed this barrier in 1911 to keep shifting sands from the dunes out of the harbor. People of all ages were crossing with ease, it appeared, leaping in places from one angled surface of rock to the next. But once I got out a ways, I starting thinking about how long it might take to make it all the way there and back (it is said to take one to two hours each way, depending on your pace) and what would happen if I turned an ankle. The reward for making it all the way across is a walk on Long Point, a curving strip of beach less than two miles long, with lighthouses on either end, but I didn't make it.

At dawn the next morning, I was back in the woods.

Walking the trails, you may not see every sight Mary Oliver's eyes have taken in, but you will be hard-pressed to find anything she hasn't turned into verse. I thought of this as I watched a half-dozen little white butterflies flitting around the sunlit spots on a trail in front of me, then looked through her books to see if she had written about them. Indeed, in the collection *Blue Iris,* I found "Seven White Butterflies": "Seven white butterflies / delicate in a hurry look / how they bang the pages / of their wings as they fly. . . ."

After a few days in the Province Lands, just before leaving, I stopped back at good old Blackwater Pond. Birdwatchers were quietly making their way along the Beech Forest Trail, stopping to aim their binoculars at orioles and black-throated blue warblers. I sat beside the water under a bunch of pines and opened Oliver's *American Primitive* to reread "In Blackwater Woods" and imagine this landscape in other seasons, when "the trees / are turning / their own bodies / into pillars / of light" and "cattails / are bursting and floating away," part of the cycle of life here that Oliver has watched so many times. Her appeal to her audience seems especially clear here—her sharp eye, her tugs of emotion as she relates the outer world to a deeper interior experience:

To live in this world

you must be able
to do three things:
to love what is mortal;
to hold it

against your bones knowing
your own life depends on it;
and, when the time comes to let it go,
to let it go.

Originally published in July 2009.

Mary Duenwald is an editor at *Bloomberg View.*

Finding the Spirit of H. P. Lovecraft in Providence

Noel Rubinton

To walk through the streets of Providence, particularly those of the city's verdant, historic East Side, is to be deep in Lovecraft-land.

Though H. P. Lovecraft was not widely appreciated during his prolific but brief writing career in the early 1900s, his love for and connection to his Rhode Island hometown were near absolute. His stock has risen dramatically in the worlds of horror and science fiction literature in recent years, and so has his place as a local hero.

When I moved to Providence not long ago, I was compelled to learn more about Lovecraft. It proved a fateful decision, because to know Lovecraft is to know a great deal about the city.

The year 2015 marked the 125th anniversary of his birth, and it's clear that Lovecraft is more studied and more hip than ever, certainly far more than during his relatively short life (he died at forty-six in 1937). More than two thousand people from around the world came that summer to a four-day

NecronomiCon (named after the fictional book Lovecraft created) with more than a hundred programs.

In summer 2016, the city's first H. P. Lovecraft Film Festival in Providence debuted, showing short and feature-length films based on his life and work, along with walking tours and Lovecraft-inspired gaming.

Lovecraft's higher visibility has come after a radical reassessment by literary critics. He has gone from an eccentric minor author of fantasy and horror tales for the pulp magazines of the 1920s, to one of the seminal figures in the development of horror and science fiction genres. He is credited as an influence on many writers, including Stephen King and Robert Bloch, best known as the writer of *Psycho.* As Lovecraft's reputation has grown in recent years, so has the recognition that some of his writing was racist; as a result, the World Fantasy Awards last year stopped using his face as a model for their trophy.

In his lifetime, Lovecraft's work gained little attention. He worked ceaselessly, spending his days and nights writing stories with layered and complicated prose, and he was paid a pittance to rewrite the fiction of others. On top of that, he spent many hours each day writing letters to fans and favorite correspondents. Estimates are that he wrote a staggering eighty thousand letters in his lifetime.

When he wasn't writing, Lovecraft took long walks. His fiction, full of high-styled descriptions based on many Providence places, shows that he must have been looking and thinking hard on those rambles.

"As a historian and preservationist, I love how he writes about Providence," said Sarah Zurier of the Rhode Island Historical Preservation & Heritage Commission as she led a Lovecraft-like walking tour. "That's what he loved to do, go for long walks and show off Providence to his friends."

It seems fitting to do as much as possible of a modern-day tour through Lovecraft's historic and architecturally rich Providence on foot, a feat made easier because many of the essential sites are packed into a compact area.

A Lovecraftian journey has a new starting place these days, the Lovecraft Arts & Sciences store that opened the summer of 2015 in the Greek Revival Providence Arcade downtown. Niels-Viggo Hobbs and Carmen Marusich are the proprietors of a shop that is part bookstore (Lovecraft and beyond in horror and science fiction) and part tourist information bureau for Lovecraft pilgrims from around the world.

"Providence is a peculiar town," said Hobbs, who is also director of NecronomiCon. "It is really embracing of weirdness."

Downtown Providence is not too different now, building-wise, than in Lovecraft's time. The iron, brick, and granite City Hall is the same place where Lovecraft has the main character in his novel *The Case of Charles Dexter Ward* do research.

The former Industrial Trust tower—often a character in Lovecraft stories and also called the "Superman Building" because the twenty-six-story skyscraper closely resembles the Daily Planet building Superman leapt over in the television series—has been empty since 2013. Yet it remains a towering presence on the city's skyline and, each night, on goes its large beacon, a recurring motif for Lovecraft, including, menacingly, in his story "The Haunter of the Dark."

One of the great changes in Providence, helping to fuel its renaissance in the last two decades, happened in the 1990s, when two rivers, the Moshassuck and the Woonasquatucket, were moved and a wide bridge covering a third, the Providence River, was removed, creating a wonderful walkway downtown. (This is the site of the spectacular WaterFire on the rivers many Saturday nights each summer.)

Near the river, Zurier led me to the Market House, the stately brick landmark built in 1773 and now a classroom building for the Rhode Island School of Design. Lovecraft wrote of the spot in a story: "He liked mostly to reach this point in the late afternoon, when the slanting sunlight touches the Market House and the ancient hill roofs and belfries with gold, and throws magic around the dreaming wharves where Providence Indiamen used to ride at anchor." The shipping trade is gone, but the late-day natural light show continues, showing off many of Providence's remarkable buildings.

A block up College Hill on majestic Benefit Street, we went to the Providence Athenaeum, an independent library whose origins date back to 1753. It was a place Lovecraft spent many hours, and where his great inspiration, Edgar Allan Poe, had sat before. The Athenaeum welcomes visitors and is home to a bronze bust of Lovecraft. As a child, he had also visited the nearby Rhode Island School of Design Museum, particularly enjoying ancient Greek and Roman artifacts that now share space with more contemporary works.

Farther up the hill took us into the picturesque environs of Brown University. Lovecraft dropped out of high school, yet Brown was a center of his universe, as he walked among its buildings most of his life. His writing is infused with the results of his prodigious research in its libraries. Sometimes the school is mentioned by name in his work, though more often it is Miskatonic University, Lovecraft's creation with Brown at its roots.

Nearby is Brown's John Hay Library, the rare book repository whose archives include the largest collection of Lovecraft materials in the world, including original manuscripts, books, magazines, letters, and items from his personal library. The library, a center of international research about Lovecraft, also mounts occasional exhibitions about him.

Lovecraft was generous in helping many young writers, as his letters show. Robert Barlow started as a teenage fan and eventually became Lovecraft's literary executor, donating Lovecraft's materials to the John Hay. Lovecraft made several trips to visit Barlow in Florida by bus, debunking what for years was a common image of Lovecraft as a sickly person who rarely left home and confined most of his outside activity to nighttime. A broader picture, of a man full of curiosity who loved to travel, has emerged.

An exception to his joy of travel and other places was the two-year period he spent living in Brooklyn after he married Sonia Greene at Saint Paul's Chapel in Manhattan in 1924. He raged about New York and its crowds, and returned to Providence alone in 1926, never to live anywhere else again.

Providence has embraced him. Next to the John Hay Library is a memorial plaque installed for the centennial of his birth in 1990. A sign at the next corner, the intersection of Prospect and Angell Streets, declares it H. P. LOVECRAFT MEMORIAL SQUARE.

Nearby, at 65 Prospect Street, is Lovecraft's last home (though the house was moved a few blocks from College Street, where Lovecraft lived in it). There he wrote "The Haunter of the Dark," the last of his stories. He lived on part of the upper floor of the handsome 1825 house.

"Providence was a place of outcasts and independent-minded people," Zurier said as we approached Prospect Terrace Park on Congdon Street. Lovecraft was a regular visitor to the park, with its statue of Roger Williams, the nonconformist proponent of religious freedom who started what became Rhode Island. The magnificent view of the State House and downtown gave Lovecraft inspiration. "The vast marble dome of the State House stood out in massive silhouette," Lovecraft wrote, "its crowning statue haloed fantastically by a break in one of the tinted stratus clouds that barred the flaming sky."

Not far from the park is the house at 10 Barnes Street where Lovecraft was his most productive (from 1926 until 1933), writing two of his most legendary works, "The Call of Cthulhu" and *The Shadow over Innsmouth,* among others. The burst of energy seemed related to his return to Providence from New York.

Lovecraft had wide-ranging tastes and loved to say what he hated. The 1885 Fleur-de-Lys Building, seen as an early and important example of Arts and Crafts architecture in the United States, is back down the hill on Thomas Street. It was an example of something Lovecraft despised. But that didn't keep him from using it in his fiction, Zurier pointed out, as it became the home of Henry Anthony Wilcox, a character in "The Call of Cthulhu." He wrote, "Wilcox still lived alone in the Fleur-de-Lys Building . . . a hideous Victorian imitation of seventeenth-century Breton architecture which flaunts its stuccoed front amidst the lovely colonial houses on the ancient hill, and under the very shadow of the finest Georgian steeple in America."

That steeple across the street is of the First Baptist Church in America, built in 1775; Lovecraft liked it despite his lack of interest in religion, and despite being kicked out of its Sunday school as a child. You wouldn't know it for the brightness of the church now, but in Lovecraft's day it was a gloomy place and was crumbling, which appealed to him. Lovecraft sneaked in once with friends, intending to play "Yes, We Have No Bananas" on the church's organ, but the organ was locked.

Some Lovecraft sites are a little beyond an easy walk, so I rode with Hobbs of Lovecraft Arts & Sciences.

As a preteen, Lovecraft was smitten with astronomy. He

got a telescope and made many visits to Brown University's Ladd Observatory, built in 1891 and still open to the public. "It was a place where Lovecraft's precocious nature was allowed to develop," Hobbs said. "It's also where he started to consider the cosmos."

We visited a green, nondescript house at 598 Angell Street, where Lovecraft lived from 1904 to 1924 and wrote some of his early stories, working to develop his craft. He also lived there through the hospitalizations and deaths of both his parents.

While preservation has saved three of Lovecraft's residences in Providence, the house where he was born, at 454 Angell Street, is no more. It was demolished in the early 1960s and replaced with an apartment building, though a stone marker of his birth has recently been installed at the site. "You can imagine how heartbroken Lovecraft would be," Hobbs said. But he looked around and, seeing a coffee shop and a bookstore, smiled and said, "He would have liked those."

Hobbs and I went into Swan Point Cemetery, the beautiful place where Lovecraft is buried along with many of Providence's best-known citizens, including twenty-three state governors. Because he died nearly broke, he was buried in a family plot, unmarked for many years until admirers paid for a stone.

Lovecraft's is one of the most visited graves in the cemetery, and workers at the gate often meet foreign tourists who struggle with English except to say "Lovecraft." Offerings frequently adorn his grave, and the day we visited, there were pennies (a visitor said it's connected to Lovecraft dying penniless), a plant, and notes, including one marked with a lipstick kiss. As Hobbs talked about the regular procession of visitors, a car drove up and two men, off-duty police detectives, got out for a look. One of them said he was a Lovecraft fan and had always been curious to see the grave.

Lovecraft, like his Providence, has that effect on people. This, after all, is the legacy of a man who wrote a line that became his epitaph: "I am Providence."

Originally published in August 2016.

Noel Rubinton is a writer based in Providence, Rhode Island.

Rachel Carson's "Rugged Shore" in Maine

Frank M. Meola

When Rachel Carson built a summer cottage on the Maine coast in 1953, she had not yet written *Silent Spring,* the work that arguably inspired the modern environmental movement. It was thanks to an earlier best seller, *The Sea Around Us,* that she was able to leave her government job and fulfill a long-standing dream.

"I have loved the Boothbay Harbor area for years," she wrote to a friend, "and do look forward to having a summer place to write in such beautiful surroundings." As a marine biologist, she also hoped for ample time to observe the ocean's intricate life in the ideal natural laboratory of coastal mid-Maine.

Carson, a Pennsylvania native, quickly formed a bond with her new home, and, in a sense, it bonded with her. On a recent trip to Boothbay, I discovered that many places remain much as Carson experienced them and that the area and its residents still hold a strong connection to her.

The coast northeast of Portland indents to green, hilly peninsulas and fjord-like estuaries—"salt-water rivers, now arms of the sea," in Carson's words. I drove along one of those rivers, the Sheepscot, to Boothbay Harbor, a white-clapboard fishing village and resort, where shops and restaurants slope down to a busy waterfront. As I passed onto a swing bridge that leads to Southport Island, the location of Carson's cottage, the hectic, information-laden world began to slip away.

The island retains the pristine timelessness that attracted Carson, with its "deep dark woodland and rugged shore." I meandered five miles south to Cape Newagen, the island's tip, site of the Newagen Seaside Inn, a hotel dating from 1816 that Carson often visited. The stately white colonial building sits above "the hollow boom of the sea striking against the rocks," she wrote.

In the lobby, two books were displayed opposite the front desk: *Silent Spring* and *Rachel,* a children's book about Carson. Her portrait hung nearby.

"Carson is very important here," said Lin Koch, the desk manager. "The staff all read her books—it's not required, but she is so much a part of this place. Visitors often ask about her." She pointed toward a row of wooden rockers on the plank porch. "She would sit out there for hours, writing," she said, as if recounting a personal memory. "It was quiet and inspiring."

A walk around the grounds supported that notion. Terraced pathways look toward "rocky, forested ridges" beyond which "chains of islands jut out obliquely into the sea, one beyond another," Carson wrote. There are views of boat-dotted inlets from a higher point at the Newagen Inn's restaurant, where Carson would often meet friends.

Later, Koch asked if I'd found "the plaque," referring to the spot where the writer's ashes had been scattered. She showed me a trail flanked by wild blueberry patches leading to a stony, jagged shoreline. A cool, tangy wind blew as

I approached the simple bronze marker on a boulder, below which the tide washed "in lacy cascades of foam." It read, "Rachel Carson (1907–1964), Writer, Ecologist, Champion of the Natural World, Here at last returned to the sea," with a quotation from one of her last letters: "But most of all I shall remember the monarchs."

Seriously ill and burdened by the controversy that followed *Silent Spring*—the book had been widely attacked by both big industry and other scientists—she recalled in that letter the autumn butterfly migration at Newagen, noting that it made her aware of nature's cyclical power and brought her solace. Two white Adirondack chairs were perched near the plaque, and it was easy to imagine Carson sitting there, gazing out at the ocean and shore she cherished with a poet's vision and a scientist's acuity.

My next morning in Maine saw a silvery mistiness when, as Carson wrote, "the softness of sea fog blurs the contours of the rocks." The Newagen lobby was filled with women dressed in suffragist-era clothes, assembled for a festive meeting of the Boothbay Region Garden Club. Serendipitously, they too had a kinship with Carson. The club announced a coming tour named after *The Sea Around Us,* and members were enthusiastic about Carson's influence.

"We do much more than gardening," one member said. "Carson knew that." She quoted the author's praise for the garden club, which was founded in 1931, as "a strong constructive force for conservation." Some members even skipped a recent butterfly-collecting field trip because it would have violated Carson's principles.

At the nearby Southport Library, another plaque, framed in greenery out front, and a vibrant quilt with a planet Earth theme inside lovingly commemorate Carson. (The quilt was made to honor her one hundredth birthday in 2007.)

Linda Brewer, the head librarian, gladly shared her knowledge about Carson, some of it gleaned from locals who had met her. "Island kids still learn about Rachel," she said, smiling. Two shelves are devoted to Carson, including old clippings from Southport papers, mostly reminiscences from island residents. Reserved, kind, gently humorous, Carson would chat at the (still-operating) general store about children (single, she was raising an orphaned great-nephew), her beloved cats, and preservation efforts on the island.

The next day was clear and sunny, perfect for exploring other areas of natural splendor that Carson had enjoyed. At Ocean Point, a peninsula's nubby fingertip, I walked, as Carson had, along striated, speckled rocks and watched lobster boats dropping traps into the azure bay, renowned for indigo-vermilion sunsets.

I continued east to the Rachel Carson Salt Pond Preserve, on the Pemaquid Peninsula, near an 1835 lighthouse. Carson would come here at low tide to observe and take samples, discoveries that informed her third book, *The Edge of the Sea.* Earlier that day, Barbara Vickery, the conservation director of the Nature Conservancy of Maine (Carson was a founder), had told me, as if describing a valued friend's legacy, that this sheltered tidal pool was especially popular with families who had read Carson's *The Sense of Wonder,* which urges parents to "rediscover" with their children "the joy, excitement and mystery of the world we live in."

In that spirit, I crouched to look for tidal life, with *The Edge of the Sea* as a sort of field guide. The air had what Carson described as "the salt smell of the rime that glitters on the sun-dried rocks." As if by magic, creatures invisible at high tide appeared: "periwinkles grazing on the intertidal rocks, waiting for the return of the tide"; barnacles like "a mineral landscape carved and sculptured into millions of little sharply pointed cones"; tiny crabs scuttling for shelter. Oddly shaped seaweed, with the sheen of red plastic, scattered around me. Carson, keen-eyed and patient, would sometimes stay for an entire tide cycle.

Stretching for some twenty miles along the Sheepscot, the vast Rachel Carson Coastal Greenway beckoned, a constellation of natural areas that Carson walked in and wrote about. One of her finest sketches vividly renders the view across the river to Indiantown Island, then, as now, "a dark wall of coniferous forest rising in solid, impenetrable blackness to where the tops of the spruces feathered out into a serrate line against the sky." I hiked a wooded trail with receding river vistas amid "all the heady, aromatic, bittersweet fragrances compounded of pine and spruce and bayberry, warmed by the sun."

Carson portrays an abundance of birds, like the cormorant and the hermit thrush, with its "infinite" sound. Bird populations had declined sharply here but now thrive again, thanks partly to the ban on DDT prompted by *Silent Spring,* according to Vickery of the Nature Conservancy. Even the bald eagle has made a spectacular return. Alas, no eagles appeared during my trip, but I did spot great blue herons, ospreys, and darting shore birds.

At a cove back on Southport—one of the "spits of sand" that Carson joked "pass for beaches in Maine"—families were kayaking and swimming. One small boy gazed at some discovery in the brisk, crystalline water. I glimpsed Carson's cottage nestled in spruces on "the granite rim of shore." Sitting on her porch or writing at her desk, Carson savored the view across the deep, wide Sheepscot. She excitedly recorded spotting a whale from her window. North of the house stretches a tract of evergreen spires she named Lost Woods and fought to protect. It remains as she described it, "a cathedral of stillness and peace."

Standing there, I understood Carson's annual reluctance to leave this place of beauty, wonder, and renewal.

Originally published in August 2012.

Frank M. Meola writes frequently about American culture and history, and teaches writing at New York University. He recently completed a coming-of-age novel, *Clay.*

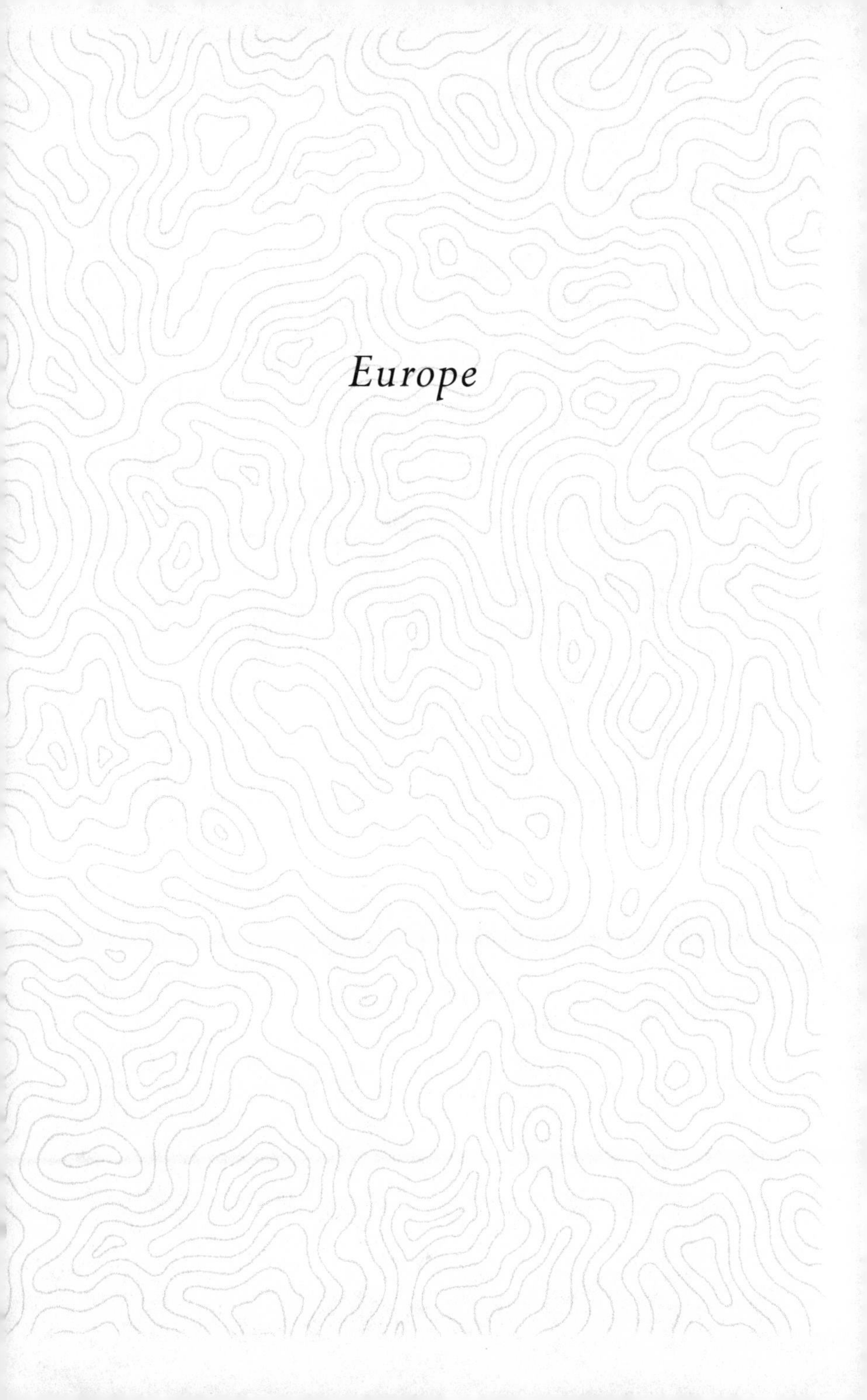

Europe

DON PATERSON
BRAM STOKER
W. B. YEATS
LEWIS CARROLL
THOMAS HARDY
JAMES BALDWIN
EDITH WHARTON
ERNEST HEMINGWAY
SYBILLE BEDFORD

CHRISTOPHER ISHERWOOD
MILAN KUNDERA
JACOB & WILHELM GRIMM
LORD BYRON & MARY SHELLEY
F. SCOTT FITZGERALD
TENNESSEE WILLIAMS
ELENA FERRANTE

In Ireland, Chasing the Wandering Soul of Yeats

Russell Shorto

I will arise and go now . . .

Surprisingly often, when I get up from a chair to leave a room, those six melodramatic words will unfurl in my mind. Somehow William Butler Yeats's poem "The Lake Isle of Innisfree," which, like millions of other people, I first read in college, stays rooted in me:

I will arise and go now, and go to Innisfree . . .

And I'm off, not to the dentist or the shopping mall but, mentally, striding emerald slopes, making for a place of myth.

Yeats named the poem after an actual place, an island in the middle of Lough Gill, a lake that spreads itself languidly across five miles of furiously green landscape in County Sligo in northwest Ireland. A few years ago, I found myself in Dublin and decided to do it for real: go to Innisfree. It would be a four-hour detour, but I had not the slightest doubt the journey would be worthwhile.

Thanks to the popularity of the poem (voted by readers of *The Irish Times* in 1999 as their all-time favorite work of Irish poetry), "Innisfree" is a bit of a brand. There are Innisfree cosmetics, an Innisfree eau de parfum, an Innisfree bed-and-breakfast, an Innisfree Hotel, and a *Rose of Innisfree* tour boat that does the lake.

But I know these things only from Google. Thankfully, none of it was evident on my drive. I didn't use a GPS; I just relied on a couple of tiny handmade-looking road signs that popped up as I entered the region, which pointed the way to LAKE ISLE OF INNISFREE. The last stage of the journey involved no tourism bric-a-brac, only small, twisty, increasingly difficult-to-navigate roads, mossy tree trunks, wind, willows, heather, cloud knuckles, and gray rock.

When I reached the lakeshore, I found the opposite of a tourist site. I could barely make my way out to the water to get a view, so thick was the shoreline with trees and brush. A farmhouse with a couple of SUVs parked outside stood nearby, and there was a little concrete dock jutting out into the lake, pointed almost directly at Innisfree a few hundred yards away. I got out on the dock, sat cross-legged facing the island, and let the wind say what it had to say. For decades, this place had reverberated in my mind; now I was actually there.

Yeats, born in 1865, the son of an artist, was a childlike intellectual. He would forget to eat, or would put food in the oven and let it burn. He was devoted to mysticism and séances. He spent decades in love with the Irish nationalist and proto-feminist Maud Gonne; after she rejected his marriage proposal for a final time, he shifted his attention to her daughter.

A few weeks after she, in turn, spurned his marriage offer, he proposed to another woman, Georgie Hyde-Lees, who, despite knowing where she ranked, became his devoted life partner. As she essentially said after his death, she saw the shimmer of his soul. "For him, every day he lived was a new adventure," she once told the Yeats scholar Curtis B. Bradford. "He woke every morning certain that in the new day before him something would happen that had never happened before."

Yeats was in his fifties when he married. "The Lake Isle of Innisfree" is a young man's poem, written when he was twenty-three. It is filled with a romantic longing for the past: the Irish past, the mythic past, and also Yeats's own. He had spent his childhood in County Sligo before moving to Dublin and then London. This countryside, the lake and its islands, this composition of greens and grays and blues, was fused within him.

When he was a boy, his father had read him Thoreau's *Walden,* and its pastoral message resonated with the landscape of his childhood. As a young man living in London, trying to make a go of it amid the industrial throb, Yeats reached back to his youth and crafted the poem. The first line signals the self-consciously antiquated style he chose. (Even back in 1888, when the poem was written, people didn't "arise.") He filled it with rhyme, pumped it with unapologetically forceful rhythm. He made it, for all its romance, compact, athletic. This is the entire poem:

I will arise and go now, and go to Innisfree,
And a small cabin build there, of clay and wattles made;
Nine bean-rows will I have there, a hive for the honey-bee,
And live alone in the bee-loud glade.

And I shall have some peace there, for peace comes dropping slow,
Dropping from the veils of the morning to where the cricket sings;
There midnight's all a glimmer, and noon a purple glow,
And evening full of the linnet's wings.

I will arise and go now, for always night and day
I hear lake water lapping with low sounds by the shore;
While I stand on the roadway, or on the pavements grey,
I hear it in the deep heart's core.

Of course, as I approached the lake, the poem was reverberating in my mind, and at first the imagery seemed to live up to it. The lake is five miles long, fringed with greenery; moody hills rise on the opposite shore. The furrowed water was dotted with little islands, some of them very atmospheric. As it happens, though, Innisfree is not one of the atmospheric ones. It's tiny, and looks like a bur, a bristling seed pod, almost angrily sprouting trees and brush from its humpy back.

Some have speculated that Yeats chose it because of the poetry in the syllables of its name, and the last syllable's suggestion of freedom. You'd have a hard time building a cabin on it, and it's too lumpen for a glade.

But to leave it at that—to say that Yeats picked a dud—would be like declaring that you had no music in your soul. The whole landscape echoes the poem. You realize, sitting there, identifying the sound of the lake water with the deep heart's core, that the Yeats who wrote the poem does not actually intend to retreat from the world and move to this spot. He is reaching for something. He is aware, at twenty-three, of death and the inexorability of change. He is searching, trying to find his balance, his center. He knows he left it somewhere in his past, as we all have done.

The poem is a mental exercise, a meditation. You could perform the exercise in a parking garage. It isn't meant to be enacted.

Then I realized that my meditation was different from Yeats's. If he was using his mind to find his center, I was using him—using history, poetry, travel—to get to the same place.

And there I was. All of County Sligo is "Yeats country." He mined it, traced its contours, translated them to verse: "black wind," "wet winds," "noisy clouds," "thorn-trees," "the clinging air." He did it so thoroughly, it's almost as if the craggy loveliness of the countryside were carved to suit his poetry, rather than the other way around.

"Where the wandering water gushes / From the hills above Glen-Car," from Yeats's poem "The Stolen Child," describes a misty waterfall to the north that seems like something out of Peter Jackson's *The Hobbit.*

A few miles away from the lake, the stupendous mountain slab called Ben Bulben rises like a natural acropolis, the home of some ancient race of Irish gods, a height whose purpose can only be to evoke awe. It became another geographic touchstone for Yeats—so much so that in his poem "Under Ben Bulben," he eerily directs the reader to his own grave, in the nearby cemetery of Drumcliffe. Actually it's the grave of another Yeats he refers to, an ancestor. But after his own death, in France, his body was transferred there, as if people treated his poem as a last will and testament.

It's only a four-mile drive from the shore of Lough Gill to Sligo town, and civilization. Sligo is an ancient and lively enough little center, dominated by its cathedral and ringed with pubs where there's nonstop rugby and soccer on the telly and you can order not just Irish stew and Guinness, but also chicken curry and New Zealand sauvignon blanc. For a tourist, it's the practical base. But pleasant as this is, it was the antithesis of why I had come. Yeats's meditations weren't urban, and neither were mine.

I am told that there are enormous salmon lurking beneath the waters of Lough Gill, and that otters make the lake their home, and that the lush forest along the banks, called Slish Wood, which Yeats in "The Stolen Child" calls Sleuth Wood, harbors rare orchids, ivies, and thistles, and that, yes, the evening can be full of the linnet's wings. I saw none of these remarkable things.

But I saw others.

Originally published in April 2015.

Russell Shorto is the best-selling author of *The Island at the Center of the World* and *Amsterdam: A History of the World's Most Liberal City.* He is a contributing writer to *The New York Times Magazine.*

Poetry Made Me Do It: My Trip to the Hebrides

Jeff Gordinier

I was about to slide down a hill when the strangeness of my situation struck me: a poem had brought me here.

"Poetry makes nothing happen," W. H. Auden once said, and yet there I was, clawing my way through the wet and lichen-encrusted tangle on a Scottish hillside, with limbs of bracken swatting me in the face and my Wellington boots failing to get a foothold, worried that I was about to face-plant into a pudding of aromatic Hebridean ooze, because of twenty-four lines of verse.

Something was happening, and the poem that had made it happen was "Luing." The poem, which opens *Landing Light,* a collection of poems by a Scottish literary star named Don Paterson, pays tribute to an obscure island cradled in the bosom of the Hebrides, a negligible nugget of land "with its own tiny stubborn anthem." Luing, Paterson writes, is a place where a visitor might be "reborn into a secret candidacy" and where "the fontanelles reopen one by one." Paterson's poem is a twenty-first-century ode to regeneration (fontanelles are those soft spots on a baby's head where the skull hasn't fully fused yet), but it's also about the deep satisfactions of disappearing. By the closing stanza, its narrator has succumbed to a sort of sweet obliteration: "One morning / you hover on the threshold, knowing for certain / the first touch of the light will finish you."

The poem had stayed with me since I'd first encountered it. Where was this strange island that seemed to promise both renewal and erasure? Even in the age of Google Earth I could find out very little about Luing, other than that its name was pronounced "ling" and that it qualified as the international headquarters for a prized breed of cattle. Now and then I would walk into a bookstore and flip through travel guides; Luing didn't appear on most of the maps.

What I found tantalizing about "our unsung innermost isle," as Paterson put it, was the very obscurity of the place. It was obscure not because it was theatrically desolate and raw, but because it was the opposite of that. It was an island that just sat there and gazed out at all the more famous islands. Luing's pretty-wallflower modesty meant that it could not compete with the grand gestures of alpha islands like Mull and Skye, and, as I would learn, it had deferentially opted not to. It had no tourist industry to speak of. It had no pubs, no hotels, no restaurants, no blood-soaked battlefields. Luing was a place that you might spy in the distance as you traveled to somewhere else.

And that's exactly what drew me to it—that and the poem, of course. My close friends, along with the owners of several independent bookstores in the New York area, know that for me, poetry qualifies as much more than a casual interest. I buy somewhere in the neighborhood of a hundred books of poetry each year, and when I find a particular poem that moves me, I'll hold that page open with a paperweight and meticulously type up the poem, line by line, comma by comma. So my friends weren't surprised when I told them a Don Paterson poem had moved me so much that I had, on impulse, booked a trip to Scotland.

A few days before I left, I met Paterson for breakfast at a diner near Penn Station. He was scheduled to read his poems at the 92nd Street Y that week, and I figured I could make use of this serendipity to ask him what I was getting myself into.

"It's a funny little place—you'll like it," he told me in a tone of voice that suggested I might not like it at all. When people in Scotland want to embark on some kind of vision quest, he said, they usually venture way out into the North Atlantic to Saint Kilda, an isolated and storm-ravaged cluster of rocks that has become "very much a place of romantic pilgrimage for people."

"You get there and it's full of librarians from Glasgow trying to find themselves," he said. "That's not what you want."

What you want, he continued, is a hidden gem like Luing, an island that's "both protected and open," close in distance to the mainland but eons away.

He paused and smiled: "I hope you have a good time. I'll feel terrible if you don't."

Getting there, at least, was not as complicated as I'd expected. I flew to Glasgow, and followed that red-eye flight with a morning train north, through the shocking beauty of the western Highlands. Next I rented a car in the whiskey-distilling port town of Oban, filled the trunk with groceries, bought a bottle of single malt and a new pair of Wellington boots, and drove south. I'd arrived in Scotland in late October, and the narrow, tangled route to Luing was flanked by a psychedelic canvas of rusts, ambers, and greens. As I began to see the signs for the ferry, a song by the National came on the car stereo, a song whose chorus went "you're so far around the bend."

When I'd gone around the bend as far as I could, I got to a village where the road simply petered out into the water. Paterson had been correct in describing the ferry as a raft. It looked like the interior slab of a small house—maybe a kitchen floor with a pantry jutting out of it—that had broken loose in one of the Hebrides' notorious storms and floated off into the channel.

A downpour strafed the wobbling boat. The trip was less than five minutes long, but the speedy way we were borne across the rain-spattered water intensified the feeling of passing through some forgotten Narnian portal. WELCOME TO OUR ISLAND, proclaimed a sign on the other side. A PLACE TO THINK . . . A PLACE TO BE.

Luing has two main villages: the small fishing hub of Cullipool on the western flank, and a quaint scrum of houses on the southeast side, called Toberonochy. The rest is a walker's utopia. Fewer than two hundred people are said to live on the island's 5.5 square miles. Some are fishermen and farmers whose families have been around since anyone can remember. Others are relatively recent exiles from the city seeking just what's advertised on that sign: a place to think and be.

For me, the weather cooperated with that pursuit. On the first morning that I woke up in Creagard, a cottage I rented in Cullipool, sunlight was already warming the island's stone walls and bracken. The tropical conditions lasted all weekend. Outside the cottage the air was ambrosial, laced with notes of coal smoke and kelp.

Upon my arrival I got some background from Cully Pettigrew, a Glasgow art dealer who had reconstructed Creagard from the ruins of a miner's house that he had found perched on the lip of a flooded slate quarry decades ago. An obsessive sailor with melancholic blue eyes, Pettigrew was using Luing as a home base from which he and his boat explored the islands in the westward scattering of the Hebrides.

His house was full of maps. Before leaving and handing me the keys to Creagard, which he often rents out to visitors, he led me from one sailor's chart to the next as he pointed out a few of Luing's brassier neighbors. To the south was the whirlpool of Corryvreckan, an oceanic spiral that once almost pulled George Orwell to his doom. Across the water to the west was a spot on the Garvellachs islands where medieval monks used to live and pray in stone beehive cells. "This whole area," Pettigrew said, "was a center of civilization when Glasgow and Edinburgh didn't exist."

In the intervening years, apparently, civilization had fallen out of favor on Luing, which had the delightful by-product of making it more civilized. Soon after I'd arrived, the island's inhabitants began inviting me into their homes for a glass of Scotch or dinner. Many of them had fled more frenzied lives in Glasgow or London, and they were an inquisitive, cultured bunch. I found myself in conversations about Japanese poetry and the New York restaurant scene. And yet life on Luing seemed to be uncontaminated by the pressures and distractions of the global marketplace. There was a single store on Luing that sold staples like milk, eggs, and bread, but that was as far as commerce went. If you wanted fresh lobster or langoustines, they were being hauled up from the sea a few yards away.

I began to feel, on Luing, like a man out of time. Somewhere out in the hills lay the remains of a couple of Iron Age forts, but Pettigrew told me they wouldn't be easy to find unless I happened to be skilled at noticing the archaeological signals in a wet heap of rocks. (I was not.) "You'll be walking on ancient roads," he said. "You get the sense of walking into the past. If you're attuned, you might pick it up."

I put on my boots and set off. I went north, I went south, I went east. I wandered between the sheer stone cliffs of old quarries, and up grassy slopes that reminded me of central California, and through spongy pastures. Every now and then I'd come around the side of a ridge and find a reddish woolly cow fixing me with a merciless stare.

No matter where I went, my gaze kept being drawn back to the center of the island. A sort of mesa rose, flat-topped and alone, out of the middle of a field. There was something magnetic about this unassuming drumlin at the heart of Scotland's most unassuming island. I decided to check out this long, lonely mound of glacial deposits, and that's how I ended up getting snared in the bracken. I approached the drumlin from a lagoon near Luing's western shoreline, but as I began walking straight up the side of the hill I realized that the slope was steeper—and sloppier—than I'd expected.

My boots began to slip away from under me in the mud. I groped around for what looked like the trunks and branches of olive trees. They were wind-gnarled and webbed with silver-green wisps of moss. It was slow going, but gradually I pulled myself up.

The climb was worth it. The top of the mesa felt like a sanctuary. Long grass covered the ground; above my head, the branches of trees were twined together like a trellis. I sat down. The rolling landscape of Luing was laid out below. Here it was—the "intimate exile," the "secret candidacy" that Paterson had written about.

I can't verify that any fontanelles reopened (that would have been distressing, anyway), but I lost track of time and let myself disappear for a while. I looked east and saw a hunter's moon rising over a hill like a levitating scoop of ice cream. I looked west and saw sailboats drifting on the Firth of Lorn and a seemingly infinite array of islands floating out into the Atlantic. I decided to stay awhile to drink it in. There I realized that Auden was right after all. Poetry had made nothing happen. But that, in and of itself, was something extraordinary.

Originally published in October 2011.

Jeff Gordinier is the food and drinks editor of *Esquire*, the author of *X Saves the World*, and a contributor to *The New York Times*, *Outside*, PoetryFoundation.org, and other publications.

Where Dracula Was Born, and It's Not Transylvania

Ann Mah

From its quay in early summer, Whitby was a sun-scrubbed idyll, fluttering with the trimmings of a typical English seaside holiday. Souvenir shops hawked postcards and sand toys, pub bartenders poured midday pints of beer, and the smell of fish and chips hung on the breeze. Along the shore, a row of rainbow-hued beach huts sheltered swimmers brave enough to take a dip in the North Sea. A group of sunburned schoolchildren raced through cobblestone streets, past antiques shops and tearooms, toward the 199 steps ascending to a cliff. I followed them, listening as their excited chatter gave way to dead silence. "Please, miss," a little girl appealed to her teacher in an unnerved tone, "I can't go up there."

It wasn't difficult to see why. At the top loomed the stuff of nightmares: the skeletal ruins of the thirteenth-century Whitby Abbey. Surrounded by gravestones, it offered the only obvious hint that this picturesque town on England's Yorkshire coast is the birthplace of one of Gothic horror's most famous villains: Dracula.

Bram Stoker spent just a month in Whitby, but those

four weeks in July and August 1890 were pivotal for his most famous book and creation. Though large portions of *Dracula* unfold in Transylvania (now Romania)—which he describes as "one of the wildest and least known portions of Europe"—Stoker himself never ventured east of Vienna. Instead, it was in this fishing-village-turned-Victorian-resort where he began work on the supernatural tale, and he honored his muse by setting key portions of the narrative within its charming streets. During my visit, I discovered that Whitby still captivates, largely because of the "beautiful and romantic bits" that inspired the Irish novelist—but it also still nurtures a dark undercurrent.

"A lot has been written about Bram Stoker," said David Pybus, the honorary manager of the Whitby Museum. "Most of it is rubbish." Take, for example, a bench perched on a bluff, dedicated with a plaque that reads: "The view from this spot inspired Bram Stoker to use Whitby as the setting of part of his world-famous novel *Dracula*."

Not actually possible, Pybus said: "That area was inaccessible to the public at the time of Stoker's visit." But at the museum, his diligent examination of Stoker's letters and other documents offers an unusually accurate account of the author's Whitby sojourn. "*Dracula* is a remarkable narrative of a Victorian upper-middle-class holiday in Whitby," he said.

On vacation from his London day job as business manager to Henry Irving, the most famous actor of the Victorian stage, Stoker spent his first week in Whitby alone, relishing the break from his demanding boss. The two men had a complex relationship rooted in admiration, sycophancy, and chats that persisted until dawn so that the actor could decompress after performances. And so, though Stoker was familiar with vampire imagery from the folklore of his Irish childhood, as well as his studies at Trinity College Dublin, some scholars have theorized that the mercurial Irving actually inspired the blood-sucking, megalomaniacal Count Dracula.

Stoker lodged at 6 Royal Crescent on the West Cliff, a stately, residential neighborhood that is today awash in bed-and-breakfasts. His wife and young son eventually joined him, plunging into a whirl of concerts, teas, and amateur theater at the Spa, the seaside pavilion at the town's social center. But Stoker preferred walking along the cliffs while howling at the wind, and researching his nascent tale—the fifth of twelve novels—at Whitby Abbey. There, in a book called *An Account of the Principalities of Wallachia and Moldavia* by William Wilkinson, he discovered the name Dracula, which means "devil" in the Wallachian dialect. "The book is still in our catalog," Pybus said. "But we can't find it."

Like the character Mina Murray Harker—the level-headed, tender-necked young lady who narrates the book's Whitby section—Stoker spent hours at the Church of Saint Mary's graveyard, which overlooks the town. He relaxed among the tombstones, admired the "myriad clouds of every sunset-colour-flame," and absorbed local lore from the retired seafarers who gathered there. Some of the lighter moments in *Dracula* are drawn from these conversations, which Stoker rendered in thick Yorkshire dialect. ("These bans an' wafts an' boh-ghosts an' bar-guests an' bogles an' all anent them is only fit to set bairns an' dizzy women a-belderin'. They be nowt but air-blebs!")

Though the bands of crusty mariners disappeared with Whitby's fishing industry around the turn of the twentieth century, the churchyard remains a popular spot for tourists and locals—a resting place both temporary and eternal. After huffing up those 199 steps that lead to it from the town's high street, I paused to admire the view of the harbor mouth sweeping open to the North Sea. In 1885, a Russian schooner crashed on the beach directly below, a dramatic shipwreck that captured Stoker's imagination. He seized the details for his book, adding a spectacular storm, a crew of corpses, and a shape-shifting Dracula bounding triumphantly to shore in the form of a black dog.

A short walk away, I gazed at a photograph of the wreckage that inspired the scene. "Stoker would have seen it in the gallery window," said Mike Shaw, the owner of the Sutcliffe Gallery, which is devoted to the work of Frank Meadow Sutcliffe, a noted nineteenth-century photographer who "captured working-class Victorian life in Whitby before industrialization." In Sutcliffe's sepia-toned prints, Whitby appears misty, moody, and—if you replace the somberly dressed fishwives with tourists—almost identical to today. "It hasn't changed much," Shaw said, "except the fishing industry is almost nonexistent. Now we're dependent on the tourist industry."

Indeed, Whitby burnishes its tourist appeal with a sense of timelessness: old-fashioned pubs, quirky boutiques, and fish-and-chip shops, which, in quintessential Yorkshire fashion, use beef drippings for frying. But the town also harbors a shadowy side as black as the masses of jet mourning jewelry it produced during Queen Victoria's reign. Twice a year, in April and October, it hosts the Whitby Goth Weekend, a music festival founded in 1994. Shaw likened the autumn event to "a global Goth gathering—thousands of [them] come." Even during my visit in the off-Goth season, I spotted Goth clothing shops dotting the side streets, and jet boutiques displaying pendants of skulls, spiders, and bats.

As the sun descended, the real bats emerged, swooping over the remains of Whitby Abbey—"a most noble ruin," as Stoker described it—and disappearing over the rooftops. I walked through empty streets, peering down narrow alleys and secret staircases that ended in pools of darkness. In one of the book's most gripping scenes, Mina runs through these same streets after dark, hurrying to save her sleepwalking friend, Lucy, as she's attacked in the churchyard by "a man or beast" with "white face and red, gleaming eyes." I headed in the other direction, away from the churchyard and any shadowy figures. When I turned to look behind me, I saw the setting sun had stained the abbey and its surrounding gravestones as red as blood.

That night I slept with my window closed.

Originally published in September 2015.

Ann Mah, a frequent contributor to the *New York Times* Travel section, is the author of *Mastering the Art of French Eating.*

Finding Alice's "Wonderland" in Oxford

Charlie Lovett

Alice leaned back in the rowboat and watched flecks of blue flicker among the branches overhead. She heard the sound of the oars splashing in the water as the boat made its way up the Thames from Oxford, and of her sisters Lorina and Edith giggling, but mostly she heard Dodgson weaving a tale about another Alice, a little girl who had fallen down a rabbit hole and was now having a wonderful adventure in a wonderful land. When the girls returned to Oxford with Dodgson and his friend Robinson Duckworth on July 4, 1862, Alice thought she would ask Dodgson to write the story down—it was one of his best.

Alice was Alice Liddell, the ten-year-old daughter of Henry George Liddell, the dean of Christ Church, the largest college of Oxford University. Dodgson was Charles Lutwidge Dodgson, a mathematics lecturer at Christ Church, a recently ordained deacon in the Church of England, brilliant logician, and consummate storyteller.

He acceded to her request, and over the next few months

recorded the story in a manuscript he eventually illustrated and gave to Alice as a Christmas gift in 1864.

Encouraged by friends, including the fantasy writer George MacDonald, he expanded the book, commissioned illustrations by the political cartoonist John Tenniel, and had it published at his own expense under the name Lewis Carroll. In the 150 years since the publication of *Alice's Adventures in Wonderland,* it has influenced creations as varied as *Finnegans Wake* by James Joyce, illustrations by Salvador Dalí, and a mock turtle soup from the British chef Heston Blumenthal. The book and its author were remarkable: the one for its utter departure from moralistic children's stories into a world of subversive nonsense, the other for talents as diverse as mathematics and logic, photography, and poetry and an ability, nurtured in his childhood home of eleven siblings, to entertain and connect with children.

Fantastic as it was, *Wonderland* was rooted in the place Dodgson lived and worked: the city and environs of Oxford with its ancient university, its "dreaming spires," and its surrounding countryside. Oxford is a city teeming with tourists and traffic, whose shopwindows overflow with Alice merchandise. But if one listens closely, if one ducks through stone arches, opens creaky oaken doors, and descends to quiet riverside paths, one can still find the Oxford of Charles Dodgson and Alice.

I set out to discover that place, beginning with the college of Christ Church, where Dodgson lived from 1851 until his death in 1898 at age sixty-five, and Alice from the time she was three until her marriage in 1880.

Visitors enter the college through the Meadow Building, erected by Dean Liddell in 1862. Dodgson's first rooms in the college were in the cloisters, and here I saw the great Norman doorway to the chapter house—now called the Queen Alice door after a similar doorway in Tenniel's illustration of Queen Alice in *Through the Looking-Glass.*

After climbing a fan-vaulted staircase made famous in the *Harry Potter* films, I entered the Great Hall under the imposing portrait of Alice's father, Dean Liddell. Dodgson wrote to a "child-friend" that he dined there "about 8,000 times." He continues to survey it: within the cavernous space with its paneled walls, stone-mullioned windows, and hammer-beam ceiling, Dodgson's portrait hangs alongside those of other distinguished members of the college. High on the left wall, a stained-glass window depicts Dodgson and Alice Liddell. But I was drawn to the andirons in the grand fireplaces. Each of these brass beauties has a woman's head perched atop an impossibly long neck—just the way Dodgson drew the nine-foot-tall Alice in his manuscript.

I made my way through waves of tourists from all over the world back down the staircase and through a stone archway into the sun-drenched Great Quadrangle, which, Dodgson quipped, "very vulgar people call 'Tom Quad' [after the bell in Christopher Wren's tower]. You should always be polite, even when speaking to a Quadrangle."

Dodgson lived in rooms in the quad's northwest corner from 1862 until his death: first in a ground-floor suite, where he wrote *Alice's Adventures in Wonderland,* then in an upper suite overlooking Saint Aldate's. Directly opposite his staircase, in the northeast corner of the quad, is the deanery, where Alice lived.

His thoughts must have drifted there often. Charles Dodgson and the Liddell family were close friends from the time he first met the family in 1855 until 1863, when the relationship cooled—a change that has led to speculation and debate among scholars and novelists alike. He continued to see the family on occasion but the former intimacy (at times almost daily visits, games, and stories) was gone. Dodgson, a bachelor who lived in college rooms for the rest of his life, went on to have scores of other child-friends, many with whom he remained on close terms after they reached adulthood. But he always remembered Alice, who inspired his greatest writings, with special fondness. Alice had three sons, two of whom were killed in action in World War I. She lived a largely quiet life until she offered the original manuscript of *Alice* at auction in 1928 and became known as "the original Alice." As such, she traveled to New York in 1932 to receive an honorary degree from Columbia University. She died in 1934.

Ducking from the brightness of Oxford's largest quadrangle into the gloom of a narrow passage Dodgson once compared with a railway tunnel, I passed a sober reminder of Alice's later life—her son Leopold Reginald Hargreaves is listed on a memorial among the Christ Church dead of World War I.

In the cathedral, among vergers sharing bits of Christ Church history with groups of visitors, I found a possible inspiration for Dodgson's pseudonym, Lewis Carroll. Dodgson created this moniker by Latinizing his names—*Charles Lutwidge* to *Carolus Ludovic*—then reversing the order and de-Latinizing them to *Lewis Carroll.* As I studied the 1823 memorial in the north transept commemorating Charles Lewis Atterbury, whose Christian names in Latin on the stone tablet are rendered CAROLUS LUDOVICUS, I wondered whether this was the place that inspired Dodgson to play with Latin as he created his nom de plume.

Much of the cathedral's stained glass is Victorian, and I basked in the vibrant colors and bold designs of several windows commissioned from William Morris's design firm. At the east end of the south aisle is one of particular note: an 1878 Pre-Raphaelite–influenced window by Edward Burne-Jones depicting Saint Catherine. The figure is based on Alice's sister Edith, immortalized not only in stained glass but also as the Eaglet in *Alice in Wonderland.* Edith, who was eight when Dodgson told the story, died in 1876 at twenty-two. Her gravestone and those of her parents stand just outside this window.

I returned to the Great Quad through the tunnel-like passage outside the cathedral's west door, and walked along the raised stone terrace on the east side of the quad, until I came to a Gothic wood-paneled door—one of many Oxford doors that hide private places. This is the entrance to Alice's childhood home, to this day the residence of the dean of Christ Church and his family. The home is not open to the public, and the door, with its small plaque reading, THE DEANERY—PRIVATE, remained firmly shut. Dodgson first records meeting Alice in his diary on April 25, 1856, when he visited the deanery garden to take a picture of the cathedral. He soon turned his lens on the children who, he wrote, were "not patient sitters." In the years that followed, Dodgson took scores of images of the Liddell children, showing remarkable artistic prowess at the complex and difficult wet-plate method of photography.

Some of those images were on display in the Upper Library of Christ Church, not generally open to the public, in an exhibition that included photographs of the Liddell family and a wet-plate camera set up and pointed out the window. A quick glance at the plate onto which the image was focused led to a revelation—all those thousands of photographs Dodgson took were composed upside down and backward. No wonder Dodgson set his sequel to *Wonderland* in a world behind the looking glass.

Dodgson was the sublibrarian of Christ Church from 1855 to 1857, and from his office could look directly into the deanery garden. From the top of the gracefully curving stairs, I had a similar view and could glimpse a wooden door set into a stone wall. This door leads from the deanery garden to the cathedral garden, and little Alice would generally have found it locked. It is no coincidence, then, that she spends much of her time in *Wonderland* trying to find her way into the "loveliest garden you ever saw."

Among public gardens in Oxford, the one that comes closest to realizing Alice's dream of wandering "among those beds of bright flowers" is the Oxford Botanic Garden. It is a cool, quiet wonderland. Dodgson may have walked there with the Liddell girls, and drawn inspiration for the varied flora of Wonderland and Looking-Glass Land from these beds. As I strolled the gravel paths, I caught sight of a cricket match across the river and saw the occasional punt drift by, but in large sections of the garden, I was, as Alice would have been in the deanery garden, completely shut off from Oxford.

The neo-Gothic Oxford University Museum of Natural History was built from 1855 to 1860 to bring together collections within the university. Dodgson photographed many of the skeletons sent from Christ Church and almost certainly attended the great debate on evolution held there in 1860, but he also visited the museum with the Liddell children. There they found the remains of one of the only specimens of a dodo bird to survive extinction. In *Wonderland,* Dodgson portrayed himself as the Dodo who manages the caucus race—poking fun at his own slight speech hesitation that would sometimes render his name as Do-Dodgson. The museum still proudly displays the dodo remains. A case nearby holds specimens of all the animals (except mythical ones like the gryphon) from *Wonderland*—an eaglet, a lory (which represented Lorina Liddell), a duck (standing in for his friend Duckworth), and everything else from flamingos to hedgehogs.

Nearby, in the basement of the Museum of the History of Science on Broad Street in Oxford, in the midst of a panoply of photographic equipment, sits part of Dodgson's wet-plate outfit: a wooden box filled with vials, beakers, and glass-stoppered bottles. The wet-plate photographic process was enormously complicated and involved a variety of chemicals, baths, and delicate glass negatives. Yet Dodgson became a master of this "black art" (so called because the chemicals turned the photographer's hands black). His photographs of children, including those of Alice, are some of the most poignant of the era, and no doubt his ability as a storyteller helped his subjects to hold still for the thirty-second or longer exposures.

Having found relics and architecture that so clearly inspired Dodgson, I decided to turn my attention to the excursion during which he invented the tale of "Alice." So, three days later, my wife, daughter, and I set out to row upstream from Folly Bridge to Port Meadow, re-creating the trip Dodgson, Duckworth, and the Liddells took in 1862.

On our way down Saint Aldate's to the river, we came across the tiny Museum of Oxford in Town Hall, where a case holds a number of personal items that once belonged to Alice and Dodgson. Alice's calling-card case, scissors, and seal sit alongside Dodgson's pocket watch, which I could picture dangling from the kid-gloved paw of a white rabbit. The watch is stopped at 1:17—time frozen just like at the Mad Tea Party.

Farther along was Alice's Shop, in a small fifteenth-century building. The store, which now sells Alice memorabilia, was a sweets shop in Victorian days and must have held some allure for Alice and her siblings. It served as the model for Tenniel's illustration of the old sheep's shop in *Through the Looking-Glass*.

At Folly Bridge we, like Dodgson, rented a rowboat from Salter's Steamers. For the less intrepid, Salter's offers an Alice in Wonderland cruise that visits several places where Dodgson rowed with the Liddell children. Soon after leaving the bridge behind, we found ourselves on a peaceful stretch of river where trees overhung the banks and traffic was little more than a distant hum. Such stretches alternated with more urban landscape, but eventually we left Oxford behind, made our way through Osney Lock, as Dodgson and his party had done, and I pulled us upstream—the only sounds the lowing of the cattle, the splashing of the water, and the creaking of the oarlocks.

Rowing, I discovered, is a perfect metaphor for the way Dodgson composed his story. You can't see where you're going when you row, and only with the direction of my wife and daughter could I keep the boat heading in the right direction. So it was with Dodgson. As he wrote years later, he had begun by sending his "heroine straight down a rabbit-hole, to begin with, without the least idea what was to happen afterwards." Only through the prodding and interruption of the children did the story move forward.

We arrived at Port Meadow, a vast open space used for grazing for about four thousand years, graced today by geese, ducks, and the occasional blue heron. Here Dodgson's merry party landed with their picnic, and he went on with his story. After our own picnic, we pulled in at the Perch, a riverside pub opposite the meadow, for a trip to the tiny hamlet of Binsey. The walk from the riverside down a narrow country lane took about twenty minutes and led us to the isolated Saint Margaret's Church and its holy well.

According to legend, Saint Frideswide founded a place of worship on the site of Christ Church around 700 AD and later fled Oxford to avoid an unwanted marriage. She eventually arrived in Binsey where she prayed to Saint Margaret for fresh water, and a well sprang forth. In the Middle Ages, Binsey became a pilgrimage destination and the well, said to have healing powers, became known as a "treacle well"; *treacle* being a medieval word for "healing liquid." When the Dormouse tells

Alice a story during the Mad Tea Party, he places three sisters (representing the three Liddells) at the bottom of a "treacle well." Alice at first objects—"There's no such thing"—and then (no doubt thinking of Binsey) concedes that "there may be *one*."

On my last day in Oxford, I stood in the nave of Saint Frideswide's Church looking at a wooden door propped against the wall. Tradition holds that Alice, a talented artist, carved the top panel of the door in the 1880s for a church in London. Wartime bombing all but destroyed the church, and the door was returned to Oxford. The panel depicts Saint Frideswide, standing in a rowboat, returning downstream to Oxford from her exile in Binsey. When those halcyon summer days of Alice's childhood were a distant memory, she chose to carve a young woman in a rowboat on the Thames, journeying toward immortality.

Originally published in November 2015.

Charlie Lovett is the *New York Times* best-selling author of *The Bookman's Tale, First Impressions,* and *The Lost Book of the Grail.* A former antiquarian bookseller, he has written and edited several books on Lewis Carroll.

On England's Coast, Thomas Hardy Made His World

David Shaftel

It was in Lulwind Cove, an inlet on England's south coast, that the dastardly Sergeant Troy took an impromptu swim in *Far from the Madding Crowd,* Thomas Hardy's 1874 novel about an uncommonly independent Victorian woman and her suitors. The water in the cove was "smooth as a pond," Hardy wrote, until Troy "swam between the two projecting spurs of rock which formed the pillars of Hercules to this miniature Mediterranean," whereupon he was swept out to sea and presumed drowned, only to make a dramatic reappearance—this being a Hardy novel—at a most inconvenient moment.

On an evening last summer, the sun still high, my wife and I, our one-year-old daughter strapped to my chest, walked the grassy loam above the cove. The spot is actually called Lulworth Cove and is a fan-shaped bay formed by erosion of the cliffs. It and Durdle Door, an impressive limestone arch a little farther along the coast, are hallmarks of the Jurassic Coast, a ninety-five-mile stretch of shoreline where rock formations and fossils record 185 million years of geological history.

The water below the cliffs was a cerulean blue from the

mineral deposits washed into them from the crumbling stone, while the English Channel beyond retained the "clear oily polish" Hardy described. To the north lay rolling maize fields and dairy pastures, the roads and tidy plots bordered by ancient hedgerows. A few swimmers braved the water, still frigid in June, and, as on the day of Troy's swim, "a frill of milkwhite foam along the nearer angles of the shore . . . licked the contiguous stones like tongues."

Though we were in the county of Dorset, Hardy called this part of England "Wessex," using the area's Saxon name. He described it as "partly real, partly dream" country. It is a region as inextricable from Hardy as the Mississippi of William Faulkner or V. S. Naipaul's Trinidad. The term "cliffhanger," in fact, is said to have originated with Hardy, after he left one of his characters dangling from a Wessex cliff at the end of a chapter in a serialized novel.

Though Hardy country, as it is known here, is dotted with actual landmarks such as churches, markets, and villages from the author's novels, I was interested in the pastoral landscapes that he is famous for describing: the farmland and heath with sandstone cottages; sheep pastures; Roman roads ending abruptly at dramatic seaside cliffs. And since Dorset is relatively unspoiled by modern development, it isn't hard to imagine, with a squint of the eyes, the countryside as Hardy saw it.

My wife grew up near Lyme Regis, a pretty harbor town on the western end of Dorset, about 150 miles west of London. She spent her childhood in Hardy country and has been known to extol the virtues of *Tess of the d'Urbervilles,* Hardy's most enduring novel. But when I said that I wanted to see the Dorset landscape that the books inhabit—and that now inhabits a film of *Far from the Madding Crowd*—she was skeptical, thinking only of a childhood characterized by rural isolation, a lack of fashionable friends, and traffic jams caused by slow-moving tractors.

But in the twenty years since she left, Dorset has had a reversal of fortune, aided in 2001 by the Jurassic Coast earning UNESCO World Heritage status for its proliferation of fossils and the geological story told by the cliffs. It is now popular with tourists interested in more than just Victorian tragedies about fallen women and men who can't rise above their station. And though the landscape is certainly recognizable from Hardy's time, the area is increasingly home to stylish little hotels, fashionable shops, and pubs and restaurants serving modern British fare.

We based ourselves in Bridport—called "Port Bredy" by Hardy—at the Bull Hotel, in a modishly renovated seventeenth-century coaching house. A fishing and market town, Bridport has been called Notting Hill on Sea by the English press for its tasteful boutiques and restaurants. Its main street is lined with stone-and-brick Victorian buildings, connected across the high street by festive bunting.

Since we were there on a market day, we pushed the baby around the stalls selling antiques and local produce, before retreating for a creative cocktail in the luxuriant Venner Bar, supposedly the site of a sixteenth-century murder, tucked behind the hotel's ballroom.

For help with our Dorset itinerary, I contacted the Thomas Hardy Society, formed in 1968 to promote the author, as well as tourism to Dorset. In 2015, the society commemorated the 175th anniversary of Hardy's birth with a lecture, a "Hardy Walk" through Hardy country, and a wreath-laying on Hardy's grave.

"There is always another character in all Hardy's novels about Wessex, and that is the countryside," said Mike Nixon, the society's secretary. "In a way, Hardy was the first tourist officer for Dorset. And people do come to see the countryside, the towns, and the buildings he wrote about."

Nixon said Hardy pilgrimages began in the author's lifetime, aided by Hermann Lea's *Thomas Hardy's Wessex.* Compiled with Hardy's help, the 1913 book is a guide to the settings thinly disguised in his novels. I found a yellowing copy in a vintage bookshop in Bridport and used it as my guide.

Hardy was born to a builder of modest means and a former domestic servant in 1840, in the tiny village of Higher Bockhampton, about three miles east of Dorchester, the county seat. In 1885, after a nomadic period that included a stint as an architect in London, Hardy settled in Dorchester at Max Gate, an unremarkable two-bedroom brick house he designed himself and named for a nearby tollbooth.

With his balding head, gray mustache, and penchant for drab waistcoats, he was nothing like the handsome blades that appear in so many of his novels. He married a rather dour woman against the objections of her family, and their marriage eventually soured. They never had children but there was a beloved dog named Wessex, or Wessie, a wire-haired terrier known to bite.

His wife eventually moved to the attic of Max Gate, and when she died, he married a much younger woman. He lived at Max Gate until his death in 1928. Max Gate and the thatched-roof cottage he was born in are now well-subscribed tourist attractions. The author's study, however, has been removed and reassembled in a Hardy wing of the Dorset County Museum in Dorchester.

We started in Dorchester, a town of around 20,000 that lies on the site of a Roman settlement and appears as "Casterbridge" in several of Hardy's novels, most notably *The Mayor of*

Casterbridge, in which the mayor sells his wife to a sailor after too many helpings of "furmity," an "antiquated slop" of rum-spiked porridge. "Casterbridge announced Rome in every street, alley, and precinct. It looked Roman, bespoke the art of Rome, concealed the dead men of Rome," Hardy wrote. Indeed, while excavating for the construction of Max Gate, Hardy's builders discovered three Roman graves.

A preponderance of chain stores, though, has robbed Dorchester of its Roman and Victorian charms. The model for the mayor's house is now a branch of Barclays Bank, and it is hard to imagine Dorchester as the town where the by-then ex-mayor memorably wrestled his romantic rival in a granary with one arm tied to his side to make it a fair fight.

I was not disappointed, however, by the Maumbury Rings—Hardy's "Ring at Casterbridge"—the remains of a first century AD Roman amphitheater. "Melancholy, impressive, lonely, yet accessible from every part of the town, the historic circle was the frequent spot for appointments of a furtive kind," Hardy wrote in *The Mayor of Casterbridge.* It served as an artillery garrison during the English Civil War and was the site of public executions in the seventeenth and eighteenth centuries.

The once-imposing earthwork sits rather meekly amid a residential neighborhood on Dorchester's outskirts, its neatly trimmed grass now host to Roman reenactments, though a clandestine rendezvous inside its basin could still go unobserved. That it sits amid a modern residential neighborhood is a reminder of the area's long history and how the area's past was always present in Hardy's work.

A five-minute drive southwest of Dorchester is Maiden Castle, the remains of the forty-seven-acre Iron Age hill fort that Nixon said was the site where Sergeant Troy, the freeloading opportunist, performed his military sword exercise for the heroine Bathsheba Everdene, in a scene he said was "fraught with Victorian symbolism."

The fort is in the shape of a kidney bean and its earthen ramparts are covered in wild grass and ferns. The invading Romans moved the settlement's inhabitants to the site of Dorchester. These days the fort is reached by walking trails, its only residents sheep.

It took us fifteen minutes to scale the fort's outer berm from where we could see down into the pits between the ramparts, like the one where Bathsheba became "enclosed in a firmament of lights and sharp hisses, resembling a sky-full of meteors close at hand" as she watched "the marvelous evolutions of Troy's reflecting blade, which seemed everywhere at once, and yet nowhere specifically."

Since there were countless Hardy sites in Dorset, we spent the next day driving between some that were convenient to Bridport. We saw Beaminster—Hardy's "hill-surrounded little town" of Emminster in *Tess*—and the nearby Mapperton estate, where scenes in the film *Far from the Madding Crowd* were shot in the Elizabethan manor house's lovely terraced gardens.

Next we drove up to Cerne Abbas, a village that sprang up around a Benedictine abbey in the tenth century, a version of which appears in *The Woodlanders* and *Tess.* We couldn't miss the Cerne Abbas Giant, a 180-foot-high figure of a club-wielding, muscle-bound hulk cut out of the turf on a hillside and carefully maintained over the years. Its ancient origins are unknown.

In Cerne Abbas we met Will Best, who owns an organic dairy farm that hugs the hills above the village. Best credits the Hardy Society's inaugural conference in 1968 with a revival in Hardy tourism. Since Best's farm is one of the last to grow and supply wheat for use on the thatched roofs of Dorset's cottages, he was recruited to teach the cast of *Madding Crowd* how to make the large bundles of harvested wheat, common in Victorian farming, that feature in a pivotal scene. He made such an impression that he was made an extra in the movie.

Best, sixty-seven, said he developed an affinity for Hardy when he found a copy of *Tess* while away at boarding school. "I was really brought back home by it," he said. "Hardy's scenes with the country people and the way they speak reminded me of my childhood on the farm."

Twenty or thirty years ago, Best said, the cottages and villages in Dorset were still owned by the big landowners. Many were derelict, having been abandoned by laborers who left for the city when mechanized farming rendered them obsolete. But as transport links improved and Londoners started moving to the country or buying second homes there, he said, "the cottages started to emerge from scaffolding with new thatched roofs and smart porches."

Before leaving Dorset I wanted to stop in Bere Regis, about twenty minutes east of Bridport. The village has more new buildings than the prettier Dorset villages, but Bere Regis Church isn't one of them, having been built and rebuilt on the same site since 1050. It is notable for containing the tomb of the extinct Turbervilles, the "ancient and knightly" family on which Hardy modeled the d'Urbervilles in his most famous novel.

By the end of *Tess of the d'Urbervilles,* the destitute family of Tess Durbeyfield—thought to be descendants of the extinct landowning d'Urberville clan—take shelter in the "Kingsbere" churchyard after losing their home on a tenant farm following their patriarch's death, a common occurrence in Victorian Dorset, known in Hardy's time for its extreme rural poverty. They bed down under a "beautiful traceried window, of many lights, its date being the fifteenth century."

When Tess enters the church, she encounters Alec, the

"sham d'Urberville" with a "reputation as a reckless gallant and heartbreaker," whose unwanted sexual advances have ruined her. After Alec stamps on the tomb's entrance, Tess wishes for her own death, lamenting, "Why am I on the wrong side of this door!"

When we arrived at the church it was empty, but the huge wooden door was unlocked, so we entered. There, in the south aisle, was the tomb, now sealed, a sign explaining that the worn-out Latin text read that the family of Robert Turberville, who died in 1559, "had been lords of the manor from ancient times."

Once inside, our daughter needed no invitation to play with the toys left there for the parishioners' children while my wife and I ate sandwiches on a pew beneath the famous window with its "heraldic emblems"—the Turberville crest. We were, for the duration of lunch, lords of the manor.

Originally published in May 2015.

David Shaftel is a freelance writer based in New York who writes frequently about travel. He is also the editor of *Racquet*, a quarterly tennis magazine.

Blood, Sand, Sherry: Hemingway's Madrid

David Farley

In the Legazpi neighborhood of Madrid, a vast complex of early twentieth-century buildings of ornate stone and brick sits near the banks of the Manzanares River. For most of the twentieth century, the Matadero Madrid, as the compound is known, was the city's main slaughterhouse; its robust stench lingered far beyond the high stone walls surrounding it and deep into the working-class neighborhood nearby.

In the late 1930s, though, that odor did nothing to deter a young bullfighting-obsessed American writer living in the city from frequenting the slaughterhouse.

"This is where the old women come early in the morning to drink the supposedly nutritious blood of the freshly killed cattle," he later told A. E. Hotchner, his biographer. "Many a morning I'd get up at dawn and come down here to watch the *novilleros,* and sometimes even the matadors themselves, coming in to practice killing, and there would be the old women standing in line for the blood."

These days, you won't find the matadors or the old women: the Matadero has been converted into a dynamic new arts center. On a recent visit, I took in an exhibition of Latin American designers—but I wasn't really there for the art.

I was instead following the tracks of that American writer, Ernest Hemingway. Hemingway is associated with a handful of places around the planet—most notably Paris, Pamplona, Havana, Key West, and Ketchum, Idaho, where he took his own life in July 1961. But none may have held a warmer spot in his heart than Madrid, which he called "the most Spanish of all cities," referring to its diverse population from every region of the country. He also titled a short story based in Madrid "The Capital of the World."

"Don Ernesto," as he was known to the Spanish, spent enough time in Madrid—he was there for chunks of the late 1920s, late 1930s, and parts of the 1950s, with his last visit in 1960—that he left a distinct, mostly booze-stained trail. With the exception of the revamped Matadero, the modern version of Hemingway's Madrid is an old-school itinerary of bars, bullfighting arenas, and restaurants. I set out to experience all that drew Hemingway back again and again to the city.

After starting my tour at the Matadero, I met up with my wife in front of our hotel, the TRYP Madrid Gran Vía, one of the spots where Hemingway stayed (the second-floor breakfast room, named for the writer, displays photos of him in various acts of masculinity, like firing a gun or pulling in a huge fish from a boat).

From there we headed down the Gran Vía, a wide boulevard Hemingway described as Madrid's answer to Broadway and Fifth Avenue combined, passing by Museo Chicote, a cocktail bar he frequented in the 1930s, when it was popular with international journalists. We then zigzagged through the streets around Puerta del Sol, crossing narrow Calle Victoria, where Hemingway often purchased scalped bullfighting tickets. We walked through leafy Plaza de Santa Ana, home to

Cervecería Alemana, a 1904 beer hall that was such a favorite of Hemingway's that he had his own table (just to the right of the entrance, the only marble-topped table overlooking a window).

A couple of twists and turns later, we reached Calle de Echegaray, its cobblestones shining from a morning rain, and entered La Venencia, an old bar where men in flat caps and tweed jackets sipped sherry from tall, narrow glasses and barkeeps wrote their tabs in chalk on the bar.

We sat down at a table toward the back of the room with Stephen Drake-Jones, who has lived in Madrid for thirty-five years. "Welcome to the civil war," said Drake-Jones, a sixty-one-year-old former University of Madrid history professor, referring to the three-year period, 1936 to 1939, that pitted left-leaning Republicans against the Fascists. Drake-Jones runs a tour company called the Wellington Society of Madrid. A native of Leeds, England, Drake-Jones gives a popular Hemingway-themed tour and has an encyclopedic knowledge of the writer's time in Madrid.

As he pushed glasses of crisp Manzanilla sherry toward us, Drake-Jones explained that La Venencia was—and, in some ways, still is—a haunt for Republican sympathizers. "During the civil war," he said, "this bar was frequented by Republican soldiers. Hemingway would come here a lot to get news from the front"—in the late 1930s, he was reporting on the war for the North American Newspaper Alliance—which would later inform *For Whom the Bell Tolls,* his novel about the war.

"This place hasn't changed in seventy years," he added. "It's like walking right into Hemingway."

He pointed to an old sign on the wall and translated: IN THE INTEREST OF HYGIENE, DON'T SPIT ON THE FLOOR. This was, he said, only the first rule of La Venencia. The second rule—no taking photos—prevented Republican visitors from being incriminated by possible Fascist spies during the war. The third rule: absolutely no tipping. "The Republican loyalists considered themselves all workers—they were all the same—so there was no point in tipping," Drake-Jones said.

Just then his eyes squinted and narrowed in on my wife, who was taking a sip of sherry. "Stop!" he cried. There was a fourth rule he hadn't gotten to yet. "If this were during the civil war, you'd be arrested right now," he said, his eyes surveying the room to see if anyone was watching. She put her glass down. "You just gave yourself away as someone who wouldn't have belonged here. But if you would have held your glass like this"—he picked up his glass by the stem—"the regulars wouldn't take alarm. Otherwise, they would have thought you were a foreign spy."

Schooled in correct sipping technique and fortified by the sherry, I bid adios to Drake-Jones and headed to Las Ventas arena, one of the most prestigious bullfighting rings in the world, where I joined a guided group tour. The tours, given daily from 10:30 a.m. to 1:30 p.m., in both English and Spanish, take guests into the seats (Hemingway liked sitting in Section 9, Drake-Jones had told me earlier) and onto the sand in the middle of the stadium, where brave matadors stare down massive horned beasts in front of 24,000 fans. When the tour finished, I asked the guide, Sean Marcos, twenty-four, if he was a bullfighting aficionado.

"No, not really," he said. "The people of my generation don't like bullfighting. It's mostly for older people."

When I asked if he thought that didn't bode well for the future of bullfighting in Spain, he shrugged and said: "Who knows? Maybe when we're older we'll become interested."

Don Ernesto would most likely have been crushed that successive generations were losing interest in his beloved bullfighting. But he'd be happy to know that interest in his other

Madrid love is far from waning: he was also a regular patron of the Prado, home to one of the world's great art collections.

The analogy he drew to viewing art at the museum was pure Hemingway: "The tourist should be introduced to an attractive woman quite unclothed with no draperies, no concealments and no conversation and only the plainest of beds."

The Prado was one of the main reasons he sometimes chose to stay at the Palace Hotel (now the Westin Palace Hotel), across the street from the museum. Hemingway would often begin his evenings with a martini or two at the stuffy bar inside the hotel, which appears toward the end of his 1926 novel, *The Sun Also Rises.*

Like Jake and Brett, the novel's protagonists, my wife and I cozied up to the bar and ordered our own round of martinis. When asked for a dining suggestion, the bartender pointed up toward Plaza de Santa Ana and said the streets were crammed with restaurants. I had a different spot in mind, though: El Sobrino de Botín, Jake and Brett's next stop in the final scenes of the novel.

Botín, open since 1725 on a tiny street behind Plaza Mayor, claims to be the oldest restaurant in the world. Jake and Brett turned up here—like Hemingway himself often did—to dine on the house specialty, roast suckling pig, and drink several bottles of Rioja Alta. Botín isn't above playing up the association: the front window displays an image of the writer and a quote from *The Sun Also Rises* that mentions the restaurant. (Until recently, the owners of a nearby restaurant, presumably trying to differentiate themselves from Botín, hung a large sign above its door reading: HEMINGWAY NEVER ATE HERE.)

We asked for a table upstairs, the place where Hemingway put Jake and Brett, and where he preferred sitting as well. And like our fictional counterparts, we dined on juicy roast suckling pig, though we stopped at just one bottle of Rioja. Afterward,

I introduced myself to Antonio and Carlos Gonzáles, the third generation of their family to run Botín. The brothers hadn't been born when Hemingway was a regular guest at their restaurant, but they've heard plenty of stories.

"Don Ernesto once wanted to make paella," Carlos said. "And so our grandfather allowed him to go into the kitchen to make it."

Was it any good?

"Apparently not," he said, laughing. "It was the last time they let him cook anything."

Gonzáles's grandfather, however, did give Hemingway the privilege of making his own martinis. "He would get here early in the day and write upstairs until his friends showed up for lunch," Antonio said.

We bade the brothers Gonzáles farewell and, like Jake and Brett in the last scene of *The Sun Also Rises*—and most certainly the man whose trail I'd been following the last four days—we hailed a cab and drove into the warm Madrid night.

Originally published in June 2011.

David Farley is the author of the nonfiction book *An Irreverent Curiosity* and writes regularly for *The New York Times* and *Afar.*

James Baldwin's Paris

Ellery Washington

One bright afternoon in Paris, on the terrace of the café Deux Magots, in Saint-Germain-des-Prés, I found myself engaged in an increasingly animated conversation about the writer James Baldwin and the notorious feud that broke out between him and his fellow African American expatriate Richard Wright.

It was late July, and the café's terrace hummed with the casual banter of lounging tourists and residents. All the while a small battalion of crisp-collared waiters shuffled elegantly between the tightly ordered tables and stiff wicker chairs, their every gesture backed by the steady cadence of white porcelain cups tapping against saucers and the gentle clank of Art Deco silverware.

Having spent nearly a decade living in Paris, I'd eaten at Les Deux Magots many times. That afternoon, however, I had a specific purpose in mind. I was retracing James Baldwin's steps through Paris, while asking myself where Baldwin might be living if he were in the city now. To further my search, I had invited the expatriate African American novelist and Baldwin enthusiast Jake Lamar to join me at Les Deux Magots, hoping he would catch any gaps in my itinerary.

"It started right here," Jake said of the dispute between Baldwin and Wright, as our waiter swept away our plates to make space for his forthcoming espresso and my café allongé. Jake was reminding me that Baldwin and Wright's quarrel had begun upstairs from where we sat, facing the cobblestone Place Saint-Germain-des-Prés and l'Église Saint-Germain-des-Prés itself, the oldest church in Paris.

Had we been actually sitting inside the café that day, in the winter of 1948, he explained, we would have surely caught a glimpse of an earnest young Jimmy Baldwin, slightly disheveled from having arrived from New York only hours before, climbing the narrow steps to the café's second floor, where he was greeted by Wright and the editors of *Zero* magazine, a rather small but important literary journal that would shortly publish Baldwin's essay "Everybody's Protest Novel."

Baldwin was only twenty-four when he arrived in Paris, with just $40 in his pocket. Virtually unpublished, he had left New York to escape American racism—an escape that he believed literally saved his life and made it possible for him to write. His first essay in *Zero* argued forcefully against the idea of the protest novel, claiming, among other things, that it was inherently sentimental, and therefore dishonest. Wright, who had already established himself as an international literary force based on the critical success of several novels, was deeply offended by Baldwin's essay, reading it as a direct attack on the validity of his work. Shortly after the essay was published, the two men ran into each other at Brasserie Lipp, less than a block from Les Deux Magots, and Wright immediately lit into Jimmy, who by all accounts held his own.

Baldwin has maintained a grip on my imagination ever

since my freshman year of college, when I read his novel *Giovanni's Room.* Set in 1950s Paris, the novel tells the story of an ill-fated love affair between the narrator, David, a young American ex-soldier, and a darkly handsome Italian barman named Giovanni. As a young, gay black man growing up in the 1980s, I found this to be the first novel I'd encountered with the subject of homosexuality placed front and center, and written by anyone who remotely resembled me. I was inspired in equal parts by the depth and style of Baldwin's prose, and the fact that he, a gay black man, had written so boldly and lived so openly at a time when there was such deep social hatred and opposition aimed at those of us who shared either Baldwin's race or sexual identity, let alone both. What's more, the fact that he had found a way to live and write freely in Paris made the city feel like an essential destination for me.

In the fall of 1998, a few months shy of the fiftieth anniversary of Baldwin's arrival, I, too, finally moved to Paris, settling in a quaint—if not cramped—one-bedroom apartment on the Left Bank, in the Fifth Arrondissement. Seduced by the idea of chasing Baldwin's literary coattails, I dedicated myself to rereading *Giovanni's Room,* allowing the texture and mood of Baldwin's (and Giovanni's) Paris to overlap with the version of the city I was newly discovering. Now, some fifteen years later, having left Paris, ultimately for New York, I was excited to see the city through Baldwin's eyes again, which meant returning to the Left Bank.

For my first day on Baldwin's trail, I caught the Métro from my apartment in Batignolles—a recently trendy neighborhood in the once working-class northeast corner of the Seventeenth Arrondissement—south, across the Seine, to the Sixth Arrondissement and Saint-Germain-des-Prés. I was headed to Café de Flore, the place where Baldwin had spent endless hours on the second floor, drinking coffee and cognac to keep warm while working on his first novel, *Go Tell It on the Mountain.*

It was a mild, sunny day, and exiting the Métro station I was struck by how little had changed in Saint-Germain since I'd caught my first glimpse of the neighborhood back in the late '90s. At once I felt I'd returned to the model-version of Paris, the district that, as the author Diane Johnson noted in her book *Into a Paris Quartier,* the American imagination has tended to "fasten" itself onto for over a century. Surely, this fastening is largely due to Saint-Germain's fabled expatriate history, beginning with Thomas Jefferson's stay on what is now Rue Bonaparte. But for me that afternoon, I was experiencing a renewed vision of the Paris that seems to effortlessly weave the rich vitality of city life together with the ease of vacationing in a small French village. To my left a continuous stream of cars, motorcycles, taxicabs, and bikes flowed steadily down the broad, tree-lined Boulevard Saint-Germain, while on my right, the ponderous row of classic stone facades was pleasantly broken up by stylishly quaint bookstores, shops, sidewalk cafés, and side streets meandering toward the Seine.

During the late 1940s and early '50s, Saint-Germain-des-Prés was the center of a thriving artistic and literary community and a place where nightclubs and bars of varying reputations flourished, allowing Baldwin to openly explore both his literary craft and his sexuality.

At Café de Flore I took a seat on one of the crimson-and-green wicker chairs on the terrace and began planning my next steps on Baldwin's trail. Café de Flore sits on the corner of the Boulevard Saint-Germain and Rue Saint-Benoît. Its location places it directly across Saint-Benoît from its chief rival, Les Deux Magots. Founded in the late 1890s, both cafés are adorned with Art Deco details, red moleskin banquettes, mahogany tables, and mirrored walls. Both have rich intellectual and literary histories, boasting a list of luminaries—writers, artists, actors, and philosophers—that includes Ernest Hemingway, Alain Delon, Jean-Paul Sartre, Simone de Beauvoir, Pablo Picasso, and Albert Camus. Both have similar menus and prices. Even the difference in ambience is barely perceptible, though residents and frequent visitors to the quarter are quick to say that the Flore attracts a slightly more fashionable clientele. When my waiter finally made his way to my table, I ordered a croque monsieur and a citron pressé, my favorite pairing at the café. Handing the menu back to him, I wondered how a starving young writer, as Baldwin had been when he first visited the Flore, might afford the same, somewhat pricey croque today.

I rounded out the afternoon in Saint-Germain by wandering down Rue de Verneuil, a short, rather tight street of low seventeenth-century facades where Baldwin lived in various third-rate hotels during his early years in Paris, before continuing on to the Café Tournon, on Rue de Tournon, near the formal Luxembourg Gardens, and the Brasserie Lipp, back on the Boulevard Saint-Germain. Baldwin was known to visit the Café Tournon and the Brasserie Lipp, albeit infrequently, often stopping in before heading off to eat and drink in one of the cheaper neighborhood brasseries or bars. Both restaurants, their Art Deco mosaics still brilliantly maintained, were hot intellectual and creative nightspots during the 1950s and '60s, the Tournon largely considered the place where the Saint-Germain neighborhood jazz scene got its start, providing the stage on which Duke Ellington made his Parisian debut. Meanwhile, the Lipp had a perpetual waiting list of A-list celebrities and politicians jockeying for a corner table.

Baldwin's main nightlife posse included the painter Beauford Delaney, the composer Howard Swanson, the dancer Bernard Hassell, and the writer Ernest Charles Nimmo, known as Dixie, according to sources like Monique Wells, founder of the blog *Entrée to Black Paris.* She added that the group's favorite spots were Le Montana on Rue Saint-Benoît, Gordon Heath's L'Abbaye on Rue de l'Abbaye, and Inez Cavanaugh's Chez Inez, a soul food restaurant on Rue Champollion. As is the case with nearly all of the restaurants, bars, and cafés in Saint-Germain, the rambunctious, often decadent spirit that inhabited these places during Baldwin's time has been replaced by a somewhat staid, upper-middle-class mood of luxury and tourism, one that seems to radiate out from Le Bon Marché, the oldest and most palatial department store in Paris, penetrating even the smallest of shops, bistros, and watering holes in the neighborhood. Of Baldwin's main hangouts there, Le Montana is one of the few that still exist and is currently one of the most exclusive clubs in Paris. I didn't even attempt to get in.

On my second day following Baldwin's trail I made my way to Montparnasse and settled into a comfortable leather bench at Le Select, yet another well-preserved Art Deco café, the place where Baldwin wrote much of *Giovanni's Room.* If ever there was an American expatriate hub in Paris, Montparnasse was certainly it during the postwar years, largely owing to the sheer number of American students who moved to the Left Bank in the late 1940s and throughout the 1950s. Baldwin associated with many of these students, mostly ex-GIs, writing about his experiences with them in the essay "A Question of Identity."

A sudden rainstorm that morning had delayed my trip to Montparnasse, but by three o'clock, the time I arrived at Le Select, the torrential streaks had subsided to a misty drizzle, and the café's green-trimmed awning, the words AMERICAN BAR printed on the corner bend, was fully extended, affording cover to a small cluster of leisurely smoking patrons huddled on the terrace. (The French government banned smoking indoors years ago, making it difficult to conjure up an image of Baldwin at Le Select, chain-smoking while scribbling furiously on a yellow legal pad in one of the tight rear booths.) In spite of an extensive urban renewal project in the 1960s and '70s that led the city to raze many prewar buildings in Montparnasse, Le Select remains intact, its Art Deco decor virtually unchanged since the 1920s. Le Select sits in the shadow of La Tour Montparnasse, which for many years held the title for the tallest building in France. Decried by Parisians as "grotesque" upon its completion, the tower became the symbol for the indiscriminate destruction of locally cherished buildings, empowering a movement to ban all skyscrapers within the city limits and to preserve historic places like Le Select.

The clientele that afternoon consisted largely of French students earnestly discussing politics and philosophy, a handful of American tourists and local businessmen having a late lunch, and people I took to be neighborhood regulars reading newspapers and books, or simply staring out at the boulevard. As I nibbled off a plate of bread and charcuterie, I couldn't help overhearing the nearby students as they discussed the lagging French economy, the weaknesses of their president, François Hollande, and the highly publicized conservative protests against gay marriage. I was captivated by the youthful sense of French entitlement in their speech, and my thoughts returned to the question of which neighborhood in Paris a young, foreign, black—and struggling—James Baldwin might currently reside, especially considering that Le Select and his other haunts on the Left Bank have all become so chic.

Clearly, Baldwin had explored Parisian neighborhoods beyond those on the Left Bank. In a May 1961 article in *Esquire* magazine, "The New Lost Generation," he attested to the joy he felt discovering Paris. "The days when we walked through Les Halles singing, loving every inch of France and loving each other . . . the jam sessions in Pigalle, and our stories about the whores there . . . the nights spent smoking hashish in the Arab cafés . . . the mornings which found us telling dirty stories, true stories, sad, and earnest stories, in grey, workingmen's cafés."

As for Pigalle, still the largest red-light district in Paris, I had walked through the quarter earlier that week on my way to a dinner party at a friend's apartment in Montmartre. The sun had already begun to set, its final rays fading into the variegated shimmer cast by a long procession of dim Art Nouveau lamps and bright storefront neon. Along the Boulevard de Clichy, I strolled past the Moulin Rouge and a vivid array of sex shops, strip clubs, adult movie theaters, and hotels for prostitution (which is still legal in Paris). It seemed with every step there was yet another barker calling out to me from the entrance of a neon-lit doorway, attempting to sell a lap dance, an XXX-rated film, a girl—or possibly a boy—for hire. That night the spectacle of Pigalle made it easy to imagine the scenes of decadence and freedom Baldwin described when reminiscing about his trips to the area. Unfortunately, this wasn't the case with Les Halles.

In *Giovanni's Room,* Baldwin describes Les Halles as a place with "choked boulevards and impassable streets, a place where leeks, cabbages, oranges, apples, potatoes, cauliflowers stood gleaming in mounds all over, in the sidewalks and streets in front of metal sheds." The restaurants, bars, and cheap workmen's cafés that Baldwin spoke of with such joy were demolished and replaced in 1977 by an underground transportation hub and shopping district—a modern monstrosity of metal and mirrored glass whose underground tunnels connect an intricate series of Métro and suburban train lines, while housing a subterranean shopping center. The extensive transportation and shopping options have allowed Les Halles to remain one of the most ethnically diverse neighborhoods in Paris, much like Downtown Brooklyn's Fulton Street Mall—in terms of daily traffic, at least, in spite of the planners' intentions to draw more exclusive retail and dining to the area. Still, the cost of living in the center limits the neighborhood's actual diversity.

In 1999, my second year in Paris, I lived beside Les Halles, in the First Arrondissement, on the pedestrian Rue du Cygne, and, more recently, I'd heard that the entire complex was being redeveloped. Curious to see the changes before leaving Paris, I invited my friend Walid Nouioua to dinner at Le Père Fouettard, my favorite restaurant in Les Halles, beside the hub's main entry. That night, I was disappointed to find the new facade of Les Halles hidden behind wide construction panels and such extensive scaffolding that it was impossible to see what the new structure might look like. Walid and I took a table on the large bustling terrace. A doctor by profession, Algerian and French by birth and citizenship, Walid happens to be an avid Baldwin reader, and so midway through our meal, I asked his thoughts on the possible whereabouts of a young James Baldwin in contemporary Paris. Other friends and colleagues, I explained, had made suggestions based on one characteristic or another: Le Marais, given Baldwin's nightlife and homosexuality. Ménilmontant or Place des Fêtes in response to a notion of creative affinity. Belleville or Château Rouge for ethnic diversity. The suburbs of Paris such as Montreuil, Saint-Ouen, Aubervilliers, and Saint-Denis, where artists and writers were currently moving. After weighing the options carefully, Walid simply shook his head and agreed that the reasons offered for each of these districts made them all viable possibilities.

And so I spent my final days in Paris visiting bars and cafés in Beaubourg and Le Marais, notably Café Beaubourg on Rue Saint-Merri, L'OPEN Café on Rue des Archives, and L'Étoile Manquante on Rue Vieille du Temple. I discovered the smartly gentrified redbrick-and-masonry town houses hidden in the alleyways near Place des Fêtes. I wandered through a string of charming studios and galleries in and around Belleville and the picturesque Rue des Cascades. I revisited the African markets at Château Rouge and toured a handful of galleries and artists' workshops housed in old factories, garages, and warehouses in the trendier corners of Montreuil, one of the eastern suburbs of the city. I even visited the northern suburbs of Paris, investigating La Maladrerie, an elegantly conceived public housing project in Aubervilliers, where writers' and artists' studios were located alongside general housing. And yet I couldn't actually picture a young James Baldwin living in any of these places. As I reflected on the idea behind my search, it dawned on me that the key elements that conspired to bring Baldwin to Paris all those years ago no longer existed in Paris, nor did the same overriding impulses to leave America.

In the spring of 1984, during an interview for *The Paris Review,* a nearly sixty-year-old Baldwin was asked why he had chosen to live in France, to which he replied: "It wasn't so much a matter of choosing France—it was a matter of getting out of America." The problem of racism in America was for Baldwin so consuming and, to his mind, deadly that he feared he wouldn't have survived it if he'd stayed, let alone been able to isolate himself enough to write. And yet upon arriving in France, he had no illusions that Paris was among the "most civilized of cities," nor did he consider the French among the "least primitive of peoples." During those early years he stayed in France because, as a black man, he perceived that the ruling-class whites there simply left him alone, unlike those in America, and that's what allowed him to develop as a writer.

But I arrived in Paris generations after the time when the French were inclined to leave people of color alone. Baldwin himself pointed out the changes in French feeling toward all minorities after the furious Battle of Dien Bien Phu, signaling the loss of colonial Vietnam, and the brutal Algerian war. Over the years this change has grown in step with the influx of blacks and North Africans from France's former colonies and outer departments, including Guadeloupe and Martinique.

As the French historian Michel Fabre noted in his book *From Harlem to Paris: Black American Writers in France, 1840–1980,* France may have served as "a place of shelter from what Baldwin called, 'the American madness,' " but that time has clearly passed. What was once a haven for American blacks is now no longer needed. Of course, during the near decade I lived in Paris, I certainly experienced occasions of French racism firsthand. And yet that didn't dissuade me during my recent trip. Even if France is no longer a haven for people of color, Paris remains a beacon, a vital connection to a time when, for many of our most important artists, writers, and political thinkers, a much-needed shelter was sought and found.

Originally published in January 2014.

Ellery Washington is an associate professor of creative writing at the Pratt Institute. He is at work on a novel, *Buffalo*.

Edith Wharton Always Had Paris

Elaine Sciolino

Like many of the characters in her novels, Edith Wharton made frequent use of concealment, reserve, and deception in her life.

So it was fitting that the leading American female writer of the early twentieth century experienced her first and most likely only passionate love affair in the city of Paris, far removed from her homes in New York and New England.

The pleasure she found in Paris in the years before World War I became a cover for the pleasure she took from her clandestine relationship with William Morton Fullerton, a handsome, Frenchified, well-read American cad who worked as the Paris correspondent for *The Times of London*.

"I am sunk in the usual demoralizing happiness which this atmosphere produces in me," Wharton wrote in a letter at the end of 1907. She added, "The tranquil majesty of the architectural lines, the wonderful blurred winter lights, the long lines of lamps garlanding the avenues & the quays—je l'ai dans mon sang!" ("I have it in my blood!")

For Wharton, Paris was a place of liberation. Intellectual

women like her were listened to in this city. The setting was both aesthetically beautiful and logistically enabling for her romance, which she embarked upon in her mid-forties and kept secret from both her husband and her circle of friends.

"Theirs was a discreet adultery," said Hermione Lee, a professor and the author of *Edith Wharton,* the definitive biography of the writer. "It worked in Paris in a way that it never would have in America."

She and Fullerton plotted their encounters via the text-message technology of the era: a furious exchange of brief notes delivered often several times a day by the Paris postal system.

"At the Louvre at one o'c in the shadow" of Diana, she wrote in one note. Today, the white marble sculpture of Diana, the goddess of the hunt, nude and reclining, her right arm wrapped around the neck of a stag, sits in a little-visited room up four sets of stairs off the Louvre's Marly sculpture court. It is an excellent meeting place for a private rendezvous.

Wharton's relationship with Paris and things French began early and ran deep. She had begun studying French with a tutor and visited Paris with her family as a young child. She spoke flawless if old-fashioned French as an adult. She wrote the first draft of *Ethan Frome* in French to perfect her style. Unlike most Americans in Paris in those days, she immersed herself in French literature, mastered French bureaucracy, and had close French friends.

In 1913, when she divorced Teddy Wharton, who had gradually succumbed to mental illness, she did it in a French court. (It avoided the public nature of the American court system.)

Her apartment hotel, when she needed temporary lodging, was the Hôtel de Crillon, recently opened in a late-eighteenth-century building on the Place de la Concorde, which catered, she felt, to a cultured crowd. She detested the Ritz, where the newly rich but uncultivated Americans stayed, calling it the Nouveau Luxe in her fiction.

There is no Wharton suite or bar in the Crillon. My search of the Crillon's guest books, kept in the safe, turned up the signatures of several other luminaries who stayed in the early years: Andrew Carnegie in 1913, Theodore Roosevelt in 1914, King George V of Britain in 1915. But there is no entry by Wharton.

Since she had described her Crillon space as "a very nice apartment up in the sky, overlooking the whole of Paris," the hotel management believes that she must have rented what is now the Bernstein Suite, the sixth-floor set of rooms named after Leonard Bernstein, the American composer and conductor, who lived there off and on until his death in 1990. Inside, two terraces give out onto the Place de la Concorde, and the Pleyel grand piano that he played stands in the living room.

For the most part, Wharton's Paris was grounded on the other side of the Seine in a neighborhood village known as the Faubourg Saint-Germain in the Seventh Arrondissement. With its private mansions hidden behind walls and doors, it was grand, formal, and difficult for outsiders to access. It was here she met Fullerton in early 1907—at the salon of the Countess Rosa de Fitz-James, now the Swiss Embassy.

I went walking through the neighborhood early one morning with David Burke, an American author of a book on writers in Paris. He pointed out the apartment at 58, Rue de Varenne, not far from Rue du Bac, which Edith and Teddy Wharton sublet from George Vanderbilt. It now serves as an annex to the Hôtel Matignon, the prime minister's office, just across the street.

Most of Wharton's years in Paris were spent in the most prestigious floor of a late-nineteenth-century stone building just down the street at No. 53. A plaque on the outside of the building describes her as "the first writer of the United States to settle in France out of love of the country and its literature."

The outer door was open. Just inside the doorway, we peeked through the long glass doors that gave onto her building's entrance hall, with its marble floor, shiny grand urn on a pedestal, and red-carpeted staircase. We walked into her courtyard with its twisted vines and row of private garages (once stables) adorned with a clock.

We could see that the back of her apartment looked out at a private, narrow residential mews known as the Cité de Varenne and a formal garden that now is part of the Italian Embassy, and on the other side, the much larger garden of the French Prime Ministry.

Today, a sign in French at the entrance to the mews announces that access is forbidden to "every unknown person," but we were there when the concierge was off duty, and no one stopped us from strolling in and out.

The Italian Embassy garden and the Prime Ministry grounds are closed to the public, but the garden of the Italian Cultural Institute across the street is not. The building once housed France's first Foreign Ministry, and Napoléon Bonaparte met Madame de Staël here.

The liveliest spot on the street is the site of the Hôtel Biron, which now serves as the Musée Rodin, near the Hôtel des Invalides. The writer Rainer Maria Rilke and his friend and former boss, Auguste Rodin, lived and worked there at the same time that Wharton was writing down the street, but there is no indication they knew each other. The two men wouldn't have been her type.

The sculpture garden and café are my neighborhood refuge, particularly early in the morning when they are mostly empty. With its one-euro entry (and free toilet), the garden is one of the best bargains in Paris.

Wharton's relationship with Fullerton worked particularly well when they acted like ordinary tourists. In just one day, they met at the Louvre, visited the nearby Church of Saint-Germain-l'Auxerrois, went to the ancient Roman Arènes de Lutèce near the Jardin des Plantes, and walked around the Luxembourg Gardens.

They saw each other in theaters like the Comédie-Française and the Marigny. They dined in restaurants in obscure corners of the Left Bank, which she described as "the end of the earth . . . where there is bad food & no chance of meeting acquaintances."

Paris was also the headquarters from which she could plan what she called their "motor flights" out of town. One day they headed by car to the fortress town of Montfort-l'Amaury, west of Paris.

With its sixteenth-century stained-glass windows, the Church of Saint-Pierre is still just as dazzling as when those two lovers visited. I followed the path they took up the hill to the ruins of the stone-and-brick tower that date from the eleventh century, with their view of the forest of Rambouillet, and then visited the seventeenth-century cemetery with its arcaded cloister and vaulted wooden roofs.

On another occasion, Wharton and Fullerton took the train to Senlis, north of Paris. The lovers wandered through the narrow cobblestone streets with their medieval and Renaissance houses. They strolled into the garden containing the ruins of medieval buildings and massive Gallo-Roman ramparts. They visited the Gothic Notre-Dame Cathedral, dating from the twelfth century, and had an early dinner in town. On the train back, Wharton later wrote in her secret diary, "I knew then, dearest dear, all that I had never known before, the interfusion of spirit & sense, the double nearness, the mingled communion of touch & thought."

But Fullerton became distant and unreliable, and by 1910 the affair was over. Crushed, alone after her divorce, Wharton nevertheless decided to stay on in Paris. With the outbreak of World War I, she fell "in love with the spirit of France," wrote Professor Lee, and poured herself into charities she created. She started in her neighborhood with sewing workshops that eventually employed more than eight hundred women, opened hostels for tuberculosis patients and refugee children, hosted benefit concerts, sent dispatches from the war front. For her war work, she was made a chevalier of the Legion of Honor.

After the war, she turned against Paris. It was filling up with Americans drunk with the buying power of the dollar. "Paris is simply awful—a kind of continuous earth-quake of motor-busses, trams, lorries, taxis & other howling & swooping & colliding engines, with hundreds & thousands of U.S. citizens rushing about in them," she wrote.

She died in 1937 at her home in Saint-Brice-sous-Forêt, north of Paris; her grave in the Cimetière des Gonards at Versailles is little visited and little tended.

But Wharton's Paris endures in her fiction—in *Madame de Treymes, The Reef,* and *The Custom of the Country.*

And one of the saddest and most frustrating scenes in her fiction, the denouement of *The Age of Innocence,* was set in the City of Light. There, the fifty-seven-year-old widower Newland Archer cannot bring himself to join his son in calling on Countess Ellen Olenska. Decades earlier, Archer and the countess had fallen deeply in love, but never consummated what was an impossible relationship.

After hours of wandering alone on foot through Paris, he meets his son and they walk together from their hotel to the Place des Invalides across the Seine. "The dome of Mansart floated ethereally above the budding trees and the long grey front of the building: drawing up into itself all the rays of afternoon light, it hung there like the visible symbol of the race's glory," Wharton wrote.

Father and son walk along one of the avenues radiating from the Hôtel des Invalides and find the little square with horse chestnut trees and a view of the gold dome of the Invalides, where Countess Olenska lives. As the day fades into a "soft sun-shot haze," Archer sits on a bench in the square and looks up at what he surmises is her apartment and imagines what's going on inside. "It's more real to me here than if I went up," he finally realizes.

Wharton does not tell the reader the name of the square, but I have gone searching for it several times. (In his 1993 film version of the novel, Martin Scorsese put it in another neighborhood, at the Place de Furstenberg in the Sixth Arrondissement.) Certainly, there are places that evoke it: a wooden slat bench in the Musée Rodin garden in front of *The Burghers of Calais,* with a view of the gold-plated dome of the Invalides and of a fifth-floor window across the street; a leaner wooden bench in the garden of the Musée de l'Armée, with a close-up view of the dome and a street of six-story residential buildings farther off.

The closest I came to the square was a long oblong: an expanse of lawn lined with plane trees that runs between the two sides of the Avenue de Breteuil. Late one afternoon I found a park bench there and, with the dome of the Invalides to my left, watched the sun pierce the upper windows of the odd-numbered buildings nearby.

I don't believe the square exists outside the pages of *The Age of Innocence.* If it does, I don't think Wharton wants us to find it.

Originally published in October 2009.

Elaine Sciolino is a contributing writer and former Paris bureau chief for *The New York Times* and the author of the *New York Times* best seller *The Only Street in Paris: Life on the Rue des Martyrs.*

Amid the Menace of War, Sanary-sur-Mer Was a Refuge Under the Sun

Antonia Feuchtwanger

It is afternoon in the garden of a white Belle Époque town house shaded by two umbrella pines, the rocky shore just a short walk away. Cicadas buzz. Young men windsurf in the shimmering water. The place is Sanary-sur-Mer, in the South of France, thirty miles from Marseille, and an inviting spot for present-day travelers.

But for those who know the history of this small, sunlit town, there is a powerful pull of the past, an undercurrent from the extraordinary time when Hitler was in the ascendant and Sanary was, for a few years, the capital of German literature in exile.

That world is evoked by Sybille Bedford, the English German novelist, in her autobiographical novel *Jigsaw* and in *Quicksands,* her memoir. In the books, the first of which was short-listed for Britain's prestigious Booker Prize, she recalls her life during the 1920s and '30s in this little fishing port that became, briefly, a safe haven for those whose lives were at risk.

Sanary, on a bay shielded from the wider Mediterranean

and circled by hills, is not far from the Riviera's fancier destinations, but it is little known outside France. It attracts virtually no Americans and few Britons, and has no high-rise hotels. But a visitor can drink an espresso alongside locals reading their local newspaper in cafés on the quay, take a small motorboat to explore the coastline, watch the fishing boats bringing in their catch, head for the nearby beach at Portissol, or wander through narrow, car-free backstreets lined by boulangeries and boutiques.

In the era chronicled in *Quicksands,* the Côte d'Azur was already a playground for sun worshippers, writers, artists, and the fashionable, but when the Nazis began to strip political opponents of their citizenship, little Sanary was still peaceful and affordable.

Aldous Huxley—always Aldous to Bedford—had bought a house in Sanary in 1930. In 1933, Thomas Mann took a villa there, encouraged by his son Klaus, who, according to Bedford, used to smoke opium with Jean Cocteau at Toulon, nine miles away. In a garden above the Sanary bay, the exiles clustered together as Bertolt Brecht, with his leather jacket and Bavarian accent, sang his latest anti-Reich songs.

Sybille Bedford, born von Schoenebeck, lived in London up until her death in 2006 at the age of ninety-five. She had always written in English—much, she wrote, to Thomas Mann's pained disapproval. Her father was a Southern German Catholic baron and her mother was English and partly Jewish—as for "how partly," she wrote, "no one cared much—or had to."

Her life began in the splendor of Kaiser Wilhelm's Berlin. In time her mother disappeared to Italy, leaving the young Sybille to aristocratic poverty with her father in a Baden country house. As a young adult, her peripatetic life took her to Rome, Touraine, and Mexico; to Ischia with Martha Gellhorn; to Paris, where she knew Jane Bowles and Truman

Capote. And to Sanary. She writes in *Quicksands:* "Chance, often choice had led me to spend the squandered years in beautiful or interesting places: to learn, to see, to travel, to walk in nocturnal streets, swim in warm seas, make friends and keep them, eat on trellised terraces, drink wine under summer leaves, to hear the song of tree-frog and cicada, to fall in love."

A few months ago, with *Quicksands* in one hand and a book on the exiles in Sanary from the local tourist office in the other, I relished retracing the streets and paths she had walked.

The first stop was the group of harborside cafés where the émigrés used to congregate. A plaque on a wall, visible from the Place Michel Pacha, in front of the Church of Saint-Nazaire, implores the visitor to lend an ear to pick up echoes of the poems composed there seventy years earlier to mock Goebbels and Hitler, or the buzz of talk on Goethe or Stalin, or just the gossip about how to get from one day to the next. It must have been hard, keeping up appearances and the commitment to write, when politics and life itself had become so terrifyingly uncertain.

In Sanary, however, the horrors of Hitler's Germany must have seemed far away. They still do. As I explored in the brilliantly clear morning light, the residents and French tourists in the market, with its fruits and vegetables and a curious kind of charred chickpea polenta, were getting on with the business of enjoying everyday life.

A few blocks away, outside the Villa Roge, where the pacifist writer Wilhelm Herzog once lived, I stopped in a little stone-paved alley, almost envious of his life in exile in this small town house with an enclosed garden of bamboo and bougainvillea, in a pleasant backstreet not far from the harbor. Herzog, who was among the first German writers to predict the rise of Nazism, settled in Sanary in 1930 and left Germany forever in 1933, after being hunted by Nazi storm troopers while visiting Berlin for a speaking engagement.

I walked slowly up the Montée de l'Oratoire, a wide uphill lane, free of cars and an easy climb with a view across the bay. On one side were borders and private gardens stocked with palms, rosemary, and pink oleander. On the other, the bay was busy with motorboats and sporty catamarans from the sailing school.

I reached the little Notre-Dame de Pitié Chapel, which dates back to 1560. Once it was inhabited by a hermit whose job it was to ring a bell when he sighted storms, fog, or enemy vessels. Now I sat on a pew and read in *Quicksands* that the Villa la Tranquille, in this part of Sanary, had once been refurbished by Bedford's stepfather for an old German family friend called Mamoushka in the book. In 1933, Mamoushka had left France, and Bedford and others arranged for Thomas Mann, who by then had realized he could no longer stay in Germany, to rent the villa. In a strange twist, Mamoushka's son-in-law was already one of Hitler's ambassadors.

After the fall of France the Villa la Tranquille was destroyed to make way for a German antiaircraft battery. Still intact on this high point, however, is the Moulin Gris, a picturesque old watchtower that Franz Werfel, author of *The Song of Bernadette,* and his wife, Alma, the widow of Gustav Mahler, made their home in 1938. The tower, with all its windows, suited Werfel very well, but his wife wrote in her autobiography that the rooms near the kitchen were unbearably hot.

My last stops were the two villas of Lion Feuchtwanger. He was the best-selling author of the novels *The Oppermanns* and *Jew Süss,* a prominent critic of the Nazis, and also the uncle of my father, Edgar. Bedford disliked Lion's conceit and womanizing, but he was a generous host to the émigré circle in Sanary and, later, after they had all fled France, in Pacific Palisades, California.

I found the first Sanary house that Lion had occupied, the Villa Lazare. It was charmingly set among pines above a tiny bay. But his next, the Villa Valmer, on a gently climbing road, was exceptional, with commanding bay views. In the Valmer garden—then full of fig, cherry, almond, and olive trees—Brecht sang his songs and Bedford endured my great-uncle's rudeness about her German writing style. And it was there that Bedford's American friend and Lion's mistress, the Munich-born painter Eva Herrmann, drew cartoons of them all.

Lion wrote movingly of returning from Paris on the night train to his beautiful Mediterranean garden. In 1939 he lingered too long in his villa and was briefly interned by the French government. When the Germans invaded in 1940, he was interned once more as German nationals were rounded up again, this time for real.

Some of the ambivalence he had felt about living a charmed life, in comfort while his fellow Jews in Germany were enduring daily humiliation and persecution, comes through in *The Oppermanns,* written during the Sanary years; it describes the impact of Hitler's rule on a long-established Berlin family.

That, after all, is the peculiar tension that one feels as one follows the path of Sanary's exiles in paradise, as they are often described. To modern eyes, they seem astonishingly fortunate to have reached such a place, getting by on their wits or on capital or reputations created elsewhere. Anyone retracing their steps can only feel grateful that they should have found such a refuge. But it could not last.

After writing critically of the Nazis in *Die Sammlung,* the periodical published by Klaus Mann and Thomas Mann's novelist brother, Heinrich, Bedford was stripped of the income from her German inheritance. As she puts it, "By September 1939, all existences snapped in two." In Sanary, Wilhelm Herzog wrote in his diary that month: "Hitler is attacking Warsaw. Met the Werfels in the Café Nautique. Is this the Decline of the West?"

Lion and his wife, Marta, along with the Werfels, Heinrich Mann, and Golo Mann, another son of Thomas Mann, escaped across the Pyrenees with the help of the American Varian Fry and his Emergency Rescue Committee. Thomas Mann was already in the United States, and Bedford was soon there too. It would be five years before peace was restored to a scarred and devastated Europe.

Sanary was just a temporary haven—one that could not last forever. But today it is still possible to picture the civilization that the émigrés had brought with them, the political argument, literary endeavor, and hospitality, surviving for a few years under the welcoming sun.

Originally published in October 2005.

Antonia Cox (née Feuchtwanger) is an elected member of Westminster City Council in London and a former lead writer for the *Evening Standard* and *Daily Telegraph.*

On the French Riviera, Fitzgerald Found His Place in the Sun

Nina Burleigh

Unless you happen to be on a billionaire's yacht requiring a deepwater port, or are a paparazzo stalking Leonardo DiCaprio along the Riviera, you might have no reason to find yourself near Antibes or its charming little sister village, Juan-les-Pins, on a summer evening. And that would be unfortunate, because among the legendary diversions of Cap d'Antibes is exploring the rocky playground peninsula on the French Riviera that inspired one of America's greatest writers.

It's been almost a century since F. Scott Fitzgerald lived here, in a rented seaside house called the Villa Saint Louis with his almost-mad wife, Zelda, and their towheaded daughter, Scottie. A few years after the Fitzgeralds left in 1927, the house on the seawall in Juan-les-Pins was expanded into a hotel called the Belles Rives, now with forty rooms and five stars.

Fitzgerald and the rest of his Jazz Age set have been "borne back ceaselessly into the past," as he predicted in the most famous of his *Great Gatsby* lines, but the essential nature of Cap d'Antibes outlived them. The "diffused magic of the hot sweet South . . . the soft-pawed night and the ghostly wash of the

Mediterranean far below" that Fitzgerald described in *Tender Is the Night* is as palpable now as then, even as the demographics of the rich set that so intrigued him are now less Anglo-American and more Russian, Chinese, and Arab.

From all the terraces of the hotel and from the restaurant perched on the low seawall, one can still see the small blinking green lighthouse, just a hundred yards off, warning ships about the shallow rocky shore. The lighthouse, which Fitzgerald had seen on previous visits to the area, may have been the model for the green light on the dock that symbolized Jay Gatsby's longing for the elusive Daisy, and his ephemeral goal of belonging to the moneyed set.

During a recent stay in Antibes, I spent a few evenings at the Hôtel Belles Rives's Fitzgerald Bar, a jewel box of a room with a grand piano, mirrored tables, little leopard-upholstered Art Deco chairs, and French doors opening onto the sea. I ordered a single "Green Therapy" cocktail of gin, cucumber, and egg white, and settled in to observe the swells swanning through the lobby.

The shimmery demographics of Riviera money are as varied as the schools of shiny fish flitting beneath the waves nearby. A diminutive young Russian woman in a white lace romper sprayed herself liberally with expensive perfume in the bathroom while her hulking boyfriend with his wraparound shades and security entourage waited.

Eight British financiers talked business around a table for four hours, drinking throughout and never seeming drunk. An elegant French couple of a certain age, his yellow cashmere sweater thrown over his shoulders in the universal sign of Euro-maleness, studied the wine list carefully. A wedding party of Africans and African Americans waltzed through, decked to the nines, some in gleaming white linen and tapestried skullcaps. Everywhere, women with freshly lacquered nails and sequins and lip-liner. Finally, a family of sportif Americans, discussing whether to sell New York and keep Hawaii and Colorado, or just stay right there and figure it out later.

Out on the bay bobbed the great yachts, most notably the enormous *Ecstasea,* built for the Russian oligarch Roman Abramovich in the early 2000s, and reportedly sold several times, including once to the crown prince of Abu Dhabi (it even has its own Wikipedia page). On land, villas once owned by literary stars like Jules Verne and W. Somerset Maugham are now inhabited by wealthy Arabs and Russians.

The Cap is still democratic enough that many stretches of waterfront, usually rocky, occasionally sandy, are public. Here, among ruined walls and shallow, pale emerald waters, middle-aged men and women snorkel and sunbathe topless, utterly careless about their flab. Beneath the waves, sunlight is cooled to heatless, quivering bars of gold.

Fitzgerald was famously obsessed with the mysteries of great wealth, what people do with it and what it does to them, big money's glorious power and ruinous effects, and the irreconcilability of the lifestyles of the rich with those of the rest of us. It became one of his great themes. In Antibes today, visitors can still watch, speculate, and wonder about the demigods behind the villa walls and on the yachts, much as the author of *The Great Gatsby* did, who supposedly concluded that the rich "are different from you and me."

Fitzgerald had spent time on the Riviera before, finishing *Gatsby* there. He lived in Antibes full-time for two years and would later call them the happiest of his life.

Happy he was, but tormented, too. He started writing *Tender Is the Night* in Antibes, modeling his characters Dick and Nicole Diver on real-life friends, the wealthy Americans Gerald and Sara Murphy, who had bought a property on the western rocky cliffs of Antibes that they named Villa America.

The Murphys' elegant, exceedingly bohemian scene included a who's who of literary and artistic stars, from Gertrude Stein and Picasso to John Dos Passos, Dorothy Parker, Hemingway, and the Fitzgeralds.

He opened *Tender Is the Night* with a description of what is clearly today's Hôtel du Cap-Eden-Roc, a legendary pleasure palace built in the 1870s that Fitzgerald named Gausse's Hôtel des Étrangers and painted rose instead of white. "Deferential palms" still "cool its facade," and there are white marble steps that descend to a Versailles-like allée shaded by perfectly symmetrical Mediterranean umbrella pines and vast, pristine gardens (including a dog cemetery carved out a hundred years ago for a wealthy and grieving guest).

The allée leads from the main hotel building to the beach house, with a wisteria-draped porte cochere, grand pillared entryways, and a deck cantilevered like an ocean liner above an infinity pool carved out of a white cliff. The nautical design of the beachfront restaurant mirrors those of the great yachts bobbing just offshore. Waiters in striped French boater T-shirts deliver pricey cups of Nescafé.

One of the charms of Antibes is that in spite of all the ostentatious, iron-gated mansions tacked to the edges of its rocky shores like glorious sea urchins, one is far more likely to encounter a regular Joe or Jacques than a millionaire on the streets of its two towns. Morning and afternoon, natives gather at the cafés, or play *pétanque* in the great dusty square near La Pinède Park, with its playground and strange, old, round stone building charmingly signed BIBLIOTHÈQUE POUR TOUS.

At night, when the sea breeze isn't blowing inland, Juan-les-Pins smells faintly like North Africa, a combination of diesel, dust, cooking oil, and cloying flowers. The entertainment district has a seedy edge, with sidewalk seating at nightclubs like the Pam Pam and snack shops with all-American names—Monster Burger and Wall Street.

By day, on the other side of the peninsula from Juan-les-Pins in Old Antibes, the medieval city center, the covered Marché Provençal offers another democratic diversion. Long rows of tables display a cornucopia of cheeses, olives, oils, bright vegetables and fruits, honeys and jams, and, of course, Marseille soaps. The fishing industry that existed in the 1920s and '30s is gone, but fishermen from other regions still take their catches to the fish market just beyond the covered market.

Aromas of bread waft from boulangeries like the Veziano, where the round-bellied proprietor, Jean Paul Veziano, sweats over the same bright yellow and black bread snacks that his grandfather made, using corn flour and squid ink. But this generation's Jean Paul is known to global chefs like Alain Ducasse, and his breads turn up in their restaurants as well as in the Cap's finer establishments.

Along the edges of the *marché,* native Antibeans drink beer at metal tables and pull goodies from their market baskets—sausage and fried zucchini flowers and *socca,* the Middle East–influenced flatbread of chickpea flour and olive oil. In their clear enjoyment and simplicity, this crowd is reminiscent of the peasants and fishmongers immortalized in Picasso's drawings on display at the nearby Musée Picasso. The market is also lined with pricier bistros, proffering fine wines, foie gras, and risotto or duck confit to hungry tourists.

The Greeks settled Antibes more than 2,300 years ago, and colonized and lived here in a city they called Antipolis, the city opposite, because it faces Nice across the bay. In 1200, a church and medieval fortifications went up, and are still intact.

The Greco-Roman history is visible in the foundation blocks of the city walls, and in excavated underground ruins visible through Plexiglas portholes in some of the streets. Picasso drew many scenes at Antibes of bare-breasted women dancing with fauns, and of centaurs and nymphs. He said: "Whenever I come to Antibes I'm always attacked by the itch of antiquity."

Modern visitors to Antibes are more likely to be attacked by an itch for luxury, and at Fitzgerald's former villa, they find it. The current owner of the Belles Rives, Marianne Estène-Chauvin, gave up a career as an art dealer in Casablanca to take charge of the hotel in the early aughts. It had been in her family for three generations, since her grandfather, a Russian émigré, bought the original villa in the 1930s and set about expanding it into a beachfront hotel. The Belles Rives has since hosted celebrities, including Ella Fitzgerald, Jean Cocteau, and Josephine Baker (a photograph of her on the dock with a pet cheetah hangs in the bar).

Estène-Chauvin is proud of her property's Fitzgerald connection. "He was happy here," she said. She has worked to cement the connection with him in part because local real estate agents have incorrectly identified a house next door on the beach, La Villa Picolette, as Fitzgerald's former dwelling.

To ensure her hotel's link to the author, Estène-Chauvin hangs black-and-white portraits of Fitzgerald and Zelda in the lobby, with its Art Deco elevator cage. She has posted a large, framed quote from a 1926 letter he sent to Hemingway beside a potted palm: "With our being back in a nice villa on my beloved Riviera (between Nice and Cannes) I'm happier than I've been for years. It's one of those strange, precious and all too transitory moments when everything in one's life seems to be going well."

Fitzgerald might have been happy in Juan-les-Pins, but Zelda apparently was not. She was having a breakdown and eventually had to be institutionalized in the United States. Besides being a record of Jazz-Age expat American life in Antibes and elsewhere in Europe, *Tender Is the Night* is also a mercilessly observed chronicle of a marriage collapsing. Eventually, the rich wife's madness is transferred to the once-sane husband.

Fitzgerald left Antibes with his family after 1927, never to return, heading eventually for Hollywood and the alcoholic decline that killed him in his early forties. He took eight years to finish *Tender Is the Night,* partly because he had to keep stopping to earn money to pay for sanitariums and psychiatrists treating Zelda.

On the fiftieth anniversary of Zelda's 1948 death, Estène-Chauvin hosted a dinner at the hotel for two hundred people, including Zelda's two granddaughters, and some members of the Fitzgerald Association. The granddaughters told stories that their mother, Scottie, had shared about Zelda and Scott's life in Antibes.

According to them, the villa was a place where the couple fought bitterly and constantly. Zelda kept fully packed luggage in every room, threatening departure at the slightest grievance. After one fight, she walked out in the noonday sun with all her luggage and tried to hail a taxi. Then, as now, Antibes taxis were impossible to come by, and she was eventually persuaded to come home. But their life together was coming to an end.

"They talked about how Zelda was not happy in her life here," Estène-Chauvin recalled of the granddaughters. "And how they left and never came back."

Estène-Chauvin showed old sepia prints of the property to the descendants, including one of an anonymous small blond child playing by the breakwater. The granddaughters realized that the child was their mother. "Everyone was crying," Estène-Chauvin recalled.

Five years ago, Estène-Chauvin created the literary Prix

Fitzgerald. Annually since then, a jury of French writers and critics has selected an author working in a style or addressing themes that interested Fitzgerald. Past winners include Jonathan Dee, whose novel *The Privileges* satirized a modern New York hedge fund family; and Amor Towles, whose 2011 novel *Rules of Civility* looked at Manhattan's upper crust in the late 1930s. In 2014, the writer-filmmaker Whit Stillman won the prize for his 1998 film and 2000 book, *The Last Days of Disco,* about a group of upper-class New Yorkers coming of age in the 1980s. In 2015, Robert Goolrick won for his novel *The Fall of Princes.*

Each year, Estène-Chauvin hosts the winner for a night in Fitzgerald's old room. The award ceremony, which includes a dinner and a midnight plunge, also relates to a bit of lore from the author's Antibes days.

The story goes that one night, husband and wife had been fighting and drinking hard. Enraged by Zelda's taunts about his professional and personal failures, Fitzgerald stormed out to a Juan-les-Pins bistro down the street that employed a full-time orchestra, and persuaded the musicians to come home with him. He herded them into a room, then slammed the door and locked them in, ordering them to play all night if they hoped to be released by dawn. He then asked Zelda if she still thought he was a loser.

The legend doesn't include her response. But to commemorate the story, Estène-Chauvin sends musicians upstairs to privately serenade the winner of the Prix Fitzgerald for a few moonlit hours.

Originally published in May 2015.

Nina Burleigh is the national politics correspondent at *Newsweek* and author of *The Fatal Gift of Beauty: The Trials of Amanda Knox.*

Lake Geneva as Shelley and Byron Knew It

Tony Perrottet

Switzerland is rarely thought of as a wild artistic center. Most of us recall the harsh verdict of Harry Lime, the character played by Orson Welles in *The Third Man,* who declared that the country's most creative achievement was the cuckoo clock.

It wasn't always so.

A few centuries ago, Europe's most adventurous bohemians flocked to Lake Geneva on the Swiss-French border to savor its inspiring mountain scenery and liberal political climate. The most notorious group arrived from England in May 1816, led by the twenty-eight-year-old celebrity poet George Gordon, Lord Byron. Having earned the moniker "mad, bad and dangerous to know," thanks to his debauched behavior and operatic romances with men and women (including his half-sister, Augusta), he was fleeing England in the wake of a scandalous separation from his wife.

His mode of transport was a replica of Napoleon's coach, and with him were a bevy of footmen, his personal physician (an emotionally troubled young doctor with a bookish bent named John Polidori), a peacock, a monkey, and a dog. He and his entourage were met in Geneva by a fellow group of literary wanderers helmed by the struggling poet Percy Bysshe Shelley, who, by the age of twenty-three, had gained his own notoriety in England as an advocate of atheism and free love. He was accompanied by his brilliant and beautiful eighteen-year-old mistress, Mary Wollstonecraft Godwin (she married Shelley later that year), and her alluring stepsister, Claire Clairmont. (Also eighteen, she had been Byron's lover back in England, and, for a time, Shelley's; it was Claire who had orchestrated the holiday meeting in Switzerland when she heard that Byron was traveling there.)

Byron and Shelley got on famously and soon decided to rent adjacent summer houses in the hamlet of Cologny, about four miles north of Geneva. Byron took a grandiose villa with his doctor and servants, while Shelley, Mary, and Claire settled into a more humble house by the lakefront.

The coterie was "the most brilliant and romantic circle of poets, writers and personalities which Switzerland—and Europe—has ever seen," wrote the historian Elma Dangerfield in *Byron and the Romantics in Switzerland, 1816.* The claim may be a little overblown, but there is no question that it was a dazzling alignment of talent. When the group wasn't sailing on Lake Geneva or making horseback excursions to medieval castles in the Alps, they were writing. That summer produced Mary Shelley's Gothic classic *Frankenstein; or, the Modern Prometheus;* an array of revered poems from Byron, including "The Prisoner of Chillon"; and a sinister short story called "The Vampyre," written by John Polidori and inspired by Byron, which would years later influence Bram Stoker's *Dracula.*

Hoping to get a sense of how Lake Geneva inspired such creativity, I spent a week last summer tracking down some of the places in which the Romantic poets spent their time—a task that entailed visiting one ravishing lakeside village after another.

Croissant-shaped Lake Geneva is the largest, deepest, and bluest of Swiss lakes, and its beauty is only heightened by its surroundings—thriving vineyards, historic architecture, and, in the distance, peaks dipped in snow all year round. The winters are mild and the summers hot and dry, earning it the title "Swiss Riviera." There are even palm trees by the eastern shore, and the water is warm enough to swim from pebble beaches from June to September.

But for me, it was the legacy of Byron and the Shelleys—and the juxtaposition of such larger-than-life characters in such a pristine, buttoned-down place—that gave Lake Geneva its most powerful allure.

Because Cologny, where Byron and his coterie stayed in 1816, is primarily residential, I took a small apartment in a slate-gray cottage high above the fashionable town of Montreux on the far eastern side. As luck would have it, the Montreux Jazz Festival was in full swing when I visited, and the waterfront promenade—normally lined with quiet gardens and cafés with majestic views—had been transformed into an open-air mall, with the well-heeled crowds moving between booths selling handicrafts, clothing, and edible treats. Jazz and every other musical genre wafted through the warm night air, although finding live events was a challenge, since they are mostly held in pricey indoor venues. Instead, I got a shot-size glass of local wine—carefully measured out at "one deciliter"—found a Brazilian DJ in a bar overhanging the water, and lost myself in the tanned throng.

Climbing the 343 steps back up to my cottage, I reminded myself that, bon vivant though Byron was, he didn't come to Switzerland for the nightlife.

The next morning, I headed straight for the water. Lake Geneva, at forty-five miles long and nearly nine miles wide, is so well served by impeccable Swiss railways that one can get from almost any point to another in less than an hour. A network of elegant antique ferries also plies the lake, for more leisurely excursions. For my voyage, I waited for one of the paddle steamers, which date from the Belle Époque. Mary Shelley raved in her letters about the near-tropical color of the lake, "blue as the heavens which it reflects," and used an array of scenes from Lake Geneva in *Frankenstein*.

Today, many of the views of tiny villages and coastal crags are unchanged, although Byron and his friends, who traveled in open sailing boats and along rutted carriage trails, would be astonished at how the once-impoverished Swiss republic has become one of the wealthiest corners of Europe. In my polished ferry was a mint-condition dining room of inlaid walnut paneling and fine linen, so I took lunch in aristocratic style, gazing at the terraced vineyards while sipping Swiss sauvignon blanc.

After a two-hour boat ride and twenty-minute hop by train, I arrived in downtown Geneva, now home to United Nations bureaucrats and bankers. Back in 1816, Byron and Shelley had seen no reason to linger here; Byron complained in a letter that he was followed about his hotel garden by "staring boobies"—or, more politely, English tourists. So the two groups relocated to the secluded farming village of Cologny near Geneva—Byron to the spectacular Villa Diodati and the Shelleys to the more modest Maison Chapuis just below.

A short bus ride took me past the Jet d'Eau, Geneva's trademark fountain, to the manicured main square of Cologny. Today, the village is essentially a Geneva suburb, and one of the most exclusive residential addresses in Europe, divided into the magnificent estates of chief executives, sheikhs, and assorted celebrities. As I strolled past iron fences and hedges, security guards in glass booths eyed me with frank suspicion. To my relief, I soon spotted 9, Chemin de Ruth, where the word DIODATI was discreetly engraved into an antique stone gatepost.

The salmon-pink villa is still in private hands (now divided into luxury apartments), but there are good views of it from the street and the public park next door. Its exterior has changed very little from the depictions in nineteenth-century engravings, including the expansive balcony where Byron finished the third canto of his epic poem *Childe Harold's Pilgrimage,* although the vineyards that once tumbled down to the water are now flower-filled gardens, and Maison Chapuis is gone.

The gate was open, so I blithely strolled into the estate intending to knock on the door. As I drew near, I could easily imagine the bohemians of 1816 gathering by candlelight in the upstairs dining room to debate and carouse. Byron's initial resistance to resuming his affair with the dark-eyed Claire did not last long. ("I never loved her nor pretended to love her," he later wrote, "but a man is a man—& if a girl of eighteen comes prancing to you at all hours—there is but one way.") Sexual tensions festered as Dr. Polidori fell in love with Mary, and wild rumors began to spread among English visitors to Geneva. Curiosity seekers passed by in boats to peer at the women's underwear on the washing lines—evidence, it was believed, that the Villa Diodati was a virtual bordello. Others would stop Byron on his evening rides to accuse him of corrupting the local girls and youth. The whole Swiss setup, one British newspaper reported back in London, was a sordid "league of incest."

But the summer of 1816 was historic not only in a literary

sense. A huge volcanic eruption of Mount Tambora in Indonesia in 1815 (far more powerful than Krakatoa would be sixty-eight years later) sent a pall of volcanic ash across the Northern Hemisphere, bringing so much cold weather and torrential rain to Europe that 1816 was nicknamed the "Year Without a Summer." In Switzerland, it was mid-June when the freakishly bad weather began—"an almost perpetual rain," Mary recalled, with terrific thunderstorms rippling back and forth across the lake. Wine flowed copiously, as did laudanum, a form of liquefied opium. One night, when Byron read aloud a haunting poem, Shelley leapt up and ran shrieking from the room, having hallucinated that Mary had sprouted demonic eyes in place of nipples. It was in this surreal, claustrophobic atmosphere that she experienced the famous nightmare that became the lurid plot of *Frankenstein* (as she later recounted in the preface to the 1831 edition of her book), about a scientist who creates a creature from stolen body parts and infuses it with life. The next night, she told the gloomy fable in the Villa Diodati to a rapt audience.

As visitors do today, Byron and his cohort loved to explore the lake. When the rain finally eased, Shelley and Byron set sail for a weeklong literary pilgrimage of their own. The first stop was the village of Clarens, where the most beloved novel of their era, Jean-Jacques Rousseau's epistolary love story, *Julie, or the New Héloïse,* was composed and set. In Lausanne, they paid their respects at the house of Edward Gibbon, where he penned his revered, epic *History of the Decline and Fall of the Roman Empire.* (It was already a ruin, and would be knocked down in 1896 for the Lausanne post office.) On their way home, the pair were caught in a storm that broke their rudder and nearly sank their boat—presaging the sailing accident that would end Shelley's life six years later in Italy, since despite his love of boats, he never learned to swim.

But the highlight of the trip, according to Byron's letters, remains one of Switzerland's most thrilling attractions: the Château de Chillon, a medieval fortress whose turrets rise dreamlike from the waters. The castle became notorious in the sixteenth century as a political prison, and the two poets were deeply moved when a gendarme showed them the dungeon, where an outspoken cleric, François Bonivard, had been chained to a pillar for six years.

For my visit, I strolled the two miles along the lakefront from Montreux (ferries also make the journey). The dungeon is still a major attraction, as is the pillar where Byron's name is carved (although Byron's friend John Hobhouse, who traveled with Byron later in the summer and revisited the castle in 1828, believed that the inscription was made by a drunken guard to attract sightseers). Stairs lead up through endless chambers, many with traces of the original medieval frescoes, into the highest keep, where every arrow slit offers a stunning lake view.

After their visit, Byron and Shelley stayed at a guesthouse in Ouchy, the port below Lausanne, where Byron stayed up late into the night writing "The Prisoner of Chillon" while Shelley worked on his "Hymn to Intellectual Beauty." Today, Lausanne is the most spectacular and vibrant city on Lake Geneva, whose steep hills, crowned by a Gothic cathedral, can be ascended without strain in high-tech funiculars. The old waterfront inn still exists, although it has been expanded into a glamorous business hotel, the Hôtel d'Angleterre, with bloodred velvet armchairs and contemporary art on every wall.

But perhaps the most evocative relic from 1816 is one that was entirely deserted when I went: the mansion of Madame de Staël, in Coppet, whose salon was the only one in Switzerland that Byron would deign to attend. The formidable fifty-year-old de Staël was famous in Europe for her best-selling novels, her collection of famous lovers, and her outspoken liberal politics (she was exiled from Paris by Napoleon in 1804), and her soirées attracted the greatest minds of Europe. Today the château, a five-minute stroll from the railway station, remains in the family. The tenth-generation owner, Count Othenin d'Haussonville, aged seventy-nine, lives in one section, but opens many rooms to the public. These are filled with the original furnishings, including Madame de Staël's personal bathtub and pianoforte.

Fascinated as the Romantics were by the spiritual power of untrammeled nature, not even the self-absorbed Byron could visit Switzerland without experiencing the Alps. At different times over the summer, he and his cohort made grueling excursions by horse and mule, to be totally overwhelmed by the sheer scale of the peaks and waterfalls, the rumbling avalanches and the unearthly glaciers—"like a frozen-hurricane," Byron wrote admiringly in his journal.

The most ambitious Alpine jaunt was undertaken by Byron and his visiting Cambridge chum Hobhouse, into the breathtaking Bernese Oberland. But while Byron and "Hobby" spent days on horseback, the trip can now be made in a few hours on one of Switzerland's most stunning train rides, which climbs from Montreux to Interlaken in the German-speaking region. The panoramic carriages offer sweeping views from Montbovon over the whole of Lake Geneva, then delve through tunnels and switchbacks into the heart of the Alps, where the three signature peaks of the Jungfrau, Eiger, and Mönch loom like a Lindt chocolate box cover.

Even the tormented Byron seemed to enjoy himself in this celestial mountain scenery. On one occasion, crossing a high pass, he apparently lightened up so much that he "made a snowball and threw it at Hobhouse," reports Elma Dangerfield. And on finding a lush glade, "I lay down in the sun enjoying myself most entirely," Byron wrote to his half-sister, "and dared to write down in my pocket-book that I was happy."

The climax came at the village of Lauterbrunnen, stunningly set in a deep gorge lined with waterfalls, one of which Byron described as "the tail of a white horse streaming in the wind."

Today, Lauterbrunnen's dramatic setting is entirely intact, although instead of lodging with a local curate, as Byron and Hobhouse did, I took a room in one of many efficient bed-and-breakfasts on the main street. For the next few days, instead of hitching a mule, I rode cog railways and cable cars high above the clouds to hike along breathtaking ridges, then returned to the village for fortifying cheese fondue dinners. One morning, I got up at dawn to enter a tunnel carved beneath the Staubbach Falls just outside town and gazed out through the torrent at the surrounding mountains while slowly being soaked by glacial spray. Who, I thought, needs laudanum?

In the age before contraception, "free love" worked better for men than for women. The Diodati idyll went awry in August, when Claire revealed that she was pregnant. "Is the brat mine?" Byron wondered gallantly in one letter, before reluctantly concluding that it must be. The Shelleys departed for England on August 29, with Byron promising to support the child. He lingered on at the Villa Diodati until the beginning of October, but finally left Switzerland for Italy, to throw himself deeper into sensual abandon.

In retrospect, the "Frankenstein summer" seems a fantastical interlude of happiness in lives marked by tragedy. In 1822, Percy Shelley drowned in Italy, at age twenty-nine; Dr. Polidori had committed suicide the year before, at age twenty-five. Claire's daughter with Byron died at age five, and only one of Mary Shelley's four children with Percy survived. Byron died in Greece in 1824, at the ripe old age of thirty-six.

The last survivor was the audacious Claire Clairmont, who lived to age eighty. At the end of her life, she started a bitter memoir denouncing the practice of "free love," which, she says, turned Byron and Shelley, "the two finest poets of England" into "monsters of lying, meanness, cruelty and treachery." (The scrawled pages were discovered in 2009 by the biographer Daisy Hay in the New York Public Library.)

Today, such morbid ruminations are hard to sustain in the brilliant summer light reflecting from Lake Geneva. On my last night in Montreux, I headed down to the jazz festival and drank as many thimblefuls of wine as I could afford. Carpe diem—Byron and the Shelleys surely would have concurred—for how many summers do we have?

Originally published in May 2011.

Tony Perrottet contributes regularly to *The New York Times, The Wall Street Journal Magazine,* and *Smithsonian Magazine*. He is the author of *The Sinner's Grand Tour: A Journey Through the Historical Underbelly of Europe.*

Looking for Isherwood's Berlin

Rachel B. Doyle

When Christopher Isherwood moved to Berlin in 1929, the twenty-five-year-old British novelist could not quite bring himself to settle down in one place.

At one point he changed addresses three times in three months. There was the room he could barely afford next to the former Institute for Sexual Research in the leafy Tiergarten. There was the cramped, leaky attic flat that he shared with a family of five in Kreuzberg. And there was the apartment around Kottbusser Tor, in those days a slum (now a nightlife hub), where he was pleased to discover that he was the sole Englishman when he went to register with the police.

"He liked to imagine himself as one of those mysterious wanderers who penetrate the depths of a foreign land, disguise themselves in the dress and customs of its natives and die in unknown graves, envied by their stay-at-home compatriots," Isherwood wrote of this period in *Christopher and His Kind,* his third-person memoir of the 1930s.

Isherwood would not feel out of place in Berlin today,

which is still a destination for the young and the creative. While fashions may have changed, Isherwood's work still captures the essence of the German capital, with its art collections stashed in former bunkers, and louche nightclubs hiding behind unmarked doors.

The seductive excitement of Weimar-era Berlin—with its limitless sexual possibilities for the curious gay writer, and parties where dancers "swayed in partial-paralytic rhythms under a huge sunshade suspended from the ceiling"—quickly inspired Isherwood. He steeped himself in the sordid and the refined, the red-light bars and the villas, the decadence and the apprehension of a city whose freewheeling spirit was about to be extinguished by Nazi terror. "Here was the seething brew of history in the making," the author wrote in his memoir.

In December 1930, Isherwood finally settled into an apartment, at Nollendorfstrasse 17 in the Schöneberg district. The building was full of eccentrics who are now known through their fictional incarnations in novels like *The Last of Mr. Norris* and *Goodbye to Berlin*. He lived there with Jean Ross, the model for his most famous character, the capricious nightclub singer and aspiring actress Sally Bowles, who captivated him with her "air of not caring a curse what people thought of her." His landlady, Meta Thurau, inspired the character Fräulein Schroeder, who, in Isherwood's fiction, symbolized the typical Berliner of the time. In dire economic straits after World War I, and forced to take in lodgers, she was at first skeptical of Hitler. Eventually she adapted to popular sentiment, in which locals "thrilled with a furtive, sensual pleasure, like schoolboys, because the Jews, their business rivals, and the Marxists . . . had been satisfactorily found guilty of the defeat and the inflation, and were going to catch it."

The street Isherwood called home for two and a half years was bombed during World War II, and now the stately prewar buildings—including the one where he lived, with its pale yellow facade mounted with concrete lion heads—are mixed with uninspiring modern constructions. A fetish fashion workshop and a rare-book store share the ground floor of his former building; across the street, visitors can choose between a kabbalah center and a speakeasy-style cocktail bar, Stagger Lee, where one rings a brass doorbell to enter. Around the corner there is a relatively new 1920s-themed café with musical performances, named after Sally Bowles.

Still, Nollendorfstrasse doesn't seem all that different from how the author described it in the opening lines of *Goodbye to Berlin:* "From my window, the deep solemn massive street. Cellar-shops where the lamps burn all day, under the shadow of top-heavy balconied facades, dirty plaster frontages embossed with scroll-work and heraldic devices."

The neighborhood, in the days when Isherwood was giving English lessons and writing wry, detached stories in a front room of his apartment, was a thriving center of gay life, and remains so. Today it is not uncommon to see men in leather pants or shiny rubber boots or police costumes strolling around—there are numerous shops selling just these items, and a handful of clubs where one is not allowed in unless one is clad in them.

Isherwood immersed himself in the area's nightlife; it provided fodder for *Goodbye to Berlin,* which was adapted into the 1966 musical and 1972 film *Cabaret.* His apartment was a short distance from several iconic clubs, including the Eldorado, known for its transvestite shows. There, customers could buy tokens to exchange for dances with men and women in drag, then try to guess their partner's gender.

Masks were available for those who wished to protect their identities.

"He probably saw Marlene here," said Brendan Nash, a transplanted Londoner who gives "Isherwood's Neighborhood" tours. He was referring to Marlene Dietrich, the glamorous actress born and raised in the Schöneberg district. On a sunny summer morning we were standing in front of an organic supermarket on Motzstrasse 24, where a sign read SPEISEKAMMER IM ELDORADO ("Pantry in the Eldorado"), acknowledging that the room where transvestite performers once shimmied on stage is currently dedicated to vegetables.

We went inside to inspect a small photo gallery next to the cash register that showed how the nightclub used to look—a two-story space with gilded ceilings, chandeliers, white tablecloths, and art on the walls. Nash, who began giving the tour in 2011, said it was considered chic in Weimar-era heterosexual circles to spend the evening there, just as tourists today line up to dance with the shirtless leather daddies at the techno temple Berghain in Friedrichshain.

In *Christopher and His Kind,* Isherwood drolly described Berlin's "dens of pseudo-vice": "Here, screaming boys in drag and monocled, Eton-cropped girls in dinner-jackets play-acted the high jinks of Sodom and Gomorrah, horrifying the onlookers and reassuring them that Berlin was still the most decadent city in Europe."

Many of the author's main sources of inspiration were the seedy "boy bars" that he frequented in a canal-side area of Kreuzberg, especially one called the Cosy Corner, on Zossener Strasse 7, which became a model for the Alexander Casino in *Goodbye to Berlin.* Today, that address is next to a small piano shop and close to charming businesses like Knopf Paul, which sells buttons, including ones made from eucalyptus and deer horn, and a pharmacy called Zum Goldenen Einhorn (To the Golden Unicorn) with wooden cabinets and porcelain jars.

Yet in Isherwood's fiction, the area was a notorious place where the police regularly hunted for "wanted criminals or escaped reformatory boys." Thrill-seeking visitors flocked there on weekends. "They discussed communism and Van Gogh and the best restaurants. Some of them seemed a little scared: perhaps they expected to be knifed in this den of thieves," the author wrote.

Isherwood's genius was in fusing the private, often outré lives of the Berliners with the political events unfurling like a bloodred banner. The brownshirts carrying the swastika flag put an end to much of the scene that defined his time in the city, and hastened his departure.

"Boy bars of every sort were being raided, now, and many were shut down. . . . No doubt the prudent ones were scared and lying low, while the silly ones fluttered around town exclaiming how sexy the Storm Troopers looked in their uniforms," Isherwood wrote in *Christopher and His Kind.*

In May of 1933, the author left Berlin for several years of roving around Europe with his draft-evading German boyfriend, Heinz Neddermeyer. He returned to visit in 1952 between the war and the Wall, finding "smashed buildings along that familiar street"—Nollendorfstrasse—and "housefronts . . . pitted by bomb fragments and eaten by decay." He never saw the city restored to the familiar, welcoming, and inspiring place he would likely find it today.

Isherwood settled in Southern California in 1939, but remained both exhilarated and haunted by his time in the German capital. "Always in the background was Berlin. It was calling me every night, and its voice was the harsh sexy voice of the gramophone records," he wrote in the 1962 novel *Down There on a Visit.* "Berlin had affected me like a party at the end of which I didn't want to go home."

Originally published in April 2013.

Rachel B. Doyle is the deputy editor of *Atlas Obscura,* a website devoted to the world's hidden wonders. She was previously a travel writer based in Berlin and Nairobi.

On the Trail of Hansel and Gretel in Germany

David G. Allan

Once upon a time—about two hundred years ago, to be more precise—there were two brothers, Wilhelm and Jacob Grimm, who lived in the Kingdom of Hesse, now part of Germany. They loved fairy tales, and set about collecting and publishing them, to the delight of readers around the world, young and old, forever after.

You could celebrate the debut of *Kinder- und Hausmärchen* (*Children's and Household Tales*), the Grimm brothers' famed collection, first published in 1812, by strolling through Disney World's tidy faux castles alongside grinning, crinolined mascots.

Or you could do what I did, accompanied by my wife, Kate, and our two-and-a-half-year-old daughter, Alice, and drive along the Fairy Tale Road in Germany, an official but unmarked route designed by local tourism officials to promote sites, some authentic, some imaginary. The 350-plus-mile route between Frankfurt and Bremen snakes past locations that include the actual homes of the Grimms and the fantasy ones of Little Red Riding Hood, Sleeping Beauty, and Hansel and Gretel, along with a mix of foreboding forests, striking towers, and even some genuine castles.

Alice's introduction to the world of the Grimm tales began on our flight, as I read to her from the brothers' version of Cinderella. "Once upon a time there was a girl named Isabella whose mother had died," I started, immediately rediscovering how much death, vice, and fear are woven into the Grimms' stories. (Their first volume included a gruesome story titled "How Some Children Played at Slaughtering.") As I continued, I did some on-the-spot Disneyfication, glossing over hungry wolves and murderous stepmothers to get to the happy endings. But even sugar-coated, the stories hooked Alice. Over the week, our car rides featured her backseat-spun yarns, which began, "Once upon a time there was a girl named Alice . . ."

Our real-life journey began in the Frankfurt suburb of Hanau, the official start of the Fairy Tale Road, and where the brothers lived from birth to ages five and six. Their time in Hanau is commemorated by a statue in the main plaza and a small exhibition of personal effects in the town's grand Schloss Philippsruhe museum.

The Grimms lived another seven years in the small, formerly walled village of Steinau, about thirty-five miles northeast of Hanau, in a house that is now a museum focused on Grimm-family home life. While I toured rooms under construction for an expansion that will include interactive exhibits and international versions of the tales in various forms—books, games, illustrations, film—Alice played outside in a version of Hansel's "cage." The town's castle, where the young Wilhelm and Jacob frolicked, also had a few rooms dedicated to their belongings, including snuff bottles, inkwells, and family Bibles.

After Steinau, we veered on and off the official Fairy Tale Road, which includes a number of towns that did not meet my personal criteria of being either a Grimm residence or a fairy-tale setting. The latter is, of course, a contradiction: by definition, fairy tales do not take place on any calendar ("Once upon a time . . .") or map (". . . in a faraway castle . . ."). But in the land where the Grimms transcribed oral tales for posterity, it has been the delight of locals and visitors of the last two centuries to pair their stories with places that may have inspired the brothers—no matter how loose the connection.

Our next destination, though, did have a direct link: the rural Schwalm River valley is also known as Rotkäppchenland, or "Little Red Cap country" (after the original title of what became "Little Red Riding Hood" in English translations). The valley is home to the Museum der Schwalm, dedicated to the area's textile tradition. For many years in the region, clothes indicated social status; at the museum, faded photographs and waxen mannequins display the color-coded hierarchy. Old people wore purple and black, young married couples green, and a little girl from this area would have worn her hair tucked into a little red cap.

The valley is made up of farms, rolling hills, and plenty of wooded areas. I pulled into a parking area at the edge of a forest, ignored an ominous warning sign I couldn't translate, and told Alice the stories of Little Red Riding Hood and Snow White as we walked among spindly trees that filtered sunlight onto the fern-covered forest floor.

That night, we pulled into the pension we had booked in Kassel, farther along the route, only to find out from the owner that she had no rooms available. Holding a sleepy Alice, Kate buzzed the door a second time and convinced the owner's kindly husband to find space for us. Maybe it was my overactive imagination, but when he explained that the mix-up was his daughter's, I couldn't help but wonder if it was a wicked stepmother who had turned us away. (Throughout the trip such ordinary occurrences continually recalled the tales: a woodsman chopping, a red apple that rolled out of Kate's bag, even a vaguely troll-like man near a bridge.)

Kassel is a cornerstone in the tale of the Brothers Grimm. They first moved there to continue their studies after their father died. After college they became imperial librarians, living at what is now Brüder-Grimm-Platz, marked with a diminutive statue of the two men, and later at an address near the Brüder Grimm-Museum. In their free time they tracked down verbose storytellers.

Just outside Kassel we ate at a roadhouse restaurant, Brauhaus Knallhütte, once run by Dorothea Viehmann, a farmer and storyteller who supplied the brothers with dozens of tales, including that of "Aschenputtel," or Cinderella. Over revitalizing beers brewed on-site, we watched an earnest reenactment of the story in German by a blue-bonneted actress.

As the Grimms' popularity grew, travelers in North Hesse began hiking from the main roads to see a castle known to have two towers surrounded by woods and rosebushes. The ruins matched the setting of one of my favorite tales, "Briar Rose," or, as it's better known, "Sleeping Beauty." The castle, now called Dornröschenschloss Sababurg, is part ruins, part faded boutique hotel, and is run by Günther Koseck, a member of a regional group devoted to preserving Grimm fairy-tale heritage.

The hotel is stocked with Sleeping Beauty–themed curios, serves rose-infused pasta, and offers performances of the actual tale (the accumulation verges on kitsch). But the view from our large room—of green pastures, grazing animals, and deep forests—spurred the imagination. At bedtime I read Alice the uncensored "Briar Rose" and she paid it the compliment of asking for an encore.

The final leg of our trip, through the rustic villages of

Lower Saxony, ended in Hamelin, a movie set of a town with ornate Renaissance-era, timber-framed storefront houses lining cobblestoned, pedestrianized streets. A tour of the city is fittingly led by its famous savior-turned-avenger, the Pied Piper. Michael Boyer, one of the performers who inhabits the role, is an American expatriate who brings a combination of dignity and humor to his colorful patchwork costume and clarinet playing. The tour concluded at the Rattenfängerhaus (Rat Catcher's House), a restaurant in a 408-year-old building, where specials like pork fillet "Rat-tail Flambé" trap more tourists than vermin.

According to the Grimms, the Pied Piper is legend, but Boyer, as the Piper, makes the case for the fabled exterminator's historical existence. (Whether he actually charmed away the town's rats—and its children, when he wasn't paid for the job—is a more dubious claim.)

Speeding along the autobahn back to Frankfurt—reentering modern times from four days of small-town meanderings—I wondered if Alice appreciated the Grimms' slice of Germany more than she would have Anaheim or Orlando. She loved the castles and the zoo, and was fittingly enraptured by the Pied Piper, but I wanted her to take something more away.

As we got ready for bed at an airport hotel, my wish was granted. "I am Sleeping Beauty," she said to me. "And you are the Prince. Kiss me and wake me up!"

Originally published in June 2010.

David G. Allan is the editorial director of CNN.com's Health & Wellness section and author of the Wisdom Project column.

Trumping the Unbearable Darkness of History

Nicholas Kulish

That history has not been just a string of kindnesses and gifts of beauty for the ancient, golden city of Prague is far from apparent at first glance.

The blows of World War II and the heavy hand of Communist construction—so apparent in neighboring capitals—are barely discernible there. It is nothing like the wholesale reinvention of Bucharest, the scars of Warsaw, or the division of Berlin.

"The people of Prague had an inferiority complex with respect to those other cities," Milan Kundera wrote in his now-classic novel *The Unbearable Lightness of Being*. "Old Town Hall was the only monument of note destroyed in the war, and they decided to leave it in ruins so that no Pole or German could accuse them of having suffered less than their share."

The hall is in ruins no longer, and the city's Old Town begs a postcard from almost every angle. On a crisp fall day, the flagrant yellows and reds of the autumn trees on the lesser bank of the Vltava gild the city's already rich skyline. The Charles

Bridge remains in a permanent tourist traffic jam long past the summer high season.

The streams of visitors are not disappointed by the Gothic Týn Church or the Art Nouveau Municipal House. But the result of so much beauty is a visual amnesia that lulls even the historically versed visitor into a kind of forgetting, encouraging a Disney-castle version of the city and rendering Prague's recent wounds almost invisible.

As Tereza, a principal character in the novel, climbs the grassy Petrin Hill, Kundera wrote, "On her way up, she paused several times to look back: below her she saw the towers and bridges, the saints were shaking their fists and lifting their stone eyes to the clouds. It was the most beautiful city in the world."

But *The Unbearable Lightness of Being,* first published in a French translation from Czech in 1984, is no love letter to the city; it is a message from a time of oppression, and one worth carrying for perspective on a trip through Prague. Kundera submerges the reader in the undercurrents of political life, the rough passages of far-too-recent vintage, and the personal repercussions of an invasive, claustrophobic time.

Tereza is climbing Petrin in a dream—a dream in which she will be executed, but only if she convinces the executioners that she seeks death of her own free will. The novel returns again and again to Tereza's harrowing dreams, simultaneously erotic and morbid.

She and her husband, Tomás, are living through a most tumultuous period for what was then Czechoslovakia: the crackdown by the Soviet Union after Czechoslovakia's attempt at liberalizing reform. The Prague Spring of 1968 was a brief flowering of openness behind the Iron Curtain; what followed was a trauma hidden inside the city. The novel provides a key to remembering.

Kundera writes of a time when a former ambassador could be consigned to the reception desk at a hotel, when private conversations were not only recorded by the police but broadcast on state radio, and when the cinematographers of authority would set up bright lights and film cameras at a funeral to record the mourners' faces for study. In the novel, Tomás, a superior surgeon, is consigned by the authorities to wash windows because of a politically provocative essay he once wrote about Oedipus and the guilt of unknowing crimes.

Today, scenes of surveillance and harassment play on a permanent loop in the small video room at the Museum of Communism. The visitor is also confronted by unforgettable images of tanks on the streets outside, armed forces in Wenceslas Square, and protesters being sprayed by hoses and beaten with clubs.

Much is held at the arm's-length distance of black and white. But the scene shifts to the demonstrations in 1989 that led to the collapse of the Soviet-backed regime. Suddenly the faded jeans and bad haircuts are distinctly recognizable as—for all but the youngest of us—coming from our own time. The blows of the clubs seem to land that much harder with the realization that it could be you.

Though moving and informative, the Museum of Communism has a strangely amateur feel. Busts of Party heroes are collected in one corner haphazardly and without explanation, like knickknacks in a grandmother's attic. The texts on the walls are at times quaint, like the one that declares: "From the very beginning, Lenin pushed forward the tactics of extreme perfidiousness and ruthlessness," which earns a laugh but also cuts through the typical staleness of academic understatement.

But perhaps most surprising is that the museum itself is hidden on a commercial strip of Na Příkopě, tucked, as the museum's own literature puts it, "above McDonald's, next to

Casino." Decades of a dictatorship for an entire country, a dictatorship within the lifetime of most Czech people, is squeezed into a space smaller than another pleasant enough museum devoted to the Slavic Art Nouveau pioneer Alphonse Mucha.

There is no question that Prague has chosen—at least for its public face—not to dwell on the Communist era. In the Kundera novel, Sabina, Tomás's lover and an artist, detests when she or her work are revered or adored for her country's trauma: "The trouble was that Sabina had no love for that drama. The words 'prison,' 'persecution,' 'banned books,' 'occupation,' 'tanks,' were ugly, without the slightest trace of romance."

It is easy to understand why residents would just as soon forget the entire episode. And tourists can be forgiven for concentrating on the city's grandeur rather than hunting for odd remnants of Communism.

As much as it cherishes the decorative finery of Mucha, the city unabashedly embraces Franz Kafka as its literary laureate, with Kafka tours, Kafka cafés, Kafka restaurants, and Kafka hotels. But it is a branded Kafka commodity, stripped of the dread of *The Trial,* a quaint Kafka tailored to match the charms of old Bohemian beer halls and castle views.

The alleyways and courtyards of the city still embody the disorienting quality of Kafka's work. As cold night descends, the twisting little lanes seem to mock the city plan clutched in a traveler's numbing fingers. Prague defies maps. Prague is a place to get lost.

Kundera recounts how ordinary people across Czechoslovakia tried to foil their invaders not with cannons but by tearing down the street signs to slow and confuse their oppressors. The act feels distinctly Czech in its mixture of defiance, creativity, pacifism, and even the hint of oddness.

With Kundera's work as a point of reference, the city takes

on a different aspect. It is as if Tomás, reduced to a window washer by the regime, was wielding the squeegee on the plate-glass fronts of the luxury boutiques off Old Town Square and winking at the shoppers inside.

The novel—and the movie made after it—is best known for the erotic contradiction of Sabina, stripped down to her underwear and wearing an old-fashioned bowler hat. This single object is slowly weighted down with a series of meanings, from the functional article it was for Sabina's grandfather, a nineteenth-century mayor, to the sexually charged plaything it became to the lovers and eventually as a monument to their affair after it had ended.

"Each time the same object would give rise to a new meaning, though all former meanings would resonate (like an echo, like a parade of echoes)," Kundera writes, "enriching the harmony."

The same could be said for the city. The monumental misfit of the former Federal Assembly building, where the Slovak and Czech delegates once met, squats near Wenceslas Square, one of the lonely examples of Communist-era architecture downtown. Its colossal overhang seems to me like a giant chin stuck out for an uppercut from architecture critics. It was built on top of the old Prague stock exchange without destroying the original building, a project heavy with symbolism. In another layer of historical irony the building became home, after the Velvet Revolution, to Radio Free Europe, the United States–financed service.

Though Wenceslas Square is topped by the equestrian rectitude of its patron saint, it is anything but upstanding. Preservationists would no doubt love to wipe away Casino Happy Day's light-studded facade, its neon palm tree and incongruously colored dollar signs flashing red and yellow. The square is home to drug pushers and strip-club panderers, solicitous to members of the roving packs of stag-party celebrants who descend upon the city each weekend.

The city is ripe with such turnabouts. The national martyr Jan Palach died after setting himself on fire in 1969 to protest the Soviet occupation. Now, the onetime Square of the Red Army Soldiers bears his name.

"The history of the Czechs and of Europe is a pair of sketches from the pen of mankind's fateful inexperience," Kundera wrote. "History is as light as individual human life, unbearably light, light as a feather, as dust swirling into the air, as whatever will no longer exist tomorrow."

From his exile in Paris, Kundera was less prescient about the imminent collapse of Communism, writing of "the forfeit of their nation's freedom for many decades or even centuries." The Communist era may have begun to seem like one of those passing sketches in the flipbook of history, but four decades after World War II the Iron Curtain seemed of unshakable permanence.

That is a memory worth holding onto, one that gives depth to, rather than contradicting, the city's beauty, as a place that survived its trial and came out, if not unscathed, strong and fair.

Originally published in March 2008.

Nicholas Kulish covered Central Europe as Berlin bureau chief for *The New York Times*. He is now an investigative reporter for the paper and author of the novel *Last One In*.

The Roman Seasons of Tennessee Williams

Charly Wilder

In late January 1948, Tennessee Williams arrived for the first time in Rome, a city that the playwright, then thirty-seven, would quickly call "the capitol of my heart." After more than a decade toiling in poverty and obscurity, Williams had been catapulted to national fame three years earlier when his loosely autobiographical "memory play," *The Glass Menagerie,* became an instant critical and commercial hit. Its follow-up, *A Streetcar Named Desire,* opened in 1947 to packed Broadway houses and rave reviews, cementing Williams's position as a major figure in the American theater establishment. Four months later, he set out for Europe.

After a brief, disappointing stopover in France ("I found nothing very good about Paris but the quality of the whores," Williams wrote his friend and longtime collaborator Elia Kazan), Rome provided a much-needed change of scene.

"As soon as I crossed the Italian border my health and life seemed to be magically restored," he wrote in his memoirs. Williams spent much of the next decade in Rome, which became the backdrop and inspiration for one of his most personally and creatively fruitful periods—as well as the setting for his 1950 novella, *The Roman Spring of Mrs. Stone.* Despite recurring bouts of writer's block, when the sensitive, melancholic playwright found himself "battering my head against a wall of creative impotence," he wrote many of his greatest works here, in whole or in part, including *Cat on a Hot Tin Roof, The Rose Tattoo,* and *Baby Doll,* during numerous extended visits to the city.

To search for Williams in today's Rome is to explore the vestiges of that heady, messy period after the fall of Mussolini but before the so-called Italian economic miracle of the 1950s and '60s. When he arrived in 1948, the newly open city was the epicenter of a just-dawning golden age of Italian neorealist cinema. The dollar was strong, prices were low, and, as Williams put it, "an Americano could get away with a whole lot."

Williams's first place of residence was a top-floor room at the Ambasciatori Palace, a grand neo-Renaissance hotel along the tree-lined Via Veneto. Today, like many of Williams's former haunts, both the boulevard and the hotel feel somewhat past their prime. Via Veneto is still upscale, but its touristy trattorias and chain hotels would be sadly ill-fitted to its former incarnation as the glorious main drag of *La Dolce Vita,* the 1960 Federico Fellini classic. Still, despite its depressing subterranean breakfast buffet, the Ambasciatori retains a faded elegance that makes it easy to imagine the looks of disdain Williams recalls receiving when, on his second night in the city, he brought home a raggedly dressed Roman teenager whom he calls "Raffaelo" in his memoirs.

For Williams, Rome offered freedom—an escape from the puritanism that plagued his life back home. In a 1949 letter to his publisher, James Laughlin, Williams recounted a dinner with Ingrid Bergman and Roberto Rossellini shortly after the Hollywood star and the Italian director had begun their highly publicized collaboration and extramarital affair. Their indifference to the scandal, he wrote, "is very beautiful and should have a salutary affect on discrediting those infantile moralists that make it so hard for anyone to do honest work and live honestly in the States."

Williams wasn't alone in this assessment. His social circle at the time included the poet Frederic Prokosch, Truman Capote—"that unhappy young egoist Gore Vidal"—and a number of other American writers and artists who, like Williams, were gay or bisexual, and had found in Rome a degree of creative and personal freedom unheard of back home. They also tended to share another of Williams's well-known traits: a love of drink.

"The American colony is desperately gregarious and you can only work by bolting doors and shutters," he wrote to his agent and close confidant, Audrey Wood. "Yes, some of them even climb in the window if they suspect you have a little cognac on the place!" In addition to giving house parties, Williams and his friends frequented Via Veneto spots like the Café de Paris, Rosati, and the downstairs bar of the Hotel Flora (now the Rome Marriott Grand Hotel Flora).

By now an international celebrity, Williams made regular appearances in the Roman society papers. Yet his fame was still not such as to prevent him from engaging in another activity of which Rome offered manifold new possibilities: cruising.

"In the evenings, very late, after midnight, I like to drive out the old Appian Way and park the car at the side of the road and listen to the crickets among the old tombs," he wrote to the actress Jane Lawrence Smith. "Sometimes a figure appears among them which is not a ghost but a Roman boy in the flesh!"

"The nightingales busted their larynx!" he wrote to the poet Oliver Evans of a dalliance with a Neapolitan professional lightweight boxer he picked up on one of his first nights in Rome. "I wish I could tell you more . . . details, positions, amiabilities—but this pale blue paper would blush!"

After the Ambasciatori, Williams moved into a two-room apartment in a "tawny old high-ceilinged building" just outside the Villa Borghese gardens at Via Aurora 45. There he would reside for much of his time in Rome, mostly with his longtime partner Frank Merlo, who accompanied Williams on many extended trips in the capacity of his "secretary." The building on Via Aurora has since been leveled, and today the lot is occupied by a generic taupe-and-glass office tower housing an Italian subsidiary of the BNP Paribas banking group.

So much of the Rome Williams knew and loved—the swinging, free-spirited Rome of the 1950s and '60s—is long gone, paved over by anesthetized chain stores, tourist traps, and bank branches. Some spots remain in name only—like Doney, a sidewalk café on Via Veneto that is now a bland extension of the Westin Excelsior hotel, of which the main clientele appears to be traveling businessmen and their bored-looking female companions.

But in Williams's day, Doney was a place of singular intrigue and energy, a recurring setting in his recollections and correspondences. In a 1948 letter heralding the arrival in Rome of the *New Yorker* correspondent Janet Flanner and her all-female entourage, Williams tells Gore Vidal that "the social life is considerably better than when there was just us girls, sunning ourselves like a bunch of lizards on the walk in front of Doney's." In another letter, to the *New York Times* theater critic Brooks Atkinson, he recalls passing the café and seeing Orson Welles, presumably in town for the filming of the 1949 film *Black Magic,* sitting alone and "reading a book called DECADENCE."

It was also at Doney that Williams had his first meeting in

1950 with the legendary Roman actress Anna Magnani, whom he had in mind to play the widow Serafina in *The Rose Tattoo.*

"The long-awaited meeting with Magnani has finally occurred," he wrote to the theater producer Cheryl Crawford. After keeping him waiting for forty-five minutes, Magnani sent a messenger to bring him to Doney. "She dominated the whole street," he wrote. "Her figure is the very meaning of sex. Her eyes and her voice and style are indescribably compelling."

This meeting would prove the beginning of a decades-long collaboration and friendship that would profoundly influence both of their lives. Williams and Magnani, both temperamental artists who were fearless in their determination to live unconventional lives, had a deep understanding of each other, and beyond the roles he explicitly wrote for her, from 1950 on, Williams's female characters began to resemble Magnani: passionate, sexually vital, complicated, and self-confident.

Throughout the 1950s, Williams, Merlo, and Magnani spent countless nights on her terrace above the Piazza della Minerva overlooking the Pantheon and at fashionable venues like Rosati, which is still a pleasant place to people-watch over Negronis.

They also made frequent appearances at Alfredo, the restaurant credited with inventing fettuccine Alfredo, and which today has two self-styled inheritors: Alfredo alla Scrofa, at the original location, and Il Vero Alfredo, run by the original proprietor's descendants. Both of today's Alfredos, sadly, are touristy and overpriced, though Il Vero is almost worth a visit for the hundreds of framed photos of the owners mock-feeding giant handfuls of fettuccine to celebrity visitors whose expressions range from hammy complicity (James Stewart, Sylvester Stallone) to perturbation bordering on panic (Peter Sellers, Sophia Loren).

But if Williams's recollections of a glamorous '50s bohemia seem sadly obsolete, his lyrical descriptions of the city feel abidingly apt, as in *The Roman Spring of Mrs. Stone,* when he describes "the moment before the lamps go on, when the atmosphere has that exciting blue clarity of the nocturnal scenes in old silent films, a color of water that holds a few drops of ink." Or, as in the novella's opening passage:

> *At five o'clock in the afternoon, which was late in March, the stainless blue of the sky over Rome had begun to pale and the blue transparency of the narrow streets had gathered a faint opacity of vapor. Domes of ancient churches, swelling above the angular roofs like the breasts of recumbent giant women, still bathed in golden light, and so did the very height of that immense cascade of stone stairs that descended from the Trinita di Monte to the Piazza di Spagna.*

For Williams, Rome possessed a singular mix of ephemeral grace and gaudy eroticism, softness and sex, that made it the ideal setting for the story of Karen Stone, a wealthy, recently retired American actress in the midst of an existential crisis (whose story, incidentally, could easily be seen as a superior, darker progenitor of the current retiree travel romance genre in the vein of *Under the Tuscan Sun*).

Mrs. Stone's feelings of "drift," of lostness, her "impression that she was now leading an almost posthumous existence," echo sentiments expressed by Williams himself. Like him, she found in Rome a place to disappear.

At one point in the novella, Mrs. Stone sits in the back of a car as it "twisted at random among the devious ways of the Villa Borghese" and "had a sense of arrival. This was the center. This was what the frantic circle surrounded. Here was the void . . ."

The years after his "golden time" in Rome were not particularly kind to Williams. Much of his later work was ignored by the public and panned by critics. Many close friends died prematurely, including Merlo and Magnani, who succumbed to cancer, he in 1963 and she in 1973. Returning with decreasing frequency to the Italian capital, Williams sank into depression and drug use, which contributed to his own death in 1983.

Today, the dreamy Villa Borghese gardens, with winding pathways, secretive corners, and a canopy of parasol pines, still feels just as Williams described it—like a soft abyss. And here, more than anywhere else in Rome, it's not hard to imagine him as he once was: a man of youth and creative vigor, laughing into the void.

Originally published in May 2016.

Charly Wilder is a writer based in Berlin and a frequent contributor to *The New York Times*.

Elena Ferrante's Naples, Then and Now

Ann Mah

The historic center of Naples drips with Old World charm—faded laundry strung between buildings, fish shops spilling tubs of clams and eels onto the sidewalk, *pasticcerie* tucked near Renaissance churches.

But I was looking for something else. I had come to Naples without a guidebook or even a map, in search of a disheveled neighborhood of "flaking walls" and "scratched doors," where the "wretched gray" of the buildings clashed with the passion and repression of the characters of the writer Elena Ferrante. Armed only with her series of Neapolitan novels, I was in search of a city that—through four weighty volumes, best sellers in both the United States and Italy—had become a character itself: dangerous, dirty, and seductive, the place everyone yearns to leave behind, and the place they can't shake.

As I discovered during a visit in September, the series of books offered a unique view of this complicated city, leading me away from popular tourist sites and helping to explain the city's social, economic, and geographic divisions. To view the Naples of Ferrante is to view Naples like a native.

Elena Ferrante is the pseudonym for the author of seven books, most prominently the Neapolitan Novels—gritty, unflinching portraits of female friendship set against a backdrop of political and social upheaval in Italy from the 1950s to the present. Ever since the 2012 publication of the series' first book, *My Brilliant Friend,* Ferrante has become one of modern literature's greatest enigmas—media-averse and resolutely anonymous. Even the author's gender has been cause for speculation; the publisher's official biography, however, refers to her as a woman, and offers a single personal detail: "Elena Ferrante was born in Naples."

The quartet of novels—which also includes *The Story of a New Name, Those Who Leave and Those Who Stay,* and *The Story of the Lost Child*—traces the lives of Elena Greco and Raffaella Cerullo, two girls from a dismal Naples *rione,* a neighborhood characterized by poverty, Mafia vendettas, and violence. Born weeks apart in August 1944, the girls—who call each other Lenù and Lila—are best friends and fierce competitors, each spurring the other to stunning academic achievement.

Lenù, cautious and conscientious, eventually escapes the neighborhood through diligent study (and exchanges her childhood nickname for her given name, Elena). Lila, impulsive and daring, blazes through life, eyes narrowed to cracks, a "terrible, dazzling girl" who pushes Lenù to audacious acts—as on the day the pair skip school and, for the first time in their young lives, try to "cross the boundaries of the neighborhood" to discover an invisible presence, "a vague bluish memory": the sea.

As I strolled west along a narrow street in the historic center, eyes blinded by the late afternoon sun, with the closely set buildings hemming in the sight of sky and smells of cooking, the sea felt distant indeed. My friend, Paola, said to me: "We call this 'Spaccanapoli.' It means Naples split in half."

Like many ancient Roman cities, she explained, Naples had been planned along parallel *decumani,* roads with an east-west orientation. This particular street cuts through the city's heart. "The farther east you go," Paola, a native Napolitana, said, "the poorer the neighborhoods."

I walked a block or two, and the Gulf of Naples flashed before me, all turquoise twinkle. Was it plausible that ten-year-old Lenù and Lila could have gone their whole lives without glimpsing this port city's defining feature? The answer, I knew, lay beyond the tourist district, in the shabby streets of their *rione.*

With the help of Irene Caselli, a Naples native and journalist now based in Buenos Aires, I had come close to identifying their neighborhood: it was almost certainly the Rione Luzzatti. But, she warned me: "It has a dangerous, dirty reputation. Don't go after dark. Don't walk alone."

Rione Luzzatti is bordered to the east by the central train station and to the north by Poggioreale. "It's not so far," said Paola—in fact, it's less than five miles from the historic center—"but it's a mental distance." Given the area's reputation for crime, I hired a local guide, Francesca Siniscalchi, who, like virtually all the women I met in Naples, is an avid Ferrante fan.

As we meandered through the city in a taxi, Siniscalchi pointed out sites referred to in the books: the "Rettifilo," a shopping street where Lila buys her wedding gown; the sprawling Piazza Municipio, where Elena's father works as a porter; the hulking gray bulk of Liceo Classico Garibaldi, Elena's high school.

"Her portrayal of Naples isn't just a postcard—it's a mosaic of strong, disruptive emotions," Siniscalchi said of the books. "She gives an excellent description of all the opportunities lost by every single generation in the south of Italy. When I finished the last book, I cried."

In the Rione Luzzatti, we found a cluster of dingy, dirt-streaked buildings, their narrow windows curtained by laundry, patches of unkempt grass, litter-strewn sidewalks empty despite the late-summer sunshine. Voices clashed deep within one of the apartment buildings, a hint that people were home and, perhaps, watching us. The bar–pastry shop and shoemaker from the books were missing; a fruit-and-vegetable vendor displayed wares from a truck instead of a horse-drawn cart. But despite these small differences, I needed no leap of imagination to see Elena and Lila's neighborhood. Here in this "dim and distant rockpile" of "indistinguishable urban debris," the sea did seem like a fantasy.

After the *rione,* the glossy elegance of Chiaia, the city's well-heeled shopping district, hit me like the blow of a stick. As teens, Elena and Lila's first foray here leaves them astonished by the chic women who seem "to have breathed another air," Ferrante writes, "to have learned to walk on wisps of wind." Though the outing ends in violence, when a pack of wealthy boys calls their group "hicks" and a bloody fight ensues, these streets play a role throughout the series—the luxurious yin to the *rione*'s desolate yang.

After wandering down the Via Chiaia amid a crowd of stylish locals, I paused at Piazza dei Martiri to look for the Solara brothers' shoe shop that Lila decorates with a gigantic, disfigured copy of her bridal portrait, creating an artistic image of her body "cruelly shredded." Instead I found a Salvatore Ferragamo boutique and, across the majestic plaza, the Feltrinelli bookshop, displaying stacks of Ferrante's books.

As Elena and Lila advance from girlhood to middle age, they face an era of tumultuous social upheaval—radical feminism, the 1968 demonstrations, friends who dabble in militant Communism—and their youthful hope eventually turns to disillusionment. "I've felt the same way—guilty, self-critical," Annamaria Palermo, a professor at the University of Naples "L'Orientale," told me. We were in her airy apartment, encased in book-lined walls, terra-cotta tile floors, and large windows framing views of the Gulf of Naples. "In 1968, we had so many feelings of power. I was sure we would change everything."

Palermo was born in 1943, one year before Ferrante's protagonists, to a bourgeois Naples family. Still, she identified with the books. "There is a Neapolitanness that cuts through social levels. She communicates this very well. These novels go deep into our souls," she said. "I am very attached to this city, but it is like the mermaid of Capri—something enchanting you, but something disgusting you inside," she said, referring to the sirens from the *Odyssey,* who bewitched sailors to death with their sweet songs.

In the books, Elena and Lila's battle against the Camorra, the inescapable local Mafia, is their life's mission, their greatest conflict, depicted as a hopeless, grinding struggle. "The Camorra is part of our history," said Siniscalchi. "It dates to the seventeenth century. Today, it's even been linked to the central government. To grow up in Naples is an everyday fight."

From Palermo's sun-splashed terrace, however, the city's persistent and violent Mafia presence seemed a dark and distant fantasy. In Posillipo, a wealthy residential quarter that faces the gulf, the sea is inescapable, dazzling from every angle.

I thought of a scene in the series' third book, *Those Who Leave and Those Who Stay,* when Elena takes a solitary walk through Naples at dawn, reflecting upon the city's landscape and its influence on her entire identity. "Who knows what feeling I would have had about Naples, about myself, if I had waked every morning not in my neighborhood but in one of those buildings along the shore," she muses.

Before me, the gulf sparkled, an undulating expanse of blue capped by the looming mass of Vesuvius. From here, the *rione* had completely disappeared.

Originally published in January 2016.

Beyond

ALICE MUNRO
L. M. MONTGOMERY
JAMAICA KINCAID
AIMÉ CÉSAIRE
GABRIEL GARCÍA MÁRQUEZ
PABLO NERUDA
JORGE LUIS BORGES

ALEKSANDR PUSHKIN
The Alpine Path
ORHAN PAMUK
Hundred Love Sonnets
MARGUERITE DURAS
ARTHUR RIMBAUD
PAUL BOWLES

Alice Munro's Vancouver

David Laskin

In Alice Munro's Vancouver nobody eats sushi. Nobody jogs along the seawall or browses Granville Street galleries or shops for organic herbs at the Granville Island market. Munro, the eighty-five-year-old Canadian whom the novelist Jonathan Franzen dubbed "the best fiction writer now working in North America," set a handful of her marvelous short stories in the damp British Columbian metropolis, and the urban geography is so exact you can practically map the city off her fictions. But though the addresses match, the vibe is unrecognizable. Young but hopelessly uncool, lustful without being sexy, dowdy, white, yet blind to its own staggering beauty, Munro's Vancouver is an outpost where new wives blink through the rain and wonder when their real lives are going to begin.

Which is pretty much what Munro herself was doing when she came here as a bride of twenty. A small-town beauty from a poor southern Ontario family, Munro moved reluctantly to Vancouver in 1952 after her husband, Jim, landed a job in a big downtown department store. She brought with her two years of university education and a few published stories, a perfect

1950s cinched-waist figure, and a fierce sense of irony that she kept carefully hidden.

Alice and Jim moved into the dark downstairs of a three-story rental on Arbutus Street right across from the beach in the Kitsilano neighborhood. The building, No. 1316, is still there, in need of a paint job, on a street of "high wooden houses crammed with people living tight." Cross the street, stroll out on the packed sand, and the brooding immensity of Burrard Inlet and the coastal mountains engulfs you; a ten-minute drive across the Burrard Bridge and you're cruising through downtown's smorgasbord of world cuisine and high-end retail. Yet Kitsilano seems blithely unaware of its world-class setting.

"Winter in Vancouver was not like any winter I had ever known," Munro writes in "Cortes Island," a story in her 1998 collection *The Love of a Good Woman* that matches detail for detail with her first months in Kits. "No snow, not even anything much in the way of a cold wind." After a day of wandering the city vaguely looking for work, the story's nameless narrator (dubbed "little bride" by one of the other characters) returns to Kits Beach at dusk as "the clouds broke apart in the west over the sea to show the red streaks of the sun's setting—and in the park, through which I circled home, the leaves of the winter shrubs glistened in the damp air of a faintly rosy twilight."

The clouds were scarcer, the light stronger on the January afternoon I prowled around Kits—but otherwise Munro has nailed the scene. I can perfectly imagine the struggling young writer stretched on her bed in the tiny dark bedroom, bolting down Colette and Henry Green, or bending over a notebook at the kitchen table, as the little bride in "Cortes Island" does, "filling page after page with failure."

However, there was no sign of anguished artistes the day of my visit. Fit young women jog through the park. A spread of fruit and pastry awaits a hungry movie crew outside the trendy Watermark Restaurant (Vancouver has become a big movie-making town in recent years). I stroll a few blocks up from the beach to Fourth Avenue—thirty years ago the main drag of Vancouver's counterculture (the scoundrel hippie brother in Munro's story "Forgiveness in Families" lived around here in a house full of smiling Hare Krishna–type priests), but now as bright and tony as New York's Columbus Avenue or San Francisco's Fillmore Street. The one holdover from Munro's time is Duthie Books—a literary bookstore that once had branches all over the city but has recently retreated to this one last thoroughly gentrified location.

The Munros' Kitsilano chapter was brief. By 1953 the couple had decamped to the North Shore suburbs just across the Lions Gate Bridge—first to a rather drab tract house in rainy North Vancouver, and then to a nicer place with a big front garden perched on a slope in the Dundarave section of West Vancouver. Two daughters arrived in quick succession (a third died the day she was born). The family lived in Dundarave for the next seven years, Jim commuting to his job downtown, Alice attempting to keep her art alive while managing the household.

The West Vancouver setting crops up again and again in Munro's stories—but it's always colored by the strain she was under in those years. "When I got home from school my mother would be sitting in that chair in the living room in the dark," Munro's daughter Sheila recalls. "She had great promise—she had published some stories—but she didn't know if she would continue to do it. She just wanted to be left alone to write."

The Dundarave house is still there, and so is the shopping block on Marine Drive where Munro used to walk (she never learned to drive) to do her marketing or to work in the office she rented for a while or to take Sheila to ballet class. Sheila remembers the block of shops as wonderfully ordinary—a hardware store, grocery store, cleaners, and a Chinese restaurant.

But some of Vancouver's newfound cool has wafted across the water and today downtown Dundarave has a bit of the air of Sausalito—galleries and coffee places, chowder and sushi, a scattering of petals on the sidewalk outside the florist. In summer it would be the perfect place to grab a cappuccino, assemble a picnic, and then head for the beach, two blocks away at Dundarave Pier or a hop east at Ambleside.

"Kath and Sonje have a place of their own on the beach, behind some large logs," opens "Jakarta," one of Munro's most memorable Vancouver stories from *The Love of a Good Woman*. It's unmistakably Ambleside Beach—though faux Mediterranean palazzi have muscled out most of the cottages that line the shore in Munro's story. From their outpost behind the logs, Kath and Sonje clutch their D. H. Lawrence and Katherine Mansfield and eye the gaggle of blowsy, noisy housewives they dub the Monicas:

> *These women aren't so much older than Kath and Sonje. But they've reached a stage in life that Kath and Sonje dread. They turn the whole beach into a platform. Their burdens, their strung-out progeny and maternal poundage, their authority, can annihilate the bright water, the perfect small cove with the red-limbed arbutus trees, the cedars, growing crookedly out of the high rocks. Kath feels their threat particularly, since she's a mother now herself. When she nurses her baby she often reads a book, sometimes smokes a cigarette, so as not to sink into a sludge of animal functions.*

This is pure Munro: the social anxiety, the fusing of insecurity and disdain, the heavy tug of ordinary life, the way dread can rise and spread until it erases everything lovely. "She's always dead-on," Sheila Munro says when I ask if the descriptions of places ring true to her childhood memories. And yet it strikes me when I walk out on Ambleside pier that Munro has neglected to mention this stupendous setting—the echoing curves of bridge and cove and mountain, the dull silver of the sea, the green-black hump of Stanley Park, all this grandeur of land and water so close it's as if the great northern wilderness laps at the city's feet.

But Munro was always oppressed, almost crushed by Vancouver's fabled vistas. In the story "Memorial," also set in West Vancouver, a character named Eileen challenges a wealthy foolish man who boasts about his water and mountain view:

> *"Well suppose you're in a low mood . . . and you get up and here spread out before you is this magnificent view. All the time, you can't get away from it. Don't you ever feel not up to it?"*
>
> *"Not up to it?"*
>
> *"Guilty," said Eileen, persistently though regretfully. "That you're not in a better mood? That you're not more—worthy, of this beautiful view?"*

In 1963, the Munros left Dundarave and moved to Victoria to open a bookstore. The marriage broke up nine years later, and Alice returned to Ontario and eventually remarried, but the bookstore is still there—Munro's Books, still run by Jim, still one of the finest in Canada.

Alice never again lived in Vancouver, though she does visit to collect prizes and still occasionally sets a story there.

"What Is Remembered," from the 2001 collection *Hateship, Friendship, Courtship, Loveship, Marriage,* is one of her best and touches on all of her totemic Vancouver spots. Meriel, the young wife at the center of the story, is at a funeral in Dundarave when a man unknown to her, a doctor and bush pilot from the far north, offers to drive her on a visit to a distant suburb. All afternoon, sexual tension mounts until the pilot pulls over at the Prospect Point viewing area in Stanley Park, and the two strangers get out of the car and start wildly kissing.

Munro brings them to the glass-bricked entrance of a "small, decent building" in Kitsilano, but while they consummate their mad upsurge of passion in a borrowed flat, she cuts away to describe the setting Meriel would have preferred for adultery: "A narrow six- or seven-story hotel, once a fashionable place of residence, in the West End of Vancouver. Curtains of yellowed lace, high ceilings, perhaps an iron grill over part of the window, a fake balcony. Nothing actually dirty or disreputable, just an atmosphere of long accommodation of private woes and sins."

It's just the kind of place Munro herself prefers—places like the Buchan Hotel, tucked away on a leafy side street near Stanley Park, or the ivy-covered Sylvia Hotel overlooking English Bay. By a stroke of literary magic, Munro makes an afternoon of adultery in Kitsilano all the more electric by having it happen offstage and in the wrong place, the wrong part of town, the wrong kind of bedroom.

In a way, it's a perfect metaphor for Munro's own relationship to Vancouver. For her, this was always the wrong place—the views too grand, the weather too gray, the trees too tall. She never cared for the stodgy, repressed Vancouver of the 1950s, and by all accounts she hasn't warmed much more to the sleek city of today. And yet, after you read her

Vancouver stories, you sense her watchful, uprooted presence everywhere.

It's a sign of Munro's greatness as a writer that she so pervades a place that she never really surrendered herself to.

Originally published in June 2006.

Seattle-based writer David Laskin is the author of a number of nonfiction books, including *The Children's Blizzard* and *The Family.*

Searching for Anne of Green Gables *on Prince Edward Island*

Ann Mah

My first evening on Prince Edward Island, I found myself on the shore, scrambling across sun-bleached beach grass to circle an abandoned lighthouse. The Gulf of Saint Lawrence crashed in moody bursts before me, the water reflecting the deepening gray of the sky. My feet sank into drifts of sand until I turned inland, down a spongy red clay road that edged a verdant meadow. In the distance, the cheerful lights of my bed-and-breakfast, a rambling nineteenth-century farmhouse, beckoned.

Less than an hour earlier, I had been driving past a spangly strip of tourist attractions—miniature golf courses, water theme parks—that promised "family fun" with suspicious exuberance. But on this country lane, with the roar of the gulf filling my ears, I could almost imagine myself a solitary traveler and not one of the thousands of tourists who flock every year to the green gabled house only a few miles from where I stood.

I had come to this Canadian island to follow in the footsteps of L. M. Montgomery, who made her island home famous with her novel *Anne of Green Gables.* An instant best seller when it was published in 1908, the book tells the story of the verbose, red-haired Anne Shirley—an eleven-year-old orphan who is accidentally sent to a middle-aged brother and sister instead of the boy they had requested to help with their farm. Starved for love, with a vibrant imagination and a knack for comic mishap, Anne has charmed readers for over a century, including Mark Twain, who proclaimed her "the dearest and most lovable child in fiction since the immortal Alice."

The book, which has sold more than fifty million copies and has been translated into at least twenty languages, started Lucy Maud Montgomery's career. Today it anchors the island's multimillion-dollar tourist industry, with summer musical performances, gift shops, house museums, horse-drawn carriage rides, a mock village, and more—all devoted to scenes and characters from the book and its seven sequels.

I have wanted to visit Prince Edward Island since my childhood, when I devoured Anne's escapades along with Montgomery's descriptions of the island's beauty. The landscape of "ruby, and emerald, and sapphire"—as she described it in her copious journals—is as much a character in the book as Anne herself: a temple of woods, fields, and shore, where the sunset sky shines "like a great rose window at the end of a cathedral aisle."

I worried, though, that the onslaught of Anne fans had ruined the island's secluded charm. But as I discovered during a trip in late May, it's still possible to glimpse Montgomery's island, to wander its red clay lanes and dappled woodland copses, to admire the farms fronting the silvery sea. You just have to know where to look.

Maud, as she was known, grew up in the rural community of Cavendish, on the north shore of the crescent-shaped island, a solitary child raised by her maternal grandparents on their homestead farm. Like her famous heroine, she was abandoned as a child—her mother died of tuberculosis before her second birthday, her father moved to Saskatchewan and remarried—and the girl often escaped her elderly grandparents' strict household by "fishing in the brooks, picking gum in the spruce copses, berrying in the stumps and gypsying to the shore." She later used this idyllic landscape for her fiction, renaming the area Avonlea, and borrowing as a setting the neighboring farmhouse of her cousins, an older brother-sister pair reminiscent of the book's Matthew and Marilla.

In 1937, Green Gables and its surrounding area became Prince Edward Island National Park, and child-friendly attractions soon cropped up nearby. Today the house, preserved as a historic site, welcomes over 125,000 visitors each year (about 20 percent are from Japan, where the book is a cultural phenomenon). Many dress up like Anne, donning pinafores and straw hats adorned with red braids.

The house's reconstructed rooms reflect the book with faithful accuracy, decorated in stiff Victorian furniture and scattered with details easily recognizable by fans: a black lace shawl spread across Marilla's bed; a brown, puffed-sleeve dress hung on the closet door of Anne's room. I stood for a long time in Anne's doorway, gazing at the flowered wallpaper, low white bed, and fluttering green muslin curtains. The east gable room—in fact, the entire house—was so exactly as I'd pictured it during my many readings of the book, I felt a pang of nostalgia for my own childhood.

Outside, the farmyard jolted me back to reality—both its depictions of nineteenth-century rural life, particularly grueling in the harsh Canadian Maritimes climate, as well as its incongruous surroundings, which quickly broke the spell. An eighteen-hole golf course now spreads over the former woods and farmland that abutted the home; the drone of a lawn mower accompanied my walk through the manicured grove of trees re-created as the book's "Haunted Wood," and instead of the wailing ghost of Anne's imagination, I met club-toting golfers.

At the other end of the Haunted Wood trail, I found the remains of the author's childhood home, where she wrote *Anne of Green Gables* at the age of thirty-one while living with her widowed grandmother. The object of a bitter inheritance dispute, the house fell to ruin after the death of the grandmother; today, only the stone foundation remains.

I strolled the grounds—which are lovingly maintained by a branch of Montgomery's family—admiring a fragile old apple tree ("I loved the trees around my old home with a personal love," she wrote in her memoir, *The Alpine Path*) and pausing at the spot where her bedroom window once stood. Through a screen of spruce trees, past fields and meadows, I glimpsed Montgomery's beloved gulf as she described it in an essay: "a tiny blue gap between distant hills."

In fact, I often felt as if I were viewing the writer's island as I saw that scrap of sea: slivers of beauty snatched between the carnival-style attractions peppering Cavendish. But as I ventured farther afield in my rental car, the island's splendor opened up to me. It also felt familiar from the descriptions I'd reread so many times in Montgomery's books—the "fringing groves of fir and maple," the ponds "so long and winding," the red roads that "wound like gay satin ribbons in and among green fields."

I turned off one highway, down a clay road edged by towering spruce trees, stopping at the edge of a field "starred with hundreds of dandelions," as the author wrote in her journals. For as far as my eye could see, there was only farmland, interlocking patches of red plowed fields and green meadows dotted with solitary farmhouses, a view that could have been lifted straight from the books. Indeed, as I explored the area west of Cavendish—small communities like French River, Park Corner, and North Granville—I realized I needed only a bit of imagination to picture Anne beside me. Any of these dirt roads could be "Lovers' Lane," the secluded cow path where Anne liked to "think out loud"; any of the farmhouses her Green Gables; any of the sun-splashed ponds her "Lake of Shining Waters."

In 1911, Montgomery married a minister, Ewan Macdonald, and moved to Ontario. Though she visited regularly, she never again lived on Prince Edward Island. And yet her beloved home continued to inspire her—she set nineteen of her twenty novels there—remaining her refuge throughout a life darkened by depression.

She would find today's Cavendish unrecognizable, no longer the "haunt of ancient peace," as she described it in *Anne of Green Gables.* But elsewhere, the island's "green seclusion" endures, with gulf inlets reaching in like slender fingers, fields of lupine flowers waiting to burst forth, groves of birch trees hiding eighteenth-century pioneer cemeteries—a place so rich in beauty and, in Anne Shirley's signature phrase, so much "scope for imagination."

Originally published in August 2014.

Jamaica Kincaid's Antigua

Monica Drake

The air was heavy with mist when the lights were finally trained on the stage, illuminating a set that looked as if it had been transported from a low-frills scuba diving resort. Dancers wearing short shorts—known locally as batty-riders—ground their hips with mechanical precision. Typical Carnival fare, until Dennis Roberts entered stage right in a wet suit, jutting out his rotund belly to emphasize his seal-like silhouette.

Roberts, known as Menace, glanced at the crowd through a snorkel mask, mouthpiece in place. The mere sight of this character—the clueless tourist—brought out howls of laughter. Soon he broke into his monster hit "Sand to the Beach," a song about people who are as clueless as many of the Americans and Europeans who come to this island every year. There was no better way to explain it than to evoke the type of supremely confident yet flawed interloper whom Jamaica Kincaid scolds in *A Small Place,* a slender work of nonfiction about her native country, Antigua and Barbuda:

> *An ugly thing, that is what you are when you become a tourist . . . a piece of rubbish pausing here and there to gaze at this and taste that, and it will never occur to you that the people who inhabit the place in which you have just paused cannot stand you, that behind their closed doors they laugh at your strangeness . . .*

The book, released in 1988, a mere seven years after the nation's independence, positioned Antigua's tourism industry as a vestige of colonial rule. The one-hundred-square-mile island has seen waves of settlers, from the Arawaks to the Caribs to the English, who brought kidnapped Africans to work the sugarcane fields. In Kincaid's book, the Lebanese and Syrians were moving in. Now a new wave is sweeping through: developers and hospitality companies from China, the United States, and Canada.

I explored Antigua last summer with my husband, whose family roots lie there, and my daughter, curious to get a sense of the humanity in Kincaid's books that is largely absent in Antigua's tourism marketing.

When you arrive in Antigua, Kincaid wrote, "The road on which you are traveling is a very bad road . . . You are feeling wonderful, so you say, 'Oh, what a marvelous change these bad roads are from the splendid highways I am used to in North America.' (Or, worse, Europe.)"

But anyone traveling from New York City to Saint John's, Antigua, knows that some of the rutted roads to Kennedy Airport these days are worse than those in even the most sparsely populated corners of Antigua.

The first thing you'll notice aren't the roads, which are evenly paved, but the hulking cream-stucco structure beyond the roundabout near the airport exit. This is the former headquarters of the Stanford International Bank, named for its American founder, R. Allen Stanford, who is serving time for running the bank as a Ponzi scheme. "Just down the road," to use an Antiguan directional, is a cricket stadium, also erected by Stanford, overlooking a dusty gray field that was empty each time we passed it.

The stadium stands like a great ruin on an island pockmarked with the detritus of abandoned dreams. There are crumbling sugar mills, rusted cars, and buildings subsumed by growth that was lush even during a drought. I glimpsed one man who had transformed a piece of rolling luggage into a stroller that held a napping child, and motorcycle riders who had wrapped their heads in scarves, presumably as protection against the dust.

But there was also abundance. Mangoes too ripe for trees to hold rotted in the gutters near a village called John Hughes. (When my nephew Amir, an Antiguan expat, told a friend that we'd bought some from a market, she said it pained her that we'd actually paid for them and then presented him with two dozen.) Brightly painted homes of concrete—a material Kincaid associated with Lebanese and Syrian property owners—now outnumber the modest clapboard houses in many parts of the island.

Another round of change is on its way. The Yida International Investment Group, a Chinese company, plans to open a $740 million resort on the main island's northeast corner and nearby islands. A $400 million Royalton property is slated to open in Deep Bay, and Robert De Niro and a partner are building a $250 million resort on Antigua's sister island, Barbuda. Those projects will add three thousand hotel rooms within the next five years, the government estimates.

Luxury, of course, is nothing new here. The moneyed set stays at places like the private Mill Reef Club. (In her book, Kincaid reserves a particularly sharp wrath for the place, which is effectively a stand-in for colonial rulers.) Mill Reef is so exclusive that its managers refused to give a tour during its off-season. So to sample the luxury on offer, I went to Jumby Bay, known as much for its celebrity roster as its old-money clientele.

Rather than taking a jet, I got a ride with Amir, who left for the United States two decades before our trip and had not returned until our visit. He dropped me off with his wife, Amma, and my sister-in-law, Katherine. After the brief ferry ride, we were greeted by a smiling, cat-eyed woman named Melanie Fletcher, the guest relations manager at the resort. As we walked toward the covered bar, I saw a flash of color: a lush green lawn beneath the spray of a sprinkler.

Jumby Bay, which started as a villa owners' collective, takes up just over a quarter of the three-hundred-acre Long Island. Though the capacity of the resort is about four hundred guests and it was 98 percent full, according to Fletcher, all we felt was a stillness in the air. There are no cars, only bikes and golf carts, and villas with enough space between them that you could have a conversation without being overheard by your neighbors.

Literature says that *jumby* means "playful spirit," but some Antiguans say it really means an evil one. The sugar mill in the middle of the resort was a reminder that the inhabitants had once been slaves, and left us wondering about the spirits who roamed there.

After lunch, we talked about family history and lost track of time and place. "What do you think about the history of this place?" Katherine asked, eyeing a beautiful tree whose limbs seemed sturdy enough to hold the weight borne by a noose. There is no record of lynchings on Long Island, and Jumby does not market itself as a plantation resort. Yet there was the inescapable fact that the staff was largely brown-skinned and the guests weren't, a vestige of slavery throughout the Americas and a reminder of the system of apartheid that Kincaid derides in *A Small Place.* There, as elsewhere on the island, though, I saw something I hadn't seen in *A Small Place:* upward mobility. Some of the five hundred people who worked there had managed to trade up jobs. They seemed less interested in laughing at tourists than in simply having a stable means of supporting themselves and their families.

In the resort's boutique we fingered pricey cover-ups. Somehow we managed to miss the ferry, though we were a five-minute walk away. We settled in near the bar, staring at the water—"three shades of blue," Kincaid writes in the novel *Lucy*—and nearly missed the next ferry. The tension that we'd accumulated in our daily lives seemed to float into the distance. We could have stayed forever.

Antigua can do that, Kincaid wrote. For all the drama of its history, she writes that the beauty of the place, the very thing that bewitches its tourists, renders it a time capsule to its residents. "They have nothing to compare this incredible constant with, no big historical moment to compare the way they are now to the way they used to be." And in a later passage: "The unreal way in which it is beautiful now is the unreal way in which it was always beautiful."

Her characters often flee the idyll for places where seasons change and there is hope of transformation, following the path of Kincaid and countless other immigrants from the Caribbean.

Jamaica Kincaid was born Elaine Cynthia Potter Richardson in 1949 in Saint John's. Her novels detail her biography: that her mother is an Afro-Indian from Dominica (*The Autobiography of My Mother*); that her father, an Antiguan cabdriver, abandoned the family (*Mr. Potter*); that Kincaid left Antigua in 1965 to work as a nanny (*Annie John, Lucy*).

After establishing a successful literary career in the States,

Kincaid returned home in 1986 for her first visit in two decades. But her tone in *A Small Place* led to the banning of the book there, and a self-exile as she feared for her safety.

Now, though, Kincaid is enough of an expat to long for her childhood home. She regularly took her two children, Annie and Harold, to Antigua—"I like them to see normal, boring black people going about their normal, boring lives," she said in an interview with *The New York Times* in 1996—and was there recently for an academic conference that coincided with Carnival.

She was part of what has become an exodus of Antiguans to the United States, Britain, and Canada. Every summer, many return for Carnival. And that is where I caught my best glimpses of Kincaid's Antigua.

A family friend had been enlisted to park his truck alongside the road where the procession would walk. We sat in back. Before the floats and dance troupes and steel-band drummers went through, yet another friend, parked nearby, mentioned that she'd known my husband's paternal grandmother, affectionately called Aunt Vic. I peppered her with questions, and she smiled. This sort of thing wasn't surprising to her. Meanwhile, my daughter spotted cousins dancing on the road, others marching and greeting friends of cousins, cousins of friends. It was a family reunion, made up of Antiguans and Antiguan expats returning for a dose of that small place. February is for tourists. Off-season is the time for the real Antigua.

One day, I finally found the potholed road to paradise. A pristine beach that sloped into a gentle crescent, Rendezvous Bay was all ours save for a single local family. We splashed in the turquoise water and considered a sign promising a resort on the site, which falls within a national park.

It seemed nonsensical. Until I realized that immigration to Antigua isn't only for retirees descended from the West

Africans and Europeans who lived on the island for centuries. The country recently launched a program allowing people who buy properties of $400,000 or more to become citizens. It seems that Kincaid's description of Antigua, of a nation run by foreign-landed gentry, may not be so dated after all.

If you want to find Kincaid's country and her vibrant characters though, book a trip for Carnival, in late July, hurricane season. Find a place that is not on a beach. Keep an eye out for holes in the yard where tarantulas burrow, and if you find them, close your windows when it rains. Rent a car, which you will quickly learn to drive on the wrong side of the road, and head to a little bakery for a bun-butter-and-cheese sandwich. Then drive to Saint John's during Carnival for a battle of the bands. Press to the front of the line. Don't worry about anybody stealing your wallet; you left your credit cards and trappings of being a tourist back in that home that you (thank God) remembered to seal off from the spiders as rain began to fall. You laugh when the emcee peppers her monologue with words like *stush,* for "stuck-up," and when someone onstage apes a tourist, because that's not you.

Look around—you won't find many examples of Lucy or Annie John here because they weren't allowed to come—they are at home sneaking a chance to read books after bedtime. But you will find the world that they, and Jamaica Kincaid's characters, left—the one that keeps pulling her back to her elusive, fictional universe.

Originally published in July 2016.

Monica Drake is the editor of the Travel section at *The New York Times.*

Beneath Martinique's Beauty, Guided by a Poet

Sylvie Bigar

As the stories poured out, eyes sparkled, smiles widened, hands danced. Everyone I met on Martinique harbored at least one intimate memory of Aimé Césaire—a quiet encounter or speech etched forever in their consciousness—but they all agreed: this poet, playwright, and politician, who achieved an almost monumental status on the Caribbean island, was the most humble man they had ever known.

Take, for instance, Daniel Houcou, one of two drivers assigned to Césaire in the final decade of his life. Most afternoons, Houcou would ferry the poet as he crisscrossed the forty-five-mile-long island armed with his beloved botanic treatise (its title seems to be lost to history). "He would suddenly spot a tree and ask me to stop and climb in the back so we could look it up together," Houcou said.

I first visited Martinique at age fifteen, on a tropical interlude with my Swiss parents, and was instantly engulfed in the Caribbean breath. It would be the first of many visits. As an adult, after a move to New York, I began to venture beyond the bougainvillea and the beaches. I hiked the menacing volcano Mount Pelée; I explored the rain forest; I discovered the people. And then I discovered Césaire's words and was bewitched. They gave me new insights into the painful history of Martinique.

Though raw, enraged even, his poetry is anchored in his love of his native land: "My beautiful country with its high sesame shores," he called it. When I heard that 2013 marked the one hundredth anniversary of his birth (he died in 2008), I planned a voyage through Martinique and its history, with its favorite son as my guide. In the waves, along the windy slopes of the volcano, in the banana fields, his voice unearthed for me the human tales hidden under the beauty of the island.

Born in 1913 on what was then a French colony, Césaire spent his formative years in the 1930s studying in Paris, where, with the help of other prominent black intellectuals, he established the concept of negritude, the conscious act of acceptance and pride in one's own African background and a rejection of colonial racism and oppression.

In 1939, Césaire, then only twenty-six, returned to Martinique to teach literature, shortly after the publication of *Notebook of a Return to the Native Land.* This anticolonialist surrealist scream of a poem put the idea of negritude into action, exposing the horrors of slavery and its legacy. "We are walking compost hideously promising tender cane and silky cotton," he wrote.

In 1941, a ship carrying a group of writers and artists fleeing occupied France docked on the island. Césaire's subsequent interactions with the French surrealist André Breton and the Cuban artist Wifredo Lam, whose attentions helped bring Césaire to prominence, started a lifelong network of friendship and intellectual exchange.

In 1945, Césaire was asked to head the Communist ballot in the mayoral elections of Fort-de-France, the capital, and to his surprise he was elected mayor, a position he held until 2001 (except briefly in 1983 and 1984). Days before Soviet tanks invaded Budapest in 1956, he resigned from the French Communist Party and later helped to found the Martinican Progressive Party. For forty-eight years, Papa Césaire, as many still call him, also served as deputy of Martinique to the National Assembly in Paris, where he led the peaceful transition from French colony to department.

Assisting me in my mission was the tall, elegant, and affable Houcou. We started in Fort-de-France, where even the airport is named for Césaire, and then followed the sinuous Route de la Trace, built on the site of an old trail used by Jesuits in the eighteenth century, stopping at Camp Balata, a park and nineteenth-century military fort, where the poet often strolled. To one side, the five cone-shaped peaks of the volcanic Pitons du Carbet range loomed in the distance; to the other, the bay of Fort-de-France shimmered under the sun. As I walked the "literary path" the city had recently installed along an allée of majestic mahogany trees, I paused to read markers featuring quotes from Breton and prominent Martinicans, including Césaire: "I am obsessed with nature, with the flower, with the root," one reads. "It is all linked to my situation as a man exiled from his primordial."

We headed to the Balata Botanical Garden, where I tiptoed hesitantly on the swaying aerial bridges, terrified to look down. Safely across and breathing again, I recognized the sculptural, red heliconia flower—the symbol of Césaire's Progressive Party. As we drove on, the rain forest grew impenetrable. Ripples of wind along walls of gigantic ferns brought to mind the "otherworldly chatter of the arborescent ferns" that Césaire wrote about in his poem "Rapacious Space."

I was eager to get to his seaside hometown, Basse-Pointe, where he loved to watch the Atlantic breakers, "from Trinité to Grand-Rivière, / the hysterical grand lick of the sea." Only an hour away from the tropical forest, a steep cul-de-sac led to a cove where black sand—volcanic powder, really—painted the water emerald green and the deafening surf sounded a continuous drumbeat.

By contrast, Mount Pelée, a short drive inland, was ominously silent. Around me, grassy furrows belied its buried violence. (The owner of a café on the volcano's slopes told me that "whenever we saw the sedan, we knew Césaire was back to watch the volcano and watch over us.") After five miles, we reached Saint Pierre and the Kapok Tree: "Tree non-tree / beautiful immense tree / the day on it settles / frightened bird."

The town had reigned as the chic capital of the island until the volcano erupted on May 8, 1902, killing about thirty thousand people. Carbonized, the tree had somehow revived, its now humongous branches hovering high over the stunning melancholic ruins that remain of the town. "Papa Césaire was awed by the tree's stature and resilience," Houcou said.

The next day, I headed to the small museum housed in the theater that was Césaire's old Fort-de-France mayoral office. In the formal courtyard, I spotted a bench recently installed by the Toni Morrison Society. Inaugurated in 2006, the organization's Bench by the Road Project, which places benches in various spots notable to the black experience, was inspired by Morrison's observation that there were no memorial sites at which to pause and mourn the millions of souls ripped from Africa. "There is no wall, or park, or tower, or skyscraper lobby—there is not even a small bench by the road," she said. Today, the memorials recognize transformative events and individuals in the history of the African diaspora.

I thought of slave ships brimming with chained men and women, but also of my mother and grandmother escaping through the roof of their Paris apartment building, seconds after Nazi soldiers rang their bell on July 16, 1942. I sat on the bench and, overcome by melancholy, wept.

Inside the museum, the poet's voice was piped into his office to eerie effect; photographs, artifacts, manuscripts, and even his glasses, set on his desk, perpetuated the feeling that he might suddenly appear. Instead, across the hallway, I met his daughter Michèle Césaire, the artistic director of the Théâtre Aimé Césaire. "My father created numerous cultural centers where people could study dance, music, theater, or pottery for free," she said. "And they still exist."

Later, I strolled in Fort-de-France, taking in the vibrant hodgepodge: French-accented boutiques; a market overflowing with mangoes and pineapples; the stunning Belle Époque Schoelcher Library created in Paris for the 1889 World's Fair and then rebuilt on Martinique piece by piece.

The atmosphere is very different twenty-five miles away, on the craggy Caravelle Peninsula. In her remarkable 1994 documentary, *Aimé Césaire: A Voice for History,* the Martinican filmmaker Euzhan Palcy showed Césaire in his trademark beige suit, hands clasped behind his back, walking among the ruins of Château Dubuc, a sugar plantation founded in 1725 on the peninsula. There, I listened, enthralled, as Dimitri Charles-Angèle, an erudite dreadlocked guide, brought to life the habitation, travails, and pains of the plantation's nearly three hundred slaves.

These impassioned tales were good preparation for the Cap 110 memorial at Anse Caffard, across from the Diamond Rock, on the southwestern corner of the island. For sheer beauty, I had always enjoyed Southern Martinique, with its white beaches and undulating hills clad in banana trees, but I had learned only recently that the volcanic rock that rises over five hundred feet from the surrounding water—today one of the island's best diving spots—had witnessed the devastating wreck of a clandestine slave ship in 1830. In homage to the captives who perished there, the Martinican artist Laurent Valère sculpted fifteen towering but hunched concrete figures set in a triangle (alluding to the triangular slave trade, in which slaves and goods were exchanged between Africa, the Americas, and Europe) and looking pensively toward the Gulf of Guinea off the coast of West Africa. The characters' postures seemed to strain under the weight of the past.

But I wanted to go farther south. On the coast, a few miles past the Diamond Rock, I stopped on a hill and looked back. I could clearly distinguish the profile of Morne Larcher, a bluff most often referred to as the Sleeping Woman. Césaire may have been smitten: he penned an entire poem dedicated to her. "Survivor survivor," he wrote. "You my exile and queen of this rubble / Ghost forever inapt at perfecting her kingdom." In the poet's words, I felt the pain of history: the juncture of nature and peoples, and the universality of our voyage.

Originally published in November 2013.

Sylvie Bigar, a food and travel writer, lives in New York with her three passports, two teens, and two dogs.

A Remote Colombian City That Really Does Exist

Nicholas Gill

The first time I heard of Mompós, officially called Santa Cruz de Mompox, was about a decade ago, while reading Gabriel García Márquez's novel *The General in His Labyrinth.* "Mompox doesn't exist," García Márquez wrote, "we sometimes dream about her, but she doesn't exist." For years, I assumed that to be true.

It wasn't until 2008, when an acquaintance, a British journalist in Colombia named Richard McColl, began building a hotel there, that I realized that Mompós—a perfectly preserved colonial city nearly five hundred years old, set on an island in the Magdalena River—was indeed real. In fact, the region, rich in history and ripe with romanticism, was the setting of many of García Márquez's most famous works.

There is nothing directly associated with the author in the city—no statues or plaques—but the area, and particularly the river, heavily informed his writing. Mompós, and nearby towns like Sucre, where the events portrayed in the novella *Chronicle of a Death Foretold* actually transpired, and where García Márquez, who died April 17, 2014, at his home in Mexico City, lived for many years during his youth, suddenly seemed like destinations infused with the spirit of his tales. "I traveled the Magdalena River eleven times, back and forth," he once said in an interview. "I know every village and every tree on that river."

For me, the biggest obstacle was getting there. Mompós is close to nowhere. Overland routes involve combinations of buses and ferries, and while a bridge in nearby Magangué is said to be planned for this year and roads are being improved, traveling from Bogotá still takes ten hours.

From Cartagena I took Toto Express, a pickup truck that seats five and stops at your hotel. It arrived a few minutes after 4:30 a.m., and we drove inland for nearly two hundred miles on semi-paved and dirt roads, across seven hours of tropical scrubland, until reaching the banks of the Magdalena, where a car ferry helped us across.

Mompós is home to some 30,000 residents, many of whom live within the forty blocks of colonial-era buildings that date to the town's heyday from the sixteenth to the nineteenth centuries, when it was a strategic trading route for tobacco, slaves, and precious metals on their way from the Andes to the coast. As the river silted up in the early nineteenth century and the current shifted directions, Mompós fell out of favor as a transit point and its influence began to wane. Eventually, it was all but forgotten.

During some of Colombia's most tumultuous years in the 1980s, the Magdalena Valley was accessible only during certain hours of the day. It remained that way until the mid-1990s—UNESCO named the historic center of Mompós a World Heritage Site in 1995—when the region began to open back up as threats from drug cartels and paramilitary groups began to dissipate.

During my visit, speculation was swirling on what the future holds. Along the waterfront, prices for real estate have risen. Some foresee a small boom fueled by wealthy Colombians wanting to come in and renovate old buildings. For now, though, that seems a long way off. Mule-driven carts still far outnumber cars. Outside of a jazz festival held each October and Holy Week celebrations, when every room in town is taken, on most days Mompós sees just a handful of visitors.

I checked in at La Casa Amarilla, which McColl runs with his wife, Alba Torres, whose family is from Mompós. McColl has gradually fixed up the seventeenth-century building, transitioning from a simple hostel to a proper boutique hotel, adding air-conditioning and LCD TVs. We were soon ambling along the waterfront, passing the bright yellow Santa Bárbara Church, with its baroque bell tower and gilded altars that date to 1613. A man rolled a wooden cart with freshly cut slabs of raw pork on it, as a woman beside him called out *"cerdo, cerdo, cerdo,"* like a vendor selling peanuts at a baseball game.

While we dined on fried *bocachico* (a local freshwater fish) and coconut rice at El Comedor Costeño, set right on the river, a boat appeared in the distance. Someone shouted out that it was carrying "La Virgen," a nationally famous image of the Virgin of Chiquinquirá. It was on a peace mission, I was told, traveling to towns along the Magdalena. A crowd of a hundred paraded the image through the streets, stopping at every church and singing hymns, rousing what is otherwise a sleepy place.

That drowsy rhythm is in large part due to the sweltering heat, which dictates the course of the day. At sunrise, schoolgirls in plaid skirts walked to class and men with straw hats unloaded bananas and pineapples from dugout canoes. During the peak of the day, Mompós was at its quietest. Most stay in and those who don't head to El Comedor Costeño for *limonada* sweetened with *panela,* unrefined cane sugar.

On Plaza Tamarindo, two blocks inland from the river,

women were selling *chicha,* a corn-based drink served in a gourd, while men carried trays of *queso de capa,* balls of a stringy mozzarella-like cheese, some stuffed with guava paste. At a silver filigree workshop, a handful of men sat in a courtyard making delicate jewelry, a holdout from the days when gold and silver regularly passed through.

In the evenings, when bats swoop down into the streets, locals congregate at Café Tinto on Plaza de la Concepción, where I sat in a rocking chair with a beer and listened to recordings of Beethoven and Vivaldi. For dinner, many opt for the plaza in front of Santo Domingo Church, where a dozen food and juice stalls set up each evening.

An Austrian, Walter Maria Gurth, runs El Fuerte, a surprisingly sophisticated restaurant inside the Fort of San Anselmo, which was built by slaves and was where Simón Bolívar gathered his troops for his campaign to free the continent from Spanish rule.

The leaves of banana trees hung over tables made from tree trunks, and a guadua bamboo roof covered the main dining room; all of it was made on-site by Gurth, who once made a living restoring old planes and sailboats. ("Everything is for sale," the menu read, "except our pets.") A wood-burning oven fired thin-crust pizzas with toppings like house-made speck and blue cheese. Chilean wine and Campari-and-sodas were followed by shots of homemade grappa.

On the last of my four days in Mompós, I hired a boatman named Henri to take me downriver, to agrarian and fishing villages yet more remote. We cut through streams and wetlands, where herons flew over fields of yucca and howler monkeys slept in the trees.

Henri pointed out watermarks from a flood in 2010, which stood about three feet up the walls of many houses, some still piled high with sandbags. I asked how many days the flood lasted. "Days? Seven months," Henri said. "In Mompós they thought it was the end of the world."

He added, with a straight face: "It was a good year for the fishermen, though."

Back at La Casa Amarilla, I asked McColl about the flooding. "The Depresión Momposina is an incredible but fragile and special wetland in that it acts as a sponge for the rest of the country," he said. "Over the past fifty years and more, all the lowland tropical forest has been cut back to allow for cattle grazing, which was seen as the source of economic wealth. Now, we are paying the price."

Flooding of that magnitude had not occurred in eighty years. Back then, they brought the Cristo Negro, a black Christ figure, from San Agustín Church in Chile to the Magdalena, where they washed its feet—and it's said that the waters receded. In 2010, they did the same, and the water again receded. While that may have had something to do with it being the end of the rainy season, it's nice to know there's a place where something so preposterously fantastic—the sort of thing that one might read in a García Márquez story, actually—just might not be fiction.

Originally published in May 2014.

Nicholas Gill writes frequently about food and travel in Latin America, and sometimes other places. He lives in Brooklyn and in Lima, Peru.

In Chile, Where Pablo Neruda Lived and Loved

Joyce Maynard

The idea of paying a visit to Pablo Neruda's home in Santiago had come as an afterthought. My husband, Jim, and I had been traveling through Chile, with a single day to spend in the capital.

Riding the funicular to the top of Parque Metropolitano, the classic tourist activity, seemed like a requirement. When we got to the bottom again, it deposited us a block away from La Chascona, the house the poet bought in 1951 (while still married to his second wife, Delia del Carril) for his then-secret lover, Matilde Urrutia. A promising stop, perhaps, but I kept my expectations low.

I've taken a fair number of house tours on my travels—often discovering that all the things I'd most like to see (the artist's paintings, her desk or painting studio) were either sold off or sent to museums. Take the artist out of the house and what you are likely to have, more often than not, is a collection of rooms and some old furniture.

My intention was to pick up a book of Neruda's poetry at the gift shop. These last few nights on our trip, I suggested to Jim, he and I could read poems out loud to each other and maybe memorize a few. We'd devote some time to our Spanish. That, and romance. Who better to fan the flames than Neruda?

The moment I stepped into the garden at La Chascona, I revised my plan. "I'm going to need to spend a lot of time here," I whispered to Jim, checking my watch. I was already concerned that the two hours left before closing time might not be sufficient.

I am an incurable collector of the kind of things some people may call junk. I call them treasures. Now, at the home of Neruda, the Nobel-winning Chilean poet and champion of the left, I had discovered a kindred spirit.

I hadn't even gotten through the front door of this house, but already, just at the sight of the garden, my heart was racing the way it does when I encounter a particularly enticing junk store, or a salvage yard, or a promising-looking yard sale. And this place possessed qualities of all those.

But something else, too: an element not unrelated to Neruda's poetry. If his relationship with Matilde was, as he represented it in his poems, the great love of his life, this house was the stage set against which he envisioned the two of them playing it out. "Here are the bread—the wine—the table—the house," he wrote in *One Hundred Love Sonnets.* "A man's needs, and a woman's, and a life's."

What I recognized, even at the entryway—with its ragtag assemblage of wrought-iron garden furniture and mosaic tile inlays, the mural of birds and vines winding around the arched door, the hand-forged circular staircase and glass balls from ships' buoys and orange trees and sculptures of angels—was that whatever fondness I might feel for Neruda's poetry, my truest kinship with this man who died over forty years ago would be with his sense of interior decoration.

In fact, "interior decoration" is an insufficient phrase. As much as he was a poet, Neruda was a collector of things, a builder of homes, and a designer of fantastical spaces.

La Chascona (the name refers to the wild tangle of Matilde's hair, a recurring element in his poems) is the kind of house I love best—the fabulous, wacky, excessive creation of a man for whom objects took on deep emotional meaning—not necessarily for their intrinsic value, and possibly not for their conventional beauty either, but as an expression of the dreams of the person who assembled them.

This place is also—with its never-ending birdsong, the trickling waterfall meandering through the property, the tinkling chimes—the home of a true romantic, filled with symbols and talismans and secret messages to his lover, only a fraction of which (I'm guessing) any visitor will comprehend. Up to the day of my visit, all I knew was that Neruda had written *Veinte Poemas de Amor.* But this whole house was a love poem.

La Chascona bears no resemblance to places like Monticello, in Virginia, or Versailles, or—a personal favorite—the Isabella Stewart Gardner home in Boston. Unlike those places, you won't find the rooms designed by Neruda in books of great interior design—no Louis XVI chairs, or tasteful but predictable furniture groupings. In a Neruda house, you may find a taxidermied flamingo overhead, or a life-size bronze horse, or a fifty-times-larger-than-life-size man's shoe.

And that's what I found myself loving. Those houses out of *Architectural Digest* may be lovely, but give me a room that tells something about the person who lived there—a room that displays a sense of humor, a sense of drama, and, most important, a passionate soul.

Neruda was a sensualist. You can see it in his poetry: "I crave your mouth, your voice, your hair. Silent and starving, I prowl through the streets. Bread does not nourish me, dawn disrupts me, all day I hunt for the liquid measure of your steps . . ."

But you can also see it in his living spaces. One step through the low, narrow entry to the dining room and we knew: the man who lived here loved to eat. The dining table is long, and set with English china and Mexican glassware, wonderful odd serving dishes, chairs arranged surprisingly close, in a way that suggests warmth and conviviality.

It's clear where Neruda must have presided: at the head. From my audio tour, I learned that he favored dressing up for parties. He kept a collection of hats for these occasions, and sometimes he might paint on a mustache. He liked to make an entrance, through a small special door opening into the room. The kitchen remained strictly off-limits. A magician does not display how the magic is made to happen if he wants to maintain the fantasy.

I can list here only a fraction of the furnishings and objects that stood out. By themselves, some might appear ugly—even tacky. But as the collage artist Joseph Cornell could have told us, art happens in the assemblage.

At La Chascona we found cheaply framed Caravaggio reproductions, stuffed animals, 1960s-style Formica, and a mobile (also pure 1960s) featuring staring eyes, mounted alongside African masks. There was also a leather couch from France, an original ceramic head by Léger, and a portrait of Matilde by Neruda's friend Diego Rivera, commemorating the Medusa-like red hair that gave La Chascona its name.

When we got to the bedroom, I had the sense that I shouldn't be in this place. The passion of the man for this particular woman seemed too great for a parade of tourists to pass through with headsets. ("Two happy lovers make one bread, a single moon drop in the grass," he wrote. "Walking they cast two shadows that flow together; waking, they leave one sun empty in their bed.")

The bed is covered with a simple white cloth. On the dressing table: a bottle of Chanel No. 5 and a hand mirror, not a lot more. Still, a scent of passion emanates.

In the gift shop after our tour, I stocked up on books by Neruda and purchased a Neruda-style cap for my husband. But our visit to La Chascona had left me wanting more—not of the poetry so much as the man and his houses.

We had planned to spend the remainder of the day in Santiago. But upon learning that Neruda had two other homes that he and Matilde occupied—simultaneously—over the last twenty years of his lifetime, I became a woman possessed. I suggested to Jim (no, there was more urgency than that) that we add to our itinerary a pilgrimage to those other houses—one, La Sebastiana, in the city of Valparaíso; the other, Casa de Isla Negra, a couple of hours from there, on the rocky Chilean coast.

It's one of the things I love best when traveling: those moments your well-made plans and itineraries get tossed aside for a spur-of-the-moment expedition to explore some place you never even knew existed, until you were there.

An hour later, we had the whole thing arranged: A rental car to take us to Valparaíso. A hotel room for one night. To be followed, after our visit to La Sebastiana, by a drive to Isla Negra.

We were hot on the Neruda trail now, or at least I was, with Jim at the wheel of our rented BMW convertible. It was a romantic quest, in a way (*Two for the Road,* minus Albert Finney and Audrey Hepburn). I wanted to see all three of the houses where the relationship between Pablo and Matilde had played out. But really what I wanted to know were the stories of the two who had inhabited them.

The drive to Valparaíso took us through gorgeous countryside, including many Chilean wineries. Twenty miles down the highway, with the sky threatening rain, we gave up on our top-down experience, but even so, I liked to imagine how it must have been for Pablo and Matilde, leaving behind their beloved home in the capital for the new place high on a hill known as Florida, overlooking the crazy port city of Valparaíso where no streets seem to run parallel to each other and many are one-way, though lacking the signs to tell you this.

La Sebastiana was purchased in 1959 from the estate of an architect, Sebastián Collado, who had died before construction was completed, and for whom the house is named. While Neruda bought La Chascona on his own, as a surprise for his lover, he and Matilde (now his third wife) bought La Sebastiana together. They celebrated its opening in 1961 with one of their famous dinner parties, and later with New Year's celebrations where friends gathered to watch fireworks over the harbor.

We spent an afternoon and night exploring Valparaíso—enough time for Jim to characterize the place as an intoxicating mix of New Orleans and San Francisco's Mission District, combined with a little of the Latin Quarter in Paris: pisco sours in a dive bar playing '30s jazz; cobbled streets winding down to the water; murals and funiculars and pots spilling over with flowers; dogs in the road.

Next morning, we made our way to La Sebastiana. As with La Chascona, this Neruda home features an entryway of tangled greenery and mosaic walkways, hidden gardens, staircases, low doors and ceilings that give a person the feeling of being on a ship—which was precisely Neruda's idea. Though he never took an interest in being at the helm of a boat, the nautical themes are everywhere in his houses.

Here, too, is a whole room dedicated to a bar, and a dining table set with more colored glasses, and a dressing table for

Matilde, and, at the foot of the bed, a toy sheep purchased by Neruda, late in life, to replace one he had loved and lost as a motherless child decades earlier.

There's a carousel horse and a music box and a collection of wooden ships, and maps (one dating from the seventeenth century). As always, Neruda had made himself a wonderful writing room, filled with photographs of the poet with his many famous friends (Picasso and Marcel Marceau among them) and his writer heroes (Edgar Allan Poe, Walt Whitman), along with pictures from the day in 1971 when he received the Nobel Prize.

As in his other houses, the office features a collection of bronze hands, and a sink beside the desk so he could indulge his habit of washing his hands before getting to work on his day's writing. His houses make plain: if the poet had an insatiable appetite for food, and love, and ships' models, and wine, he also possessed a strong work ethic.

He wrote in the early hours. The afternoons were reserved for seeing friends and hunting down treasures, a fact that left me imagining what a collector like Neruda would have done had eBay existed in his time. More bronze hands and ship paintings, perhaps. Fewer poems.

With little time left before our flight home, we got back in the BMW, tearing off to the last Neruda house, with the plan of touring it that afternoon, then racing back to the city to board our plane. We were cutting it close, but compulsion had taken over now.

The route to Isla Negra goes through a series of small towns before reaching the coast. Even when we arrived there, we had a hard time finding the house. No signs announce its presence in this unexceptional little beach town filled with cheap restaurants and souvenir shops.

On the advice of a local taxi driver, we made our way

down a dirt road a half-mile or so outside of town. Then there it was, on a pile of rocks overlooking a stretch of ocean so wild, Jim had to raise his voice for me to hear. Neruda's favorite house: Isla Negra.

This was the house he had purchased for his second wife, Delia del Carril (nicknamed La Hormiguita, Little Ant). He was looking, he said, for a place to write his *Canto General*. But, it could be argued, a person doesn't need a roomful of ships in bottles and a few hundred glass bottles to write a canto.

"I write for a land recently dried, recently fresh with flowers, pollen, mortar," he wrote in *Canto General*. "I write for some craters whose chalk cupolas repeat the round void beside the pure snow . . ."

Here again is the bar and the great dining table, the vast fireplace and deep soft chairs (overlooking the roiling Pacific this time), the writing room, the romantic bedroom reached by a special flight of steps—two bedrooms actually; when Pablo Neruda divorced Delia and married Matilde, the new love required a new room. At Isla Negra, the landlubber Neruda indulged his love of maritime objects more than in either of the other houses, with a dozen female ships' figureheads jutting from the walls of the living room.

Neruda celebrated Chile's Independence Day here with his many friends every September 18. It was here where he received the news of the coup that removed his socialist ally Salvador Allende from power in September 1973, and of Allende's suicide that same day.

And it was here—just three weeks later—where he spent his last night with Matilde, before being taken to the hospital where he died a few days later. The cause of death was initially reported as prostate cancer, but the Interior Ministry of Chile later released a statement saying that it was highly probable that Neruda's death "was caused by a third-party intervention."

After his death, Matilde never spent another night at Isla Negra; she returned instead to Santiago to end her days at La Chascona. First, though, she had to rebuild the house, which—like the town—had been looted and wrecked by members of the military following the coup.

A person visiting the houses now would not guess that so many of Neruda's carefully assembled treasures and furnishings had been smashed and burned in those first days. Photographs displayed on the home's walls from the aftermath tell the story—of the destruction, of the thousands who took to the streets after his death to mourn their beloved poet. There in the photographs, among the mourning masses, is Matilde herself—hair concealed under a black veil. She died of cancer ten years later and is buried at Isla Negra beside her husband.

On the plane home, I took out the volumes of poetry I had picked up at the gift shop at La Chascona. One was a collection featuring *Veinte Poemas de Amor.* I knew it so well, and the verses Neruda published, anonymously, in celebration of his love for Matilde during the early '50s when their relationship was a secret.

The other was a hefty 843-page tome with every one of Neruda's odes, in Spanish on one side of the page, English on the other ("Ode to an Artichoke." "Ode to the Dictionary." "Ode to Walt Whitman." "Ode to My Suit": "Every morning, suit, / you are waiting on a chair / to be filled / by my vanity, my love, / my hope, my body.") It's fitting for this poet who so loved material objects—less for their value, I think, than for what they represented—that he wrote 225 of these odes.

I'm no poet, and no poetry critic, but I found myself thinking, as I flew north over South America with my backpack full of Neruda, that not all of these poems are so great or memorable. The poet may have been better served writing a little less. Just as it may be said that his wonderful houses could contain one-tenth the number of amazing treasures, and they'd still be wonderful places to behold. More so, maybe.

But who am I to criticize a great poet for the excess, as I make my way back to a house filled with ample evidence of my own obsessive collecting? I know as well as the next person that it's dust-to-dust in the end. All a person takes with him to the grave are his bones.

But in the middle, between birth and death, I'd call it a glorious thing, to raise one's red Mexican glass at a fine round table set with gilt-edged china, while candles flicker and the music box plays, and the host sports a fez, and his beautiful redheaded wife whispers words of love in his ear. There's a string of rare pearls around her neck, and a ship's figurehead of a woman with her breasts spilling from her bodice, over the assembled guests, while outside, fireworks explode over a roaring sea.

Originally published in December 2015.

Joyce Maynard is the author of a number of novels, including *Labor Day* and, most recently, *Under the Influence*.

Borges's Buenos Aires: A City Populated by a Native Son's Imagination

Larry Rohter

The taxi advanced up Avenida Garay and came to a stop a couple of blocks short of the Plaza de la Constitución. The corner seemed familiar though I knew I had never been there before, and when I saw the sign for Calle Tacuarí, it came to me: in his story "The Aleph," Jorge Luis Borges had chosen a cellar in one of the anonymous buildings on this anonymous street as the location of the mystical "point in space that contains all other points" in the universe.

For any admirer of Borges, to wander about Buenos Aires is to collide with the products of his fervid imagination. His birthplace beguiled him, and he especially loved to walk its streets aimlessly, but he also complained that it had "no ghosts" and decided it was his task to populate the fast-expanding immigrant boomtown with his own phantasms. "In my dreams, I never leave Buenos Aires," he once wrote, though his dreams often were anguished ones, as expressed in one of several poems called "Buenos Aires":

And the city, now, is like a map
Of my humiliations and failures;
From this door, I have seen the twilights
And at this marble pillar I have waited in vain.

Between the anniversary of Borges's death in June and his birthday in August, the city plans readings, round tables, exhibitions, a concert, and other homages. Most of the time, though, seeking overt traces of Borges in Buenos Aires is, to use a Borgesian image, like trying to read a palimpsest: you have to look past the top layer to sense his underlying presence.

Take the street in the Palermo area where Borges grew up, known then as Serrano but now renamed in his honor. Today the neighborhood is perhaps the most chic in Buenos Aires, full of trendy bars, restaurants, and boutiques patronized by young writers, artists, and filmmakers more likely to cite Paul Auster or Martin Amis than Borges as influences.

In Borges's youth, though, Palermo was "on the shabby northern outskirts of town," as he put it, a semirural place frequented by gauchos and criminals who drank hard and fought hard at the *pulperías*, or taverns, that dotted the neighborhood. Their tales of derring-do and the sudden eruptions of violence to which they were prone impressed the bookish lad known as Georgie, and left him with a fascination with knives that would later infiltrate stories and poems like "The Dagger":

It is more than a structure of metal; men conceived it and shaped it with a single end in mind; the dagger that last night killed a man in Tacuarembó and the daggers that rained on Caesar are in some eternal way the same dagger. The dagger wants to kill, it wants to shed sudden blood.

The Borges family's Palermo homestead still exists at Serrano 2135, but it is not open to the public and there is nothing to mark Borges's passage there save for a small plaque. Just up the block, however, at the corner of Guatemala and Serrano, is the site that, in the poem "Buenos Aires," Borges imagined as that of "the mythical foundation of Buenos Aires," a city "I judge to be as eternal as water and air."

At first glance, the corner does not seem very promising: a hamburger joint, a design store, and a bar called Mundo Bizarro, whose motto is IN ALCOHOL WE TRUST, capture the current character of Palermo. But the fourth occupant of the corner is a tavern called the Almacén el Preferido, in a building that dates to 1885 and that Borges describes as the redoubt of toughs: "A pink shop, like the back of a deck of cards / It shone and in the back room they talked of tricks . . ."

Even more than taverns, however, Buenos Aires is a city of cafés, and Borges and his friends were habitués of several. Most of those have either disappeared or, like La Perla in the Jewish neighborhood known as Once (Eleven), been transformed into pizza parlors and the like or, like El Gran Café Tortoni, become tourist traps in which a wax figure of Borges is seated at a table with Carlos Gardel, the tango's greatest singer.

But the Café Richmond still preserves some of the atmosphere of the 1920s, when Borges was editing an avant-garde literary magazine, *Martín Fierro,* just around the corner and spent a lot of time there with fellow writers. As the name suggests, the feeling is that of an English club, with wood paneling and prints of fox-hunting scenes and country estates on the walls. That would have appealed to Borges, who prided himself on his English ancestry on his mother's side of the family.

Borges's circle of associates included the younger writer Adolfo Bioy Casares, with whom he wrote a series of detective stories set in Buenos Aires, and Bioy Cesares's wife, the poet Silvina Ocampo. But perhaps the most fascinating and influential of his friends was the painter and poet Alejandro Schulz Solari, whom Borges once called "our William Blake." The painter, who took the artistic name Xul Solar, was a dozen years older than Borges and shared his fondness for inventing imaginary universes and languages and exploring the esoterica of this world. In the 1950s, Borges would regularly flee the stifling atmosphere of the apartment he shared with his mother and head for Xul Solar's home at Laprida 1212, where the two men would often spend the day conversing about the kabbalah or Norse sagas.

Xul Solar's residence is today a museum devoted to his work, containing more than a hundred of his paintings as well as the fanciful objects that he created and called "heirlooms of another cosmos." Looking at the paintings makes clear the intellectual affinities between the two artists: Xul Solar's watercolors are full of utopias, cities floating in the sky, creatures that are half man and half machine, alternate universes, and other touches that we have come to think of as typical of Borges.

Visiting these and other sites where Borges lived or worked helps one to appreciate what a potent imagination he had. In 1937, for example, his once-promising literary career seemed to be stagnating, and he was forced to take a job cataloging books at the Miguel Cane Municipal Library, where he remained until 1945. There was little for him to do there, so he spent much of his time in a small, windowless room at the rear of the second floor, where he wrote many of the pieces in the collection eventually published as *Ficciones,* including the story "The Library of Babel."

"Man, the imperfect librarian, may be the product of chance or of malevolent demiurgi; the universe, with its elegant endowment of shelves, of enigmatic volumes, of inexhaustible stairways for the traveler and latrines for the seated librarian, can only be the work of a god," he wrote.

Borges later wrote that "the innumerable books and shelves that appear in the story are literally those I had beneath my elbow." But like the room in which the story was written (and which can be visited), the library itself is small, with a limited collection of books; it hardly seems worthy of the immortality Borges bestowed on it. It is in the working-class Boedo section; Borges used to ride the No. 7 tram to work there, reading Dante as he stood, and while the tram no longer exists, a bus line with the same number still runs the same route.

For a man whose personal life was often unhappy, libraries provided a kind of consolation: "I have always imagined that Paradise will be a kind of library," he wrote in a poem. After the dictator Juan Perón was overthrown in 1955, Borges was appointed director of the National Library. This was the kind of place that seems a candidate for his Babel tale—a four-story octagonal structure whose columns are engraved with the names of great writers and thinkers like Shakespeare, Goethe, and Plato.

The library, in the San Telmo neighborhood, is now the national conservatory of music and is open to visitors. Next door is the headquarters of the Argentine Society of Writers, where Borges sometimes offered public readings. The society currently shares the space with a restaurant, Legendaria Buenos Aires, whose main dining room is adorned with portraits of famous opera singers. There is, though, one reminder of Borges on a wall of the restaurant: a metal plaque listing the society's board of directors during 1942–44, including one Jorge Luis Borges.

Other than knives, perhaps the favorite motif in Borges's

work is the feline, evoked in such works as *The Other Tiger,* in which he meditates on the difference between the real beast and those that populate his imagination. From childhood on, the beasts fascinated him, and he would often go to the Buenos Aires zoo, on Avenida Las Heras on the edge of Palermo, to observe the big cats. Sometimes, well into his sixties, he would even be accompanied by a woman he was hoping to impress, and recite poetry as they stood in front of the cages:

> *It came and went, delicate and fatal, charged with infinite energy,*
> *On the other side of the firm bars and we all watched it . . .*

The feline collection is still there, and it includes a solitary white Bengal tiger, which seems to spend most of its time sleeping under a tree.

As an adult, Borges lived in various apartments in the Recoleta area, on Calle Presidente Quintana and Avenida Pueyrredón, also dutifully marked with brass plaques. But he lived the longest, nearly forty years on and off, in apartment 6B at Maipú 994, just off Plaza San Martín, which he came to think of as his true home.

When I was a young *Newsweek* correspondent in the early 1980s, I twice interviewed Borges there. I remember the apartment as being small and austere, with no television, no radio, and, most surprising of all for a man who by then was blind, no record player. Borges insisted the interviews be done in English, which he spoke with what he called a Northumberland accent, inherited from the English grandmother from whom he had learned the language, and he showed a fondness for antiquated words like "thrice."

Though the apartment is not open to the public, La Ciudad, the bookstore in the shopping gallery just across the street, where Borges would spend many of his afternoons, is still in business. First editions of many of Borges's works are in the window, along with photographs of him sitting in a chair that still occupies a spot of honor in the store, as if awaiting his return. If the octogenarian proprietor is in a good mood, she might even be persuaded to reminisce a bit about her friend and most famous client.

But perhaps the most vivid reminder that Borges was not just a literary personage but a real flesh-and-blood inhabitant of Buenos Aires is at Paraguay 521, a photographers' studio where residents still go to have their pictures taken for passports and identity cards. Look carefully at the collection of some three dozen portraits in the front window, and there, fourth from the right in the top row, is Borges, still peering out quizzically at a world that seemed so alien to him that he had to invent his own.

Originally published in May 2006.

Larry Rohter is a former culture reporter and foreign correspondent for *The New York Times*. He is currently writing a biography of the Brazilian explorer Cândido Rondon.

Where Rimbaud Found Peace in Ethiopia

Rachel B. Doyle

In December 1880, the mercurial French poet Arthur Rimbaud entered the ancient walled city of Harar, Ethiopia, a journey that had involved crossing the Gulf of Aden in a wooden dhow and twenty days on horseback through the Somali desert. Several years before, the author of the prose poems *A Season in Hell* and *Illuminations* had abruptly renounced poetry and embarked on peregrinations that would take him around Europe, Asia, the Middle East, and, finally, Africa. At age twenty-six, Rimbaud accepted "a job consisting in receiving shipments of bales of coffee" with a French trading firm in a thriving corner of what was then called Abyssinia.

Then, as now, Harar was a market town threaded with steep cobblestone alleys that wind between high limestone and tuff walls. Today those walls are painted with geometric designs in green, white, pink, and blue. As one strolls down the narrow, mazelike streets lined with single-story dwellings, the city, fortified and enigmatic, feels closed off. Donkeys carrying bundles of firewood wait patiently for their owners near the crenellated entrances of the city's historic gates. In the densely populated Old City, there are over 180 mosques and shrines, some dating to the tenth century. Occasionally one comes upon open-air markets where spices, khat leaves, and coffee beans are sold in huge sacks.

Rimbaud arrived in Harar "sick and completely helpless," according to his employer, Alfred Bardey. He rented a rough, clay-walled house with a thatched-reed roof. The man credited by many with reinventing modern European poetry would reside in this preindustrial Ethiopian city for nearly five years, during three distinct periods between 1880 and 1891, the longest time he ever stayed anywhere as an adult. It was a life he had visualized years before he began his travels. "I sought voyages, to disperse enchantments that had colonized my mind," the nineteen-year-old author wrote in *A Season in Hell,* a hallucinatory collection of nine poems that had been published seven years before his arrival in Harar, featuring a narrator who rages at, and then roams, the world. "My life would always be too ungovernable to be devoted to strength and beauty."

Rimbaud's travels had been preceded by a dramatic flameout in Europe: his lover, the French poet Paul Verlaine, had shot him in the wrist with a revolver in a Belgian hotel room. Living with his difficult mother in a farmhouse in Charleville, his constricting hometown in the French Ardennes, was intolerable for the high-strung poet. It didn't help that *A Season in Hell,* which would later bring him acclaim, was barely noticed at all when it was published in 1873.

And so it was that the poster child of the "decadent movement" ended up in Harar, a city three hundred miles from Addis Ababa that predated the Ethiopian capital by nearly a millennium.

Harar had been a Sufi Muslim center of learning closed to outsiders for hundreds of years before the explorer Sir Richard Burton entered the city in 1855. As soon as Rimbaud heard about the place, he begged his employers in the Arabian port of Aden to send him there. No matter that the region was viewed as dangerous and that several other trader-explorers had experienced run-ins with the warriors of the Danakil Desert. The adventurous Rimbaud immediately recognized Harar as an intriguing business prospect at the edge of the known world.

"In exile, life was a stage where literature's masterpieces were played out," the poet wrote in *Illuminations,* several years before moving to Harar. "I could share untold riches that remain unknown." (There is no evidence that Rimbaud wrote poetry again after his twenty-first birthday; however, he sent hundreds of evocative letters about his new life in Ethiopia to his mother and sister back in France.)

In Harar's Old City, now a UNESCO World Heritage site with a layout dating to the sixteenth century, a willingness to walk in circles, doubling back often, is a necessary precondition for exploring. There are no signs. If you're lucky, you'll come across the cheerful woman who serves cups of milky tea made from toasted coffee leaves to patrons sitting on buckets; or the man who feeds swooping falcons from his bare hand at the camel market; or the lane called Mekina Girgir, where tailors mend clothing on antique, pedal-operated sewing machines, and where vendors sell fritters and syrupy fried sweets from banana-leaf baskets.

In the center of the Old City, called Harar Jugol, a grand merchant home with a fine wooden facade has been turned into a museum dedicated to Rimbaud and his time in Harar. In a room with colored-glass panels and a painted ceiling, the small but informative exhibits include self-portraits taken by the poet with a camera he ordered from Lyon. Rimbaud's shot of a man sitting amid pottery in his storehouse was very likely the first photograph of Harar. "When he was here, he was somebody else, totally," said the museum curator, Abdunasir

Abdulahi, a Harari whose great-aunt knew Rimbaud when she was a child. "She said he was a Muslim and they used to play in his house."

The Arthur Rimbaud Cultural Center opened in 2000, and now "young people are starting to believe Rimbaud was really a white man who loved Hararis, who wanted to die in Harar, who preferred Harar to his sophisticated, nationalized Europe," said Abdulahi. "His mind was peaceful here."

Previously, many locals had been dismissive of their famous former resident because they suspected he might have been a spy. In fact, the French trader was genuinely fascinated by the city and its surroundings, and set about mastering the regional languages. "With the common people he spoke in Arabic, but with his servant he spoke in Harari," Abdulahi said. "He spoke Harari perfectly and he learned Amharic and Oromo as well."

In Rimbaud's time, Harar was a major trading hub, where prized goods from the highlands—coffee, animal hides, gold rings, and musk of civet—were exchanged for foreign goods that had arrived at the coast by wooden dhows. For his job, Rimbaud spent much of his time riding to faraway markets to source goods, or "trafficking in the unknown," as he described it to his family in a letter before he set off on an expedition in 1881.

"There is a great lake a few days' journey from here. It's in ivory country. I'm to try and get there. The people of the region are probably hostile," he informed them, before giving instructions on how to collect his back wages if he didn't return.

Rimbaud highlighted the risks and difficulties of his life in Africa in letters to his disapproving mother. "This last expedition has exhausted me so much that I often lie in the sun, immobile like an unfeeling stone," he wrote. Another trip he described as "insane cavalcades through the steep mountains of the country." Did the author remember that in *A Season in Hell,* he had written what now seems like an ode to the very landscape he was complaining about? "I loved desert, scorched orchards, sun-bleached shops, warm drinks. I dragged myself through stinking streets and, eyes closed, offered myself to the sun, god of fire."

Grumble he might, but according to Bardey, his boss, Rimbaud was "always impatiently waiting for the next occasion to set out on adventures . . . I could sooner have held on to a shooting star."

By the late 1880s, the former enfant terrible of the Parisian literary scene was at the center of much of the foreign trade in southern Abyssinia. It didn't always go smoothly: when the future Ethiopian emperor Menelik II decided he needed guns, he turned to Rimbaud, who spent months acquiring antique European rifles for the capricious king, only to be promptly swindled when he delivered them. "Menelik seized all the merchandise and forced me to let him have it at a reduced rate, forbidding me to sell it retail and threatening to send it back to the coast at my expense!" Rimbaud complained in a letter to the French consul.

Frustration aside, Rimbaud's procurement of weapons for Menelik II may have been his greatest contribution to modern African history. Scholars reckon that the guns he sold in 1887 likely helped the emperor defeat Italy in 1896 when the country's troops tried to invade Ethiopia. As a result of the rout at Adwa, Italy signed a treaty recognizing Ethiopia as an independent nation.

Rimbaud would not be around to witness this triumph. In 1891, after the pain from a swollen knee became unbearable, he was forced to leave Harar to seek medical treatment. Sixteen porters carried him on a hidebound stretcher to the port at Zeila, two hundred miles and twelve days from Harar. It was the same port where Rimbaud had first set foot in Africa, eleven years earlier. By the time his ship reached France, it was already too late: his cancerous leg had to be amputated.

From his hospital room in Marseille, the poet and explorer thought fondly of his time in "beloved Harar." "I hope to return there . . . I will always live there," he wrote that summer. In November 1891, at thirty-seven, Arthur Rimbaud died while dictating a note to the director of the Messageries Maritimes shipping line. "Let me know what time I shall be carried on board," he requested in his letter. Until the end, the brilliant polymath was determined to return to the city where he had finally found a kind of peace.

Originally published in March 2015.

In Saint Petersburg, a Poet of the Past Serves as a Tour Guide for the Present

David Laskin

Just inside the entrance of the elegant Literary Café on Saint Petersburg's Nevsky Prospekt, Aleksandr Pushkin sits alone at a table by the window. Upstairs in the dining room, china teacups clink and a Mozart sonata purls, but Pushkin is not listening. Dressed to the nines and staring fixedly into space, the poet—at least his wax effigy—broods upon love's bitter mystery and the sweet closure of revenge.

As every Russian old enough to read well knows, this artful mannequin, complete with luxuriant black curls and full romantic sideburns, has been propped up by a window on roaring Nevsky next door to the KFC, because the café was the site of Pushkin's last meal before his fatal duel in 1837.

Buttonhole one of the cake nibblers and you'll hear the whole story: how Pushkin challenged the dashing guardsman Georges d'Anthès for brazenly wooing his ravishing wife, Natalya; how the insolent Frenchman fired first, tearing a hole in the poet's abdomen; how the wounded literary hero lingered for two excruciating days before he died, at the age of thirty-eight. You may even get a sonnet or a few lines of the novel-in-verse *Eugene Onegin,* Pushkin's masterpiece, recited with eyes uplifted and breast swelling with pride.

To an American, the Russian cult of Pushkin is a little mystifying. Even though I had journeyed to Saint Petersburg expressly to pay homage to places made sacred in Pushkin—from the shadowy linden walks of the Summer Garden, where the youthful Eugene Onegin strolled with his French tutor, to the Marble Palace ballroom where the bored lady-killer danced the mazurka with the cream of Saint Petersburg society—I was nonetheless stunned by the scope and fervency of Russia's Pushkin cult. Tolstoy, Dostoyevsky, Chekhov—all far better known and more widely read stateside—are commemorated in their native land with the occasional tour or plaque, but Pushkin is everywhere, especially in the former capital. His image greets you in grand public squares, museums, and street-corner posters. Through revolution and all manner of siege, the poet's apartment, his school dorm room—even the patch of ground where the bullet felled him—have all been lovingly preserved.

This most unlikely hero—an impoverished nobleman descended through his mother from an African slave, an artist who fused Mozart's grace and Byron's ironic smolder, a political rebel addicted to carousing and dueling—has been a superstar ever since his first poems appeared. Supposedly, on the day of his funeral, mourners from all over the city jumped in cabs shouting "To Pushkin!" and drivers whisked them to the church where he lay in state—such was the poet's fame. In Russia, he's Shakespeare, Thomas Jefferson, and Bob Dylan rolled into one.

"In Russian literature, Moscow is a calm city—but Saint Petersburg is the place where all the bad things happen," Frank J. Miller, professor of Slavic languages at Columbia University, told me. "Pushkin started this theme of Saint

Petersburg madness with his story 'The Queen of Spades.'" Hermann, the cold-blooded hero of that tale, loses his mind over an obsession with a surefire gambling secret, but nearly all denizens of Pushkin's mad capital devote themselves night and day to trysting, drinking, dueling, party- and theatergoing, and debt-incurring. "One can be capable and moral with manicure upon one's mind," insists Pushkin in *Eugene Onegin,* whose hero requires the better part of five stanzas "to put his evening costume on."

A swell, as the expression was.
He used to squander many an hour
Before the mirrors in his room,
At last to issue forth abloom
Like playful Venus from her bower,
When in a man's disguise arrayed,
The goddess joins a masquerade.

Has any poet made the frivolous more delectable? Through a haze of champagne bubbles and French perfume, Pushkin conjured up an aristocratic stage set of theater and palace, restaurant and ballroom, that remains astonishingly intact today. Rarely pausing to paint cityscapes with recognizable boulevards and buildings in the manner of Gogol or Tolstoy, Pushkin preferred to let the urban scene flash by through the windows of careering carriages. Who knows or cares exactly what street we're on as Eugene dashes to yet another ball in a hired hack—

Along the housefronts past him speeding,
Down streets aslumber, fast receding,
The double carriage lanterns bright
Shed their exhilarating light

And brush the snow with rainbow flutters;
With sparkling lampions, row on row,
The splendid mansion stands aglow.

One evening, though, in the lingering twilight of the northern summer, I did manage to track Pushkin's party-sated hero to the "granite shelf" of the Neva Embankment, where, "lost in meditation," he listened to the sound of horses' hooves pounding the pavement of Millionnaya—the street of millionaires' mansions that runs from the Hermitage to the Field of Mars (a military parade ground turned public garden). I leaned over the same granite shelf in a fine rain that dimpled the river—as wide here as the Hudson and lined on both shores with the long, low facades of imperial masterpieces. As if on cue, a horse clopped down Millionnaya just as I ducked through the arch of the impossibly beautiful Winter Canal, which runs in a masonry canyon between the wing of the Hermitage known as the Large Hermitage and the Hermitage Theater.

As darkness fell at last, I ended my stroll beneath the massive equestrian statue of Peter the Great that Pushkin christened the Bronze Horseman in his great narrative poem. *The Bronze Horseman* opens triumphantly with a paean to the window Peter cut through on Europe—"I love thee, city of Peter's making; / I love thy harmonies austere"—but it ends in despondency and madness. Crazed by grief after his beloved dies in the great Neva flood of November 7, 1824, the hero imagines the "awful Emperor" spurring his horse off the wavelike granite pedestal and thundering after him through the city streets.

In the glare of floodlights and the heavy night-scent of flowers, there was indeed something nightmarish about this rearing pile of eighteenth-century bronze and stone. "Town so gorgeous, town of beggars," Pushkin wrote of Saint Petersburg in one of his haunting lines. "Air of slavery, splendid face, / Pale green archway of your heaven, / Boredom, cold, and granite grace." Everything he loved and hated about the city—beauty and absolutism, magnificence and monotony, grace and ice—stares from the chubby, imperious face of the czar, three times life size.

The Pushkin apartment museum on the Moika Embankment, a five-minute walk from the Winter Palace, is the most sacred shrine on the Pushkin circuit. After the dazzling immensity of Palace Square, the cityscape along the Moika feels intimate, melancholy—the scale of Amsterdam, the tarnished gleam of Venice, all of it washed by Saint Petersburg's watery northern light. It was typical of Pushkin to choose to live in the most picturesque bend of the city's most beautiful waterway, but to the literary pilgrim the exquisite atmosphere is poisoned by the misery of his final days.

For so worldly and cynical a man (he once referred to his wife as "my 113th love"), Pushkin could be violently sensitive to slaps. When he received an anonymous letter on November 4, 1836, initiating him into "the most serene order of cuckolds" on account of his wife's public flirtation with d'Anthès, he went mad with jealousy. At the entry to the apartment museum, adjoining rooms display Natalya's tiny, carnation-pink dance slippers and Pushkin's dueling pistols nested like Christmas ornaments in a velvet-lined box—the whole sad story of the poet's demise in a kind of visual haiku.

The suite of rooms facing the Moika is as stately and graceful as any literary aristocrat could desire—lofty ceilings and windows, carpets of red and gold, gilded lamps, ruby decanters—but to me the artist came most alive in the room where he worked and died. Some four thousand books cover the walls of Pushkin's study with the rippling brown and gold of stamped leather; his precious cane and Turkish saber are close at hand; a soft light from the three courtyard windows falls on the papers, books, and trinkets left on the huge worn desk.

Deep in the shadows beneath the bookshelves stands the heavy, walnut-sided sofa where the poet bled to death while dreaming that he was climbing up the books.

Originally published in September 2005.

Orhan Pamuk's Istanbul

Joshua Hammer

On a windswept afternoon in mid-December, the writer Orhan Pamuk stood in a leafy square around the corner from Istanbul University, absorbed in a forty-year-old memory. He walked past parked motorcycles, sturdy oaks, and a stone fountain, browsing through secondhand books in front of cluttered shops occupying the bottom floors of a quadrangle of pale yellow buildings. Sahaflar Çarşisi, Istanbul's used-book bazaar, has been a magnet for literary types since the Byzantine era.

In the early 1970s, Pamuk, then an architecture student and aspiring painter with a love for Western literature, would drive from his home across the Golden Horn to shop for Turkish translations of Thomas Mann, André Gide, and other European authors. "My father was nice in giving me money, and I would come here on Saturday mornings in his car and fill the trunk with books," the Nobel Laureate remembered, standing beside a bust of Ibrahim Müteferrika, who printed one of the first books in Turkey—an Arabic-Turkish language dictionary—in 1732.

"Nobody else would be here on Saturdays. I'd be haggling,

talking, chatting. I would know every clerk, but it's all changed now," he said, referring to the somewhat touristy atmosphere and the disappearance of characters he'd come to know, such as a manuscript seller who doubled as a Sufi preacher. These days, he said, "I come only once a year."

Pamuk was born about three and a half miles from the market, in the prosperous Nişantaşi neighborhood in 1952, the son of a businessman who frittered away much of his fortune through a series of bad investments. Pamuk grew up surrounded by relatives and servants, but quarrels between his mother and father, and the ever-present sense of a family unraveling, cast his youth into uncertainty and periodic sadness.

For most of the six decades since, Pamuk has lived in Istanbul, both in Nişantaşi and nearby Cihangir, alongside the Bosporus. His work is as grounded in the city as Dickens's was in London and Naguib Mahfouz's was in Cairo. Novels such as *The Museum of Innocence* and *The Black Book* and the autobiographical *Istanbul: Memories and the City* evoke both a magical city and a melancholy one, reeling from the loss of empire, torn by the clash between secularism and political Islam, and seduced by the West. Most of Pamuk's characters are members of the secular elite, whose love affairs, feuds, and obsessions play out in the cafés and bedrooms of a few neighborhoods.

"I did my first foreign travel in 1959, when I went to Geneva for the summer with my father, and I didn't leave Istanbul again until 1982," Pamuk told me. "I belong to this city."

After many visits, I wanted to get beyond the tourist sights and observe the city as Pamuk sees it—a place of epic history and deep personal associations. I e-mailed him and asked if he would take me on a tour of the neighborhoods that shaped his upbringing and his development as a writer. Pamuk readily agreed, and two months later I met him at his apartment in the affluent Cihangir quarter, overlooking the Cihangir Mosque, a nineteenth-century monolith flanked by minarets, and, beyond it, the Bosporus, the strait that forms the boundary between Europe and Asia.

It seemed appropriate that I was visiting Pamuk during the off-season, given his focus in books like *Snow* and *Istanbul* on winter, grayness, and melancholy. The air was crisp, the light was muted, and although the sun occasionally burst through the clouds, the city seemed largely drained of color. "I have always preferred the winter to the summer in Istanbul," Pamuk wrote in *Istanbul.* "I love the early evenings when autumn is slipping into winter, when the leafless trees are trembling in the north wind, and people in black coats and jackets are rushing home through the darkening streets." From the balcony of his apartment, he looked approvingly at the sun shining weakly through the cloud cover and pronounced it an optimal day for a walk. "If this was a hugely sunny day I would be upset," he said. "I like the black and white city, as I wrote in *Istanbul.*"

I had caught up with him during the last stages of polishing his novel *A Strangeness in My Mind,* published in English in 2015, which chronicles the life of an Istanbul street vendor from the 1970s to the present. He told me that he was grateful for a break. "I am an obsessive about my work, but I love it," he said. He put on a trench coat and pulled a black baseball cap over his brow, a halfhearted effort to render himself a little less recognizable.

In 2005, Pamuk responded to an interviewer's question about a crackdown on freedom of expression in Turkey by asserting that "a million Armenians and 30,000 Kurds were killed in this country and I'm the only one who dares to talk about it." The offhand remark, published in a Swiss newspaper, resulted in death threats, vilification in the Turkish press, and charges by an Istanbul public prosecutor of the "public denigration of Turkish identity." Pamuk was forced to flee the country for nearly a year—his longest time out of Turkey. The charges were abandoned in January 2006 amid an international outcry, and the threats have subsided. Though Pamuk sometimes travels with bodyguards, especially during his nocturnal rambles, he now feels relatively safe.

On this cloudy afternoon we followed a zigzag route that roughly paralleled the Bosporus and took us through the heart of Cihangir, once a predominantly Greek neighborhood. In the 1960s, when Pamuk was a student at the elite Robert College prep school farther up the Bosporus, rising nationalistic fervor over a looming conflict in Cyprus came to a climax in the government's eviction of the neighborhood's Greek population. Deprived of its commercial class, Cihangir became the city's red-light district.

"I wrote an early novel here in the 1970s, in my grandfather's apartment," Pamuk said. "Every night, I used to wake up to women and their bodyguards—their macho protectors—and their clients, bargaining, throwing belts out the window."

Cihangir is now a trendy neighborhood of artists and writers, elegant cafés, antiquarian shops, and sky-high rents.

One engine of Cihangir's revitalization is Pamuk's own creation: the Museum of Innocence, which opened in 2012 in a burgundy building on a steep road leading down to the curving Golden Horn, which connects the Bosporus to the Sea of Marmara. The museum is a meticulously rendered time capsule of 1970s Istanbul, and a tribute to the power of obsession. It was inspired by Pamuk's 2008 novel *The Museum of Innocence,* about an affluent Istanbul businessman, Kemal Basmaci, who falls in love with a poor shopgirl, Füsun, and becomes so consumed that he assembles a collection of every trace of contact with her.

Pamuk found the building himself, designed the exhibits, and assembled his character's fictional collection from flea markets and his own family heirlooms. Glass cases on the walls in darkened rooms are arranged chapter by chapter, filled with these supposed tokens of his character's mostly unrequited love: crystal bottles of cologne, porcelain dogs, Istanbul postcards, and 4,213 of Fusun's cigarette butts, each one encased behind its own tiny window. "I didn't publish a novel for years, but I have excuses," Pamuk told me. "I did a museum in between."

Karaköy Square, farther down the hill, is a waterfront plaza radiating outward into avenues lined with modern and Ottoman-era office buildings, food bazaars, and appliance shops. Street vendors sell pomegranate juice and *simit,* the wheel-like bread otherwise known as a Turkish bagel.

Tucked off one steep avenue is an alley of government-sanctioned brothels guarded by the police. The Karaköy area conjures vivid memories for Pamuk of his childhood. He pointed out a row of bicycle shops, where his father bought him his first two-wheeler. A bit farther on is a passageway leading to the Tünel, one of the world's oldest subterranean transit lines. The two-stop subway, built by French engineers, began in 1875 and still links Karaköy Square with the embassy district in the central Beyoğlu district. In its early incarnation the train consisted of a steam engine that pulled two wooden cars, with separate compartments for men and women. "The empire fell apart, and there was no other subway line in Turkey for 120 more years," said Pamuk, who loved riding the trains with his parents as a child.

We stopped for lunch in the shadow of the Galata Bridge, a double-decker, concrete-and-steel span, opened in 1994, with walkways, three lanes of traffic in each direction, and tram tracks. Plastic tables and chairs stood haphazardly on a muddy patch near the water, flanked by portable grills selling fish fillets on baguettes, garnished with paprika, chile powder, and chopped vegetables. A stray dog, his ear tagged as proof of his government-issued rabies shot, lay in the dirt. "He's a local monument," said Pamuk, who was bitten by a street dog during an evening walk thirteen years ago and had to undergo a painful series of rabies shots.

Across the inlet, in stunning contrast to the scruffy surroundings, rose the silver dome of Hagia Sophia, wreathed in limestone and sandstone minarets. Built as a Greek Orthodox basilica and opened in AD 537, and converted into a mosque after the 1453 Islamic conquest of Constantinople, it was secularized by Mustafa Kemal Atatürk, modern Turkey's founder, and turned into a museum in 1935.

"I had little interest in Byzantium as a child," Pamuk wrote in *Istanbul.* "I associated the word with spooky, bearded, black-robed Greek Orthodox priests, with the aqueducts that still ran through the city, with Hagia Sophia and the red-brick walls of old churches."

Legal disputes have kept this patch of waterfront property, where we were eating lunch, in limbo, resulting in a rare zone of neglect in the heart of the city. It's one of Pamuk's favorite places. "All my childhood was like this, but will it be like this in twenty years? No way," he told me, as we savored the maritime smells. He is all but certain that the rapid gentrification of surrounding neighborhoods will eventually overtake this forgotten field.

We continued across the Galata Bridge, the historic epicenter of Istanbul, stopping midway to admire the scene: tourist boats and pleasure crafts floated down the Golden Horn, past the mosques of Sultan Ahmed on one side and the steep hills of Cihangir on the other. "This was originally a wooden bridge, and when I was growing up you had to pay to cross it," he said, "but you could also hire rowboats. I remember my mother taking me across by boat in the 1950s."

Half a mile down the Golden Horn, a new bridge has just opened, a sleek white span that partly blocks views of some of Istanbul's grandest mosques. Like Prime Minister Recep Tayyip Erdoğan's aborted plan to raze Gezi Park in Taksim Square and put up a shopping mall in the style of an Ottoman military barracks, the bridge project has divided the city largely along socioeconomic lines: the city's liberal elite has strongly backed the preservation of its Ottoman-era core, while the mostly poorer Islamists have tended to welcome this sweeping away of the past.

A century ago, "all the boats that came from the Sea of Marmara, from the Mediterranean, ended up here," Pamuk told me.

As he relates in *Istanbul,* Gustave Flaubert arrived here in October 1850 for a six-month stay, stricken with a case of syphilis picked up in Beirut. He still managed to frequent the city's brothels and wrote about the "cemetery whores" who serviced soldiers by night. Another celebrated visitor of that era, the French writer and politician Alphonse de Lamartine, "described boys on the bridge shouting to the tourists, 'Sir, give me a penny,'" Pamuk went on. "Tourists would throw the money into the sea, and they would jump from the bridge and dive in and the money would be theirs."

On the south side of the Golden Horn, we pushed past crowds in the Baharat spice bazaar, and emerged on a busy street in the Eminönü neighborhood. In his childhood, Pamuk was fascinated by stories about the Ottoman sultans and pashas who ruled from this quarter of Istanbul, the site of rebellions, coups, and secret jails where fearsome punishments were meted out. "One place in Eminönü was especially constructed for what was known as the Hook," Pamuk wrote in *Istanbul.* "Wearing nothing but the suit in which he emerged from his mother's womb, the condemned was winched up with pulleys, skewered with a sharp hook, and, as the cord was released, left to drop."

Within these few square blocks, the Ottoman rulers commissioned grandiose palaces and other buildings that proclaimed the durability of their empire. "The whole bureaucracy was here," he said, pointing out the Sirkeci train station, a classic example of European Orientalist architecture, with colored tiles, Moorish-style archways, and twin clock towers, which opened in 1890 and served as the final destination of the fabled Orient Express. The age of grandiosity didn't last long. When Vladimir Nabokov alighted here in 1919, he found "a city in ruins," Pamuk said. "There was no physical destruction, but this place used to get the riches of all the Middle East and the Balkans, and then it all vanished, and it was reduced to poverty."

In *Istanbul,* Pamuk captured the melancholy, or *hüzün,* that infused the metropolis during his boyhood, when it was still suffering a long decline after the collapse of the Ottoman Empire. He described "the old Bosporus ferries moored to deserted stations in the middle of winter . . . the old booksellers who lurch from one financial crisis to the next and then wait shivering all day for a customer to return."

The autobiography, published in 2001, brought Pamuk's life story up to his decision to become a writer in 1973 and captured a very different time in the city's history. "The city was poor, it wasn't Europe, and I wanted to be a writer, and I wondered, 'Can I be happy and live in this city and realize my ambition?' These were the dilemmas I was facing," he told me. "When I published it, the younger generation told me, 'Our Istanbul is not that black and white, we are happier here.' They didn't want to know about the melancholy, my kind of dirty history of the city."

Not far away was another symbol of Ottoman hubris: the

monumental central post office, opened in 1909, shortly after a military cabal of Young Turks seized power. "Now it's just a local branch," he said with an ironic laugh, sizing up the arched entryway and the cavernous, nearly empty atrium. It has deep associations for Pamuk. In 1973, at twenty-one, he had just dropped out of architecture school to devote himself to writing. Afflicted by self-doubt and parental skepticism, he decided to test his abilities by entering a short story in a local magazine competition. The tale was a historical romance set in fifteenth-century Anatolia, the vast hinterland east of Istanbul. His friends frantically typed sections of the story, and Pamuk raced to this post office and handed the manuscript to a woman behind the counter just hours before the deadline. "The next day I received a note from her, telling me, 'You paid me too little,'" he said, gazing at the main, gazebo-like kiosk beneath the atrium's soaring central dome, where the moment played out. "But she'd understood that I was ambitious, submitting a literary work, and she paid the postage on her own." One month later he learned that he had won the contest. "So I love this place just because of that," he said.

Beyazıt Square, a windswept plaza behind the book bazaar, abuts Istanbul University, formerly the Ottoman Ministry of Defense compound: a sprawling campus of brick-and-stone buildings and newer, slapdash structures behind a monumental entrance gate. The plaza seethed with protests, riots, and army killings during the 1960s and '70s. Pamuk was enrolled at the journalism school during one of the most turbulent periods, but while his friends were risking their lives facing down soldiers, he spent most days reading at home in Nişantaşi. "I was an ambitious, brainy guy, and university seemed like a waste of time to me."

A few steps away we ducked into Vefa Bozacısı, another of his favorite places. Founded in 1876, the shop, a cozy establishment with leather banquettes and antique mirrors, specializes in *boza,* a fermented wheat drink that originated in southern Russia. Mixed with water and sugar and sprinkled with cinnamon, the creamy, butterscotch-colored concoction is served in glasses that were lined up by the dozens on polished wooden counters. Beside shelves of pomegranate vinegar, a case reverently displayed the shop's most valuable heirloom: a silver *boza* cup used here in 1927 by Kemal Atatürk.

We entered the grounds of the Fatih Mosque, built on the orders of Fatih Sultan Mehmed, the conqueror of Constantinople, starting in 1463. It was rebuilt in 1771 after an earthquake destroyed it.

In a marble courtyard beside the massive pink-sandstone mosque, considered one of the most graceful in the Islamic world, a wall poster caught Pamuk's eye. It demanded freedom for Salih Mirzabeyoğlu, a radical Islamist and author of incendiary political tracts, who was sentenced to twelve years in prison on a terrorism conviction. Pamuk—fascinated and disturbed by the rise of political Islam in Turkey and the Middle East—based one of his most memorable characters, the terrorist leader, Blue, in his novel *Snow,* partly upon Mirzabeyoğlu. Blue is an ambiguous figure: a charismatic intellectual who espouses a violent message, while avoiding direct entanglements in acts of terror. The cases of Mirzabeyoğlu and Blue were similar, Pamuk said. "Some Islamists kill, but he didn't, but he's been locked up for a very long time."

He seemed to tense up slightly as we left the mosque and wandered into one of Istanbul's hard-core Sunni neighborhoods. "We could be in a different country," he said in a soft voice. Salafist men with long beards and skullcaps sat on benches in tidy plazas; women in black abayas walked with their children down a cobblestone street past a madrassa, an Islamic school.

The sun had begun to set on this wintry afternoon, bathing the Golden Horn in shadow. We stood in the terraced garden of a mosque, gazing over the landmarks of Istanbul—the red roofs of Cihangir, the thirteenth-century Galata Tower, one of the few surviving traces of Byzantium. We had been walking for more than four hours, across half a dozen neighborhoods, peeling away Istanbul's tourist-friendly facade to expose the complex fabric beneath it.

"That's the beauty of living here," Pamuk told me. Then we descended along steep cobblestone alleys leading to the Atatürk Bridge, beginning the long journey home.

Originally published in February 2014.

Joshua Hammer is a freelance foreign correspondent and the author of *The Bad-Ass Librarians of Timbuktu: And Their Race to Save the World's Most Precious Manuscripts.*

In Sri Lanka, an Island of Detachment and Desire

Michelle Green

Lined with coconut palms and neon-hued catamarans, the bay at Weligama, Sri Lanka, is an escapist paradise. Open to the Indian Ocean, it is ninety-two miles from roiling Colombo and an infinite distance from angst. On a recent afternoon, bare-chested fishermen idled on the rocks and argued mellifluously. Bony children bobbed in the water, and tinny music drifted from a stall where glistening mahi-mahi was on offer. Not one head turned when cows stumbled into an empty beach café, scattering chairs and then wandering into the surf.

But the slow-motion beach scene isn't the attraction at Weligama. Instead, it is a dollop of an island two hundred yards offshore. Ringed by gleaming boulders and topped by a cloud-white villa, the outcrop called Taprobane is now a landmark in Sri Lanka. Created in the 1920s by a Frenchman who claimed to be an aristocrat, the property was once owned by the writer Paul Bowles.

These days, Taprobane is a privately owned home marketed as a luxury retreat with five-bedroom villas and a staff of five, including a private cook, who keep the Tanqueray flowing.

At the foot of a neo-Palladian gate, Taprobane's jetty reaches only a short way into the water. Though elephants have been employed to ferry visitors upon occasion, guests usually make their way to the house by sloshing through the shin-deep surf.

On my own pilgrimage in the spring, I slipped off my sandals and waded behind two porters with my bags atop their heads. Before I reached the elaborate gateway, a hand holding a towel appeared: "Madam, hello, madam," someone said.

I was making the journey alone, but not because I craved solitude, or splendor. Booking Taprobane for one night meant that I could explore the estate and parse the sensory landscape that made it so alluring to Bowles.

The Queens-born expatriate (who died in 1999) was a writer I knew, and who is still a touchstone for many travelers. A coolly charismatic figure who lived at a distance from his own culture, he made a lasting mark with dark, often disturbing tales about innocents who seek exotica and stumble into anarchy.

His best-known novel, *The Sheltering Sky,* is a cautionary tale for heedless adventurers: Distracted by their own small dramas, a young American couple ventures into the Sahara. Adrift among strangers, they become prey.

Norman Mailer's take on his vision became a trope: "Paul Bowles," he wrote, "opened the world of Hip. He let in the murder, the drugs, the incest, the death of the Square . . . the call of the orgy, the end of civilization."

Elegant and self-contained, Bowles would have been the last to define himself as hip. Exquisitely detached from his surroundings, as well as from his characters, he spent much of his life on the move; such distinctions hardly mattered in Tangier, the Moroccan port that became his backdrop.

In 1948, when Bowles brought his wife, the writer Jane Bowles, to Morocco, Tangier was an international zone where villas were cheap, kif was plentiful, and sex was a commodity. Decadence wasn't the draw for the Bowleses, but their relationship was opaque, and each famously took gay lovers.

Though he nominally was in retreat, Bowles's door was open; a generation of admirers made its way to Inmueble Itesa, the drab building where he lived for forty years. I began visiting in 1986, while researching a book about Bowles and other writers in Tangier. Patient and often amusing, Bowles seemed a glamorous anachronism.

By then, his time in Sri Lanka (Ceylon until long after he left) seemed impossibly distant; it had been distilled into anecdotes about devil-dancing ceremonies and the quirks of his servants. Once, however, Taprobane had been a place that fulfilled his longing for extremes. Along with the void of the Sahara, he wrote, the fecundity of the tropics could propel him into "a state bordering on euphoria."

His obsession was sparked by David Herbert, an aristocrat and close friend in Tangier. In 1949 (a year after Sri Lanka won independence from Britain), Herbert showed him an album with photographs from a family visit to Taprobane. Struck by a *coup de foudre,* Bowles made an expedition to Sri Lanka in 1950; he found the private island to be "an embodiment of the innumerable fantasies and daydreams that had flitted through my mind since childhood."

Two years later, Bowles arranged to buy the island from a local rubber planter. The cost for his "little parcel of paradise," as he called it, was about $5,000.

Climbing through the island's luxuriant jungle, I caught a whiff of Bowles's bliss. Flame trees and frangipani-lined paths strewn with fallen blossoms. Screaming house crows, hundreds of them, were a counterpoint to the booming waves. The mineral smell of the sea receded, and the perfume of overripe fruit took over.

The showstopper was the villa, where verandas take the place of outer walls. Pure white, the pavilion is a study in light and shadow. In the octagonal center room, the ceiling rises thirty feet; bedrooms and sitting areas extend beyond. Visible in all directions, the seascape is infinite.

Majordomo Carman Abeyeunga was a compact man who, like his staff, was dignified in shorts and bare feet. Service at Taprobane was swift and unobtrusive; my bags materialized in a small bedroom that, at midday, was shuttered against the heat. With heavy Dutch Colonial furniture and a four-poster draped in mosquito netting, the room was shabby but appealing.

Wandering while Abeyeunga prepared a mind-altering curry, I decided that, with its planter's chairs and posh family photos, Taprobane's look was Tatler-colonial. Library shelves were stocked with worn volumes, including *Confessions of an English Opium Eater,* but I spotted not a single book by Bowles.

The photos, it seemed, belonged to the British-born entrepreneur Geoffrey Dobbs, who bought Taprobane from a Sri Lankan mogul. A retired publisher and a high-profile figure in Sri Lanka, Dobbs has converted two colonial houses in Galle into boutique hotels and helped shore up a tourist industry enfeebled by an excoriating civil war and a tsunami. (I was transfixed by photographs of his elephant-polo team on the beach.)

By all accounts, Taprobane was less haute in Bowles's day. There was no running water or electricity and "the house would have delighted the heart of Charles Addams," in the words of Arthur C. Clarke, who visited in 1957. "Windows had been boarded up, plaster was flaking away, and though the place was perfectly livable there was a general air of neglect."

Any lugubriousness was a plus for Bowles, who delighted in the fact that the island had once served as a cobra dump. In his memoir *Without Stopping,* he described the scene when his wife first set foot on the estate. Mrs. Bowles, he wrote, instantly understood its appeal: "I can see why you like it," she shrugged. "It's a Poe story."

Jane Bowles felt besieged in her husband's house. "I had prepared her for the nightly invasion of bats . . . but she had not expected so many, she said, or that they would have a three-foot wingspread and such big teeth," he remembered.

But Bowles savored the exoticism. In a 1955 letter to his editor, David McDowell, he wrote: "The house is self-sufficient in eggs, orchids, lobsters, crabs, and that's all." He continued, "Think how much we should have to spend for our daily supply of orchids if they didn't grow here."

Hot-pink blossoms were at my place when I sat down to lunch on the terrace. Red rice, dal spiked with turmeric, curried potatoes, and freshly made *papadum* made me wildly happy.

I wanted to lie in the shade and listen to bird shrieks competing with sounds from the mainland: a flute, car honks, random firecrackers. Instead, I grabbed my camera and maneuvered down the island's south face. I leaned carefully over a twenty-foot drop to photograph the surf as it smashed into hulking boulders.

The sun was still fierce, so I headed into the tangle that canopies the walkways. Like the house, the gardens were created by Maurice de Mauny Talvande, a French commoner who declared himself a count. A debt-plagued aesthete whose marriage to an earl's daughter collapsed, he pegged the island as a kingdom in the rough. When he managed to acquire Galduwa, as it was then called, around 1925, he rechristened it with the name that the ancient Greeks gave to Sri Lanka.

Now, every step revealed a curiosity—green pods cradling bloodred seeds, or white blossoms erupting from the depths of crimson flowers. Heart-shaped leaves were veined in startling white, and orchids leapt across walkways at eye level.

Bowles, who used *majoun* (a Moroccan confection containing cannabis) to tweak his consciousness in Morocco, sensed that his garden had a life of its own. In another letter to McDowell in 1955, he described "the strange psychological effect this powerful world of vegetable life can have on the person who opens himself to consciousness of it . . . it's a rather unpleasant sensation on the whole, to feel very strongly that plants are not inert and not insentient."

Still, the setting suited him. Finishing his third novel, *The Spider House,* that winter, he established an enviable routine. After early tea, he put on a sarong and went to watch daylight take hold. He worked until noon, when the heat closed in. Afternoons were highlighted by naps and swims in the "blood warm" surf.

Bowles intended to separate himself from the world here, but he seldom was alone. Late in 1954, he arrived at Taprobane with Jane Bowles, as well as his lover, the Moroccan painter Ahmed Yacoubi, and their friend Mohammed Temsemany. It was not a happy ménage: struggling with the heat and with writer's block, his wife, always fragile, drank heavily; she returned to Tangier after two months.

Throughout, his estate was a draw for strangers who seemed to regard it as public property. Tourists from Weligama or Colombo or as far away as Bombay "hallooed and pounded" at the gate, though Bowles posted a sign warning that drop-ins would be turned away.

Over time, he developed the sense of being an interloper in Sri Lanka. By his account, visitors began advising him that he was lucky to live in a house that was part of their history, and newspapers called for Taprobane to be declared a national monument.

Along with financial worries and his wife's loathing for the place, that shift spurred Bowles to sell his one-off paradise. In 1957, it went to the Irish writer Shaun Mandy.

It's hard to say whether anything of Bowles remains at Taprobane. The portrait in the room where he is said to have slept is a likeness of M. de Mauny Talvande. But Bowles once wrote that Taprobane "spoke to him" before he bought it, so perhaps the connection lingered.

Taprobane did offer reminders of Bowles's love for the tropics, however: I thought about him as I walked barefoot on the cool floors and listened to nighttime laughter from the outdoor kitchen.

Sleep came easily at Taprobane; the banging of the waves obliterated the usual static, and not a single bat disturbed my dreams.

I woke early, opened the shutters, and saw that my terrace was deserted. I was free to do yoga, or watch the sea birds, or read in perfect peace.

Instead, I walked out to watch the ten-shades-of-turquoise ocean, where barely visible boats disappeared into the horizon.

I remembered what Bowles had said about what lay beyond: at Taprobane, he wrote, "there's nothing between you and the South Pole."

That became my mantra for the new day.

Originally published in December 2014.

In Vietnam, Forbidden Love and Literature

Matt Gross

There is no better place to have an affair than Ho Chi Minh City. Virtually every block in the city has a hotel or guesthouse whose front-desk clerk won't bat an eye as you check in with your paramour. What happens in Saigon, as it's still known, stays in Saigon.

No one understood this better than Marguerite Duras, the French writer who was born in colonial Indochina in 1914 and spent her childhood there. At the age of fifteen, Duras, then living with her mother and two brothers in Sa Dec, a town on the Mekong River, began an affair with the twenty-seven-year-old son of a rich Chinese landowner. They met on a ferryboat, and soon she was sneaking away from her boarding school in Saigon to spend hot-and-heavy evenings in his "bachelor's quarters" in Cholon, the city's enormous ethnic Chinatown.

Their scandalous affair served as the raw material for Duras's best-selling 1984 novel, *The Lover*; for a film version shot in Vietnam; and for Duras's revisitation of her past, the memoir-like 1992 novel-in-film-notes, *The North China Lover.*

But as popular as the various forms of *The Lover* are, Duras's life remains unmarked in present-day Vietnam. Still, as I discovered over the course of a few days trying to retrace some of her narrative, her world has largely survived seventy-five years of near-constant upheaval.

My hunt began on Dong Khoi Street, in the heart of Ho Chi Minh City's downtown District 1. Dong Khoi used to be known as Rue Catinat, Saigon's premier shopping and entertainment strip; it's still hopping, with boutiques and cafés leading from the Notre Dame Cathedral at one end to the Saigon River at the other. Right in the middle is a little alley lined with shelves—this is the Lan Anh Bookshop, run by a friendly sixty-nine-year-old Saigonese man who introduced himself as Mr. Thach and who tends a small collection of Vietnamiana.

In an unwieldy mixture of English, French, and Vietnamese, I described my project, and for 200,000 dong, or about $12, Mr. Thach sold me the 1953 *Annuaire des États-Associés: Cambodge, Laos, Vietnam,* an annotated directory of the colonies, complete with maps, ads for Mic Extra cigarettes, and a pamphlet that matched old French street names, the ones Duras would have known, to their contemporary equivalents. Jackpot.

While motorbikes raced down Dong Khoi and vendors offered me the previous day's newspapers, I flipped through the yellow-pages-style listings until one heading caught my eye: "Cinéma (Salles de)." Below it was the Eden Cinéma, where Duras's mother had worked as a piano player.

For Duras, the Eden represented an escape from her miserable family. Today, it has been renamed the Video Mini Dong Khoi, and sits forlornly at the rear of an arcade whose shops sell reproductions of famous Vietnamese and European paintings. Its wide, red-leather chairs have been uprooted and left in the lobby, while the theater itself is filled with rubble. The only reminders of the past are a few hand-painted movie posters (*Cleopatra*) and signs suggesting that the building is managed by an entity called the Eden Company.

Equally elated and disappointed at my discovery—and unable to find Duras's dormitory, the Lyautey Boarding School, on any map—I decided to follow Duras's lead and leave Saigon.

Cholon occupies the same space in the Saigonese imagination that Los Angeles's Chinese quarter does in the movie *Chinatown.* It's right there—Districts 5 and 6—but unknown, foreign. My Vietnamese friends had no acquaintances among its million or so inhabitants and barely knew the streets, which look just like Saigon's, only different: Chinese characters supplement the Roman Vietnamese script on signs; roast pigs and ducks hang in restaurant display cases; and the roads are lined with the low, balconied, colonial-era shop houses on which the Lover's father made his fortune.

Finding a hotel to match their ground-floor love nest—"hastily furnished from the look of it, with furniture supposed to be ultra-modern"—proved impossible. I settled for the next best thing: the Phoenix Hotel, with a faux-Bauhaus facade and a stairway that would let me bypass the front desk—an essential feature for any adulterer interested in maintaining anonymity. (Not that I was interested—and anyway, my fiancée, Jean, would not have approved.)

As the sun began to set, the night market at the intersection of Nguyen Trai and Phung Hung Streets was getting going, and although those roast ducks were enticing, I wanted a Durassian meal. The famous dinner scenes in *The Lover* take place at expensive Chinese restaurants—"they occupy whole buildings, they're as big as department stores, or barracks, they look out over the city from balconies and terraces"—where Duras's siblings get drunk on Martell and Perrier and then ignore and insult the Lover, who picks up the tab anyway.

Since Duras never names the restaurants, I turned again to the *Annuaire,* which had an ad for the Arc-en-Ciel, boasting *"une ambiance inégalable et unique"* and *"taxi-girls de Hongkong."* Amazingly, fifty years later, the Deco-ish Arc-en-Ciel remains open for business, minus the taxi-girls. It is now primarily a hotel, but with three floors of restaurants.

A wedding had taken over the rooftop garden terrace, so my friends Christine and Sita joined me on the ground floor—a neat dining room that could have been in any hotel, anywhere in the world—for sizzling scallops with crispy rice cakes. Then I gathered my courage to make Sita, a married artist from Rhode Island, a proposal. Would you like, I asked, to have a make-believe affair in Sa Dec?

Sure, she said.

The next morning, I descended from Room 205 in an Italian linen suit, the closest thing I had to the Lover's raw-silk outfit. Outside was a topless, white 1930s Citroën Traction Avant, a substitute for the Lover's black Morris Léon Bollée, which I'd hired to take Sita and me to Sa Dec and back. The driver was Mr. Chien, a fit, dashing Vietnamese in his late thirties, who gently steered the Citroën's luxurious bulk through the crammed streets to Sita's house across the river.

She emerged, looking like Marguerite Duras reincarnated. Thin as a teenager, she had on a light sundress, and her hair hung down in braids from under the fedora she wears even when she's not pretending to be someone's fictional mistress.

For fifteen minutes, we reveled in the image we presented—two stylish travelers off for a weekend in the country. Then we began to feel guilty; this was a little too neocolonial. Meanwhile, we realized we had no air-conditioning and nothing to block the dirt that gets kicked up along Vietnam's highways. The road to the Mekong Delta is not, as it's pictured in the film *The Lover,* a rust-colored path through verdant, unpopulated rice paddies. Vietnam's surging economy has brought with it urban sprawl, and factories, offices, and industrial parks were all there was to see for many, many miles.

But the eyesores did eventually come to an end, just before we crossed the My Thuan Bridge, a sparkling mile-long span over the Mekong that was built by Australia in 2000 and made obsolete the ferry on which Duras—then Marguerite Donnadieu—and her lover first met. From there, a bumpy road dotted with hive-like brick factories led to Sa Dec.

Sa Dec, population 96,000, may be the quintessential river town. Sandwiched between two branches of the Mekong, it is threaded through with streams and canals over which arc bridges of all sizes. All along the water, there are shops and warehouses sending rice flour and pigs along a trade route that has served the town for centuries.

Signs of Sa Dec's most famous residents were not, however, immediately apparent. At the Bong Hong Hotel, Sita and I checked into separate rooms (some affair!), changed out of our fancy duds, and, while Mr. Chien bathed his dusty Citroën, began our inquiries: Where could we find the riverfront house of a rich Chinese man? No one we asked gave coherent directions, but they all knew who we were talking about: Huynh Thuy Le, aka the Lover.

Still, somehow we made it to the colonial villa that served as the Donnadieu residence in the movie (it's now a Department of Education office), and then to a low house with a Chinese-style ridged roof. Was this really the "big villa" with "blue balustrades" and "tiers of terraces overlooking the Mekong" where the Lover had lived? Its current occupants, the antidrug police, did not look interested in talking to us.

Finally, our motorbike taxis took us to the Truong Vuong Primary School, which we had been told was built by the French. It did indeed look colonial, and as Sita and I stood in the quiet courtyard, a man in a white jacket and black slacks waved at us from the doorway of his office and called out, "Bonjour!"

Mr. Sang was a shy, gentle French teacher in his sixties who had spent his entire life in Sa Dec. This school, he explained carefully, had most likely been run by Duras's mother, but one could not be sure.

"There are no documents," he said. "Others have said that Madame Donnadieu lived here, since the director had a house next door in order to observe the school. But everything has changed. One cannot find the exact site."

We asked about the drug-squad headquarters, and he confirmed that it had indeed been the Lover's villa. Then he offered to be our tour guide: "You and your friend are foreigners in my country," he said, "so it is my duty as a Vietnamese to show you around." How could we refuse?

Our first stop was the tomb of the Lover and his Chinese wife, on a concrete island in an algae-covered pond near our hotel. A white gate marked with Chinese characters hung above the tombs; a neighboring isle had two more, those of the Lover's parents, who refused to let him marry Duras.

Mr. Sang next brought us to the Huong Pagoda, built in 1838, to which the Lover had donated heavily. Inside, past a turtle-filled pool, we discovered an ornate shrine displaying two photographs. They were, Mr. Sang said, Huynh Thuy Le and his wife.

The Lover looked to be in his early seventies, thin and mostly bald, but with "the white skin of the North Chinese" that once caught Duras's attention. Was there regret in his eyes? Years after their affair, he phoned Duras in Paris to tell her "he would never stop loving her for the rest of his life." Perhaps that is why his wife, in her photo, looks so uncomfortable, so unloved.

Outside, a light rain began to fall, and we hurried to the car. Mr. Chien drove us through the wet streets, then we treated Mr. Sang to a dinner of stewed pork and sour fish soup with *bong dien dien,* a kind of Vietnamese zucchini blossom. Afterward, Sita and I retreated to our respective rooms, and I put on a bootleg DVD of *The Lover.* It wouldn't play. Instead I watched *Sin City,* and fell asleep alone.

Originally published in April 2006.

Matt Gross is *The New York Times'* former Frugal Traveler columnist and the author of the travel memoir *The Turk Who Loved Apples.* He lives in Brooklyn with his wife and daughters.

Acknowledgments

Every spot on the Earth has been trod by someone. So I'd like to thank the many literary luminaries who've roamed the world and come away with language that inspires us all.

Also deserving of thanks are the many *Times* editors who came before me, conceiving the Footsteps feature and becoming guardians of it. They include Mike Leahy, who as travel editor published a James Joyce series that roughly followed the format of the column in its current form, as well as Nancy Newhouse, Stuart Emmrich, and Danielle Mattoon, my predecessors in this role who each had a vision that enlivened this column through the years. For their tireless work polishing the words that make literature of the lives of literary figures, credit goes to the editors Steve Reddicliffe, Suzanne MacNeille, Lynda Richardson, and Dan Saltzstein.

It sometimes takes editors beyond the *Times* to recognize that the wealth of material we publish would best be consumed in book form rather than in the daily newspaper. So I'd like to thank Amanda Patten of Three Rivers Press for realizing the potential of these articles and Jenni Zellner who made an anthology out of a simple collection.

And finally, the champion of this project and linchpin of the operation is Alex Ward of the *Times,* whose even, steady guidance ensured that both the newsroom and book publisher could rest easy. His execution made working on this project as enjoyable as reading it.

All these people have had a hand in putting together this wonderful treat, which I hope will inspire you to read, go, and, most of all, daydream.

—M.D.